AYN RAND NATION

ALSO BY GARY WEISS

Wall Street Versus America

Born to Steal

AYN RAND NATION

THE HIDDEN STRUGGLE FOR AMERICA'S SOUL

GARY WEISS

ST. MARTIN'S PRESS NEW YORK

 Printed in the United States of America. For information, address St. Martin's Press, 175 Fifth Avenue, New York, N.Y. 10010.

www.stmartins.com

Design by Claire Vaccaro

Library of Congress Cataloging-in-Publication Data

Weiss, Gary (Gary R.)
Ayn Rand nation : the hidden struggle for America's soul / Gary Weiss.—1st ed.
p. cm.
Includes index and bibliographical references.
ISBN 978-0-312-59073-4 (hardcover)
ISBN 978-1-4299-5078-7 (e-book)
1. Rand, Ayn—Criticism and interpretation. 2. Rand, Ayn—Influence. I. Title.
PS3535.A547Z975 2012
813'.52—dc23

2011041106

First Edition: March 2012

1 3 5 7 9 10 8 6 4 2

For Seymour Zucker and in memory
of Bill Wolman, editors and economists,
always a true and steady moral compass

CONTENTS

If religion was a thing
That money could buy,
The rich would live
And the poor would die.

—*All My Trials* (traditional)

AYN RAND NATION

INTRODUCTION

Why Ayn Rand Matters

It was early in 2009, and the horror of the financial crisis was fully evident. The shock had worn off, but little else. The hunt for villains was in full swing.

I was researching a magazine article on Timothy Geithner, the recently appointed Treasury Secretary, when I found an old photo that I thought might be a good illustration for the piece. It showed his most eminent mentor—the former chairman of the Federal Reserve, Alan Greenspan—posing in the White House with President Gerald Ford and three other people. The photo was taken in September 1974, when Greenspan had just been sworn in to his first major government post, chairman of the Council of Economic Advisors.

Standing next to Greenspan was a woman of about seventy. I had last seen her on a book jacket, younger but no less imperious, and always with a short, pageboy haircut. In her televised appearances she spoke with a Russian accent and was always precise, forming her words carefully, as if she had written them down beforehand.

Ayn Rand was a figure from yesterday. I never had any reason to write about her. In my many years as a reporter covering Wall Street, mostly its underside, she was always on someone else's beat. She inhabited a vague intersection of literature, philosophy, economics, and politics—far-right politics. My focus was the "greed beat," and her theories, I thought, had no relevance.

I was wrong. And to make matters worse, I was wrong for a long time.

Looking at that photo in 2009, I realized that Rand provided the missing piece of a puzzle I had been pondering since the depths of the financial crisis. Over the years I never thought very deeply about the *why* of it all, the moral component of the behavior to which we had all been exposed. Why did legitimate, essentially honest financiers, traders, and CEOs pursue monetary acquisition with such a single-minded intensity regardless of consequences to others? What motivated the regulators and government officials who abetted them? The usual explanations were glib: greed, status, and power, with "regulatory capture" thrown in to explain government inaction. But these explanations did not seem adequate.

I saw a pattern of behavior in the actions and utterances of the main actors in the financial crisis.

I saw it in the downfall of John Thain, the plain-spoken and supremely efficient Midwesterner who was the supposed rescuer of Merrill Lynch. To the public, thanks to his well-oiled publicity machine, he was Thain the Brain, the human calculator, a man of unquestioned integrity. Today he is mainly known for the $35,000 commode that he bought for his office with shareholder funds.

I saw it in John Paulson, the hedge fund manager who collaborated with Goldman Sachs in designing a financial instrument, pegged to subprime mortgages, that was as profitable for him as it was devastating for Goldman clients. Paulson was a brilliant man who could see the financial system racing to a precipice. Unlike other hedgies who sounded the alarm—and were pilloried as a result—Paulson placed his bets and kept silent, cashing in his chips when the system nearly collapsed. In talking with Paulson I came away with the impression that he had devoted his life to one goal: the acquisition of ever-larger sums of money. The Goldman Sachs deal was the culmination of that single-minded quest.

What made these two accomplished men so selfish, so seemingly amoral, so lacking in public-spiritedness, so thirsty for a buck? These two men and many others personified a philosophy. Whether it was explicitly adopted or implicit was not important. What mattered was that they lived it.

This underlying, unspoken philosophy was reflected in the belief, continually promulgated by Greenspan at the Fed, that the markets were supreme, a kind of fifth estate. It was an attitude toward life that pervaded the financial system and was accepted, sometimes with considerable enthusiasm, by regulators and Congress in all administrations, and a sizable portion of the media.

At first I developed a theory that this was a hodgepodge of beliefs which I called "market supremacy." But it was brought home to me by the Greenspan photograph from 1974 that this philosophy of greed had a philosopher.

Ayn Rand had been there all along, and I never noticed. This book is my attempt to correct that oversight.

My purpose in writing this book was not to tell the story of Rand's life or to recount again the much-told tale of the financial crisis. That has been skillfully depicted in numerous fine histories and by the final report of the Financial Crisis Inquiry Commission. Rand's story was thoroughly explored by Jennifer Burns and Anne Heller in their two masterful biographies.[1] John Cassidy's *How Markets Fail* was especially insightful in describing the rise of "utopian economics," and how that and the worship of unregulated markets led to the debacle of 2008.

It's all history now. Yet the failure of deregulation and untrammeled capitalism doesn't seem to matter anymore. What followed the financial crisis was not reform but retrenchment, rebuttal, denial. Led by Jamie Dimon, the outspoken chief executive of JP Morgan Chase, Wall Street struck back against the very idea of reigning in its compensation and any curbs on its ability to freely transact business regardless of societal consequences. Little reform was enacted, and what was passed into law was undermined in Congress. Even talking about such things, blaming bankers for the things they had done, was to be condemned. Greenspan went on the talk show circuit, the Oracle as in days of old, arguing that regulation was not the answer. Through it all was the spirit of the lady who stood next to Greenspan in that photograph almost four decades ago: Ayn Rand, triumphant, the first lady of the politics of reaction.

Rand has experienced an extraordinary revival since the financial crisis, and nothing seems to be stopping her. It is a struggle for the soul of America, and she is winning. She is winning because she is not considered to be very important. She is dismissed by entire segments of informed opinion as a fringe character, a nut, a cultist, and an extremist. She is ridiculed, not analyzed, engaged, or rebutted. Yes, she was an extremist, but she matters because her extremism is no longer on the fringe.

Her followers call her a serious philosopher. Some call her the greatest philosopher who ever lived. Some call her the greatest writer who ever lived and her novel *Atlas Shrugged* the greatest novel ever written. Her detractors call her a charlatan whose teachings are simpleminded, morally repugnant, and derivative. They deny that she was a philosopher at all, or that her ideology is a philosophy. In this book I utilize the term; to deny it, I think, unwisely minimizes her undeniable influence.

What's indisputable is that Ayn Rand was a novelist, playwright, essayist, and screenwriter. All those roles were secondary to her objective in life, which was to advance the cause of the most radical form of free-market, laissez-faire capitalism. She called herself a "radical for capitalism."[2] To Rand, "capitalism" and "freedom" were synonymous, as were "government" and "force."

She advanced a system of beliefs that turned the moral values of Western civilization upside down. Bad was good, the immoral was laudatory, and the laudatory was evil. She believed in individualism and opposed the institutions of society that benefited groups of people, which she condemned as the evil of "collectivism." Every man was an island. In the parallel universe of her ideas, being selfish, pursuing one's "rational self-interest," was the only truly ethical form of existence. To be selfless was *evil.* She used that word often.

Rand periodically intruded on the political scene from the 1930s to the 1980s. She was a fount of political incorrectness and her positions seemed almost maniacally inconsistent. She opposed U.S. entry into World War II and supported Israel. She opposed the Vietnam War and thought Dwight D. Eisenhower was soft on Communism. She endorsed Barry Goldwater and opposed Ronald Reagan for catering to the Christian right. She opposed racism and the Civil Rights Act of 1964. She believed that big business was a "persecuted minority," but did not speak out when big business discriminated against real minorities, including the one to which she belonged. She despised hippies and the draft. She was an elitist who adored Mickey Spillane. She was a fierce advocate of individualism and her heroes were indifferent to criticism. Yet she fell into a deep depression when her final and grandest novel, *Atlas Shrugged,* was critically skewered.

She called the philosophy that she invented "Objectivism." To Rand and her disciples, an Objectivist world would be a triumph of energy, productivity, and justice. Freedom would sweep the halls of power and the boudoir alike. Nagging relatives would be thrown out of the house. Marriage vows would be optional, just as they were for Rand in her squalid private life. Government would be reduced to three functions: the armed services, the police, and the courts. Income taxes would end, and so would almost everything the taxes paid for.

Today her vision of radical capitalism has never been more popular. She is the godmother of the Tea Party and the philosophical bulwark that stands behind the right's assault on Social Security and Medicare. Yet during her lifetime she was the leader of a cult, an adulterer, a militant atheist, a supporter of abortion, and an opponent of antidrug laws.

Rand could be abysmally ignorant of basic facts and eerily prescient.

She had an uncanny grasp of the American psyche, yet her books showed little insight into the lives of ordinary Americans.

Her most prominent critic was not a bleeding-heart liberal but the patrician leader of the conservative movement, William F. Buckley Jr. He was so appalled by her rejection of Christian morality that he assigned the turncoat former Communist, Whittaker Chambers, to write a scathing review of *Atlas Shrugged* for the *National Review.* "Since a great many of us dislike much that Miss Rand dislikes, quite as heartily as she does, many incline to take her at her word," said Chambers. In fact, he said, her vision was hateful and repulsive. "From almost any page of *Atlas Shrugged*, a voice can be heard, from painful necessity, commanding: 'To a gas chamber—go!' "[3]

"This is a story of conflict where it's equally easy to hate both sides," said *The Washington Post* in its review. "It howls in its reader's ear and beats him about the head in order to secure his attention, and then, when it has him subdued, harangues him for page after page," sneered *The New York Times Book Review* critic Granville Hicks.[4] Despite the scalding reviews, *Atlas Shrugged* sold in the millions and remains a best seller to this day.

Her two major novels are thematically very different. *The Fountainhead,* the 1943 novel that made her famous, says hardly a word about capitalism. The novel's principal character lives like a pauper and doesn't even like money. *Atlas Shrugged,* published in 1957, is entirely focused on her ideal of no-regulation, no-controls, no-government capitalism. Its heroes are ostentatiously rich. Rand had always favored radical capitalism, but her practical knowledge of economics and industry was lacking. There was a missing ingredient that Rand found after she wrote *Fountainhead.* Its name was Alan Greenspan.

Greenspan was her loyal acolyte since the early 1950s. He was a member of her inner circle, the Collective, that met with her every week and served as what today we would call a writers group, reading *Atlas* chapters and acting as a sounding board for her ideas. As the Collective disintegrated over the years, shredded by purges and defections, he never abandoned her, never doubted her even as others did, no matter how erratic her behavior.

During the 1960s and 1970s she was shunned by mainstream intellectuals and academia. Her reputation wasn't bad—it was toxic. Writing in 1972, William F. O'Neill, a philosophy professor at the University of Southern California and author of one of the few serious Rand critiques, said that writing about Ayn Rand was a "treacherous undertaking. In most intellectual circles she is either totally ignored or simply dismissed out of hand, and those who take her seriously enough to examine her point of view frequently place themselves in grave danger of guilt by association."[5]

Rand had few friends even on the far right. Her FBI file discloses that J. Edgar Hoover, on the advice of a subordinate, rebuffed her request for an appointment in 1966 to discuss an unspecified "personal-political problem."[6]

Standing in the Oval Office on that late summer day in 1974 with Greenspan next to her, Rand was still isolated, still an extremist, and had never softened her views. But thanks to Alan Greenspan, she was now posing with the President of the United States. She would come again to the White House two years later, when another acolyte named Malcolm Fraser, the prime minister of Australia, paid a visit. She rarely strayed from her apartment on New York City's East Side, emerging occasionally to give lectures. During her final years she became a fussy and bitter old woman, shuffling around her neighborhood in a housecoat.

The contrast with Ayn Rand's import and influence today could not be more dramatic. She is the darling of the conservative media and a mighty force on the Internet. Small groups of the faithful congregate on Rand blogs, Rand newsletters, Rand message boards, even a Rand-acolyte dating service. Rand is the new Benjamin Franklin, her pithy sayings trumpeted by the right, a humorless Will Rogers in reverse who knew few people she didn't dislike, an inspiration for leading political figures. Her followers meet regularly throughout the country, and her novels, once shunned by academia, are now taught in colleges and even high schools, thanks to free books provided by wealthy supporters and the Ayn Rand Institute, founded after her death to perpetuate her legacy.

Rand does not need the ARI. Her novels were on the bedstands of the baby boom long before it was founded, just as she enthralled the Silent Generation and went on to thrill Generation X and today's collegians. Her novels became a postwar American cliché, a universal teenage reading experience like *The Catcher in the Rye*. The Rand-loving advertising executive in *Mad Men* is a reflection of two Rand crazes—the one that took place on a small scale in the 1960s when she was a fringe cult figure, and the one that is taking place with considerably more impact today.

In 1975, Stanley Marcus, chairman of Neiman Marcus in Dallas, decried corporate obstruction of social legislation. "Who among the business community today," he asked, "would seriously propose that Congress repeal our child-labor laws—or the Sherman Antitrust Act? The Federal Reserve Act, the Securities Exchange Act? Or workmen's compensation? Or Social Security? Or minimum wage? Or Medicare? Or civil rights legislation?

"All of us today," he said, "recognize that such legislation is an integral part of our system; that it has made us stronger."[7]

That may have been true in 1975, but not today. The credit, or blame, lies squarely with Ayn Rand.

I read *The Fountainhead* and *Atlas Shrugged* during the early to mid-1970s. I don't remember when, nor can I say why with any precision. I'm not sure I finished either book. Back then I liked to read odd historical books and novels that were made into movies. I remember starting but never finishing *The Pickwick Papers*; I still have the copy of *Military History of the World War* that I read avidly, but partially, many years ago. I think I may have jotted down Rand's name after seeing the *Fountain-*

head movie on late-night TV. It starred a stiff Gary Cooper and a sexy Patricia Neal. I remember liking the music. I always liked Cooper. In this movie he exuded integrity but was not his usual taciturn self. This Coop was a blabbermouth. At the end he delivers one of the longest speeches in movie history. But rising above the boredom was the ingredient that made the film, and the novel, appealing to any male adolescent—sex, and plenty of it.

Rand at the time was something of a cult figure, in the mass-culture sense of the word. She had a following, though not a very visible one. I wasn't aware of it, but Rand was an outspoken opponent of the Vietnam War. She thought it was morally wrong—not for any of the usual reasons, but because it did not serve U.S. interests. It was not a *selfish* war. Since President Johnson was trying to free that far-off country from the yoke of Communism, this was an unjustifiable military adventure even though she detested Communism. The Vietnam War was, to her, "a pure instance of blind, senseless, altruistic, self-sacrificial slaughter."[8] This sounds almost like the noises that used to be made by the Bronx High School of Science SDS chapter. But she hated college protesters and hippies as much as she hated Communists.

What drove Ayn Rand into a fury was a nondescript, everyday human quality, an expression of generosity and selflessness. The prevailing sentiment in the Western world is that altruism is one of the essential characteristics of a mature, civilized person. We are born self-centered, and over time we achieve a degree of concern for others. We learn that selfishness is wrong. To Rand, the infant's me-centered view of the world is correct, selfishness is right, and altruism is the *antithesis* of everything decent and moral. Children are taught that loners needed to get with the program and join the team. "There is no 'I' in team," the saying goes. We need to share. In *The Fountainhead*, Ayn Rand teaches every alienated teenager, "It's okay to be a loner. You don't need friends. You don't have to share. It's your toy. You earned it. Keep it. Your little sister can get her own toy."

The hero of *The Fountainhead*, Howard Roark, is a loner and hyper-individualist, impervious to the opinions of others. He is not a team player. He has few friends, no family, no nurturing support group, no drinking buddies. At the beginning of the book he is celebrating his expulsion from architecture school. He doesn't care about anybody and expects no one to care about him. He is a man with no social conscience. He is totally selfish, and the mission of the book is to justify his stance as the purest expression of morality. Toward the end he blows up a public housing project when his ego is offended, and this act is justified at length. (The housing project is located in Astoria, Queens, but we get no sense of the city and its inhabitants—the Gail Wynand character is the most inauthentic child of the slums in the history of literature—and the American landscape is little more than a shadowland in *Atlas Shrugged*.)

Rand believed that the pursuit of selfishness would lead logically to a world in which government and the curse of collectivism is absent. *Atlas Shrugged* presents the case for such a paradise by showing what happens to America when the most capable people go on strike. To her, the people who mattered were the ones in charge, not slaving away at assembly lines and blast furnaces. Working people were replaceable; her "creators" were not. Her heroes were the accumulators of money; whether earned or ancestral made no difference. They were the oligarchs and technocrats, the intellectuals and the inventors. Everyone else, the wage slaves and the timecard-punchers, the vast majority of low-voltage personalities that inhabit a nation, were not Rand's people. She wanted no part of them. Their sufferings and aspirations were of no concern to her; she did not write about them unless they served to illuminate and justify her ideology. The mediocre, the weak, and the aged were clearly *untermenschen* to Rand. In one pivotal scene in *Atlas*, a train filled with the unworthy is stuck in a fume-filled railroad tunnel. It becomes a kind of gas chamber. Whittaker Chambers was blunt, but his assessment of *Atlas* was not a wild exaggeration.

Atlas Shrugged unveils her vision of the New Objectivist Man—greedy, godless, independent, uncaring, and cold-blooded. It is an alternate-universe *Modern Times* with Charlie Chaplin as the villain, 1,200 pages of daring capitalists outwitting obnoxious little tramps. It is a world of inherited wealth without philanthropy and adultery without guilt. Its central character is a thin, sexy (her heroes were always thin and sexy) railroad heiress who seeks to save her family business from a dystopian, business-hating America. The workers exploit the bosses in Rand's nightmare world. The government is not captured by industry but vice versa. Vicious stooges of the state hound and corrupt steel mill operators and oil drillers. Her principal villains are grasping bureaucrats and traitorous businessmen, shown collaborating with the Stalinist government to gain unfair advantage over their comrades.

Her ideal man is a thin, sexy inventor named John Galt. He emerges toward the end of *Atlas* the way Harry Lime steps out of a doorway halfway through *The Third Man,* only without the Welles charm. Her heroes are like Galt—steely, truthful, serious, given to philosophical monologues, purposeful, and constantly at work. If they have families they are parasitic nuisances. They do not have children.

Like a Commie in a bad 1950s Red-scare movie, Galt labors quietly to undermine America by spreading capitalist sedition and methodically pulling all the "producers" out on strike. Everybody else can just go to hell, and at the end of the book they do just that. They succumb as electrical power fails, trains are abandoned in the middle of vast deserts, and society collapses. The bureaucratic scum, crony capitalists, and blank-faced, semi-retarded ordinary people get precisely the doom they have earned.

When I read it years ago, *Atlas Shrugged* left me cold. To me it had the intellectual level of a pulp science-fiction novel. It was absurdly long and it was boring. It was far less radical than a lot of the pap that was being circulated at the time, and the novel's Objectivism made as little sense to me as the rest of the era's half-baked ideologies. I was a student at a public high school and then a public college, my tuition "looted," as Rand would have put it, from the taxpayers of New York City. In New York of the 1970s, the preoccupation of the citizenry was not the economy but crime, including real looting, and social unrest. Rand's concept of selfishness seemed to be an elaborate justification for oppressing the poor and middle class. When I thought of collectivism, I thought of the City University's free tuition and people like Jonas Salk, who otherwise would have been denied a college education. When Rand thought of collectivism, she thought of the starvation and chaos of postrevolutionary Russia.

Rand was part of the Russian bourgeoisie, a member of the privileged class. Her family was Jewish but spoke Russian and had little in common with the Yiddish-speaking, dirt-poor Jews who migrated to America in vast numbers, mostly before the Russian Revolution. They crossed the Atlantic out of necessity, for survival, in the steerage compartments of immigrant ships. They were superstitious and religious. They endured cattle-like processing at Ellis Island and then crammed into tenements to work in sweatshops and tinderbox factories. In America, a considerable number were radicalized by harsh conditions and became socialists or labor activists. But most cared little for politics and focused on work, family, and *shul*.

To Rand, they could have been Martians. She lived for politics, she wasn't interested in raising a family, and her atheism started early. Rand arrived in America in 1926, just after the immigration laws were tightened up to exclude Eastern Europeans like her. She traveled on a student visa, and her family's money meant that she could avoid the squalor of steerage (though immigration records indicate she traveled second class, not first class as contended by Randian propaganda).* She was welcomed by a prosperous branch of her family in Chicago, overstayed her visa like generations

* One cherished Rand myth is that her mother cashed in her jewelry so that Rand, née Alyssa Rosenbaum, could afford a first-class ticket to New York. It's one of the heart-tugging elements of the officially sanctioned documentary-propaganda film *Ayn Rand: A Sense of Life* (1997). She was definitely able to avoid steerage (third class). However, the ship's manifest shows her traveling in a comfortable but less luxurious second-class cabin. See entry for "Alice Rosenbaum," manifest for the SS *De Grasse*, February 19, 1926, accessed via Ancestry.com. Each page of the manifest spans two pages, and the top of the list on the second page of her listing reads: "This (yellow) sheet is for the listing of second-class passengers only."

of other unwelcome illegal aliens, and promptly fell in love with the country that didn't want her. Rand never worked in a sweatshop or factory, and was not endowed with empathy, so she saw factory owners and other capitalists not as ruthless exploiters, as they were viewed by their employees, but as heroes, the builders and brains of society.

The shabby, left-leaning masses of the Lower East Side—which elected a Socialist Party congressman a few years before she arrived—must have repelled Rand. We don't know; if she ever wrote about them, it hasn't been made public. Her heroes were businessmen, moguls, people like her father. Her family lost everything when the Bolsheviks stole her father's business. Her father's humiliation colored the rest of her life. She viewed government efforts to achieve socioeconomic parity as the use of "force" to oblige one group of people (people like her father) to help the less fortunate.

Rand used the government "gun" as a metaphor for everything the state might do that she didn't like.[9] To her there was no such thing as the violence of poverty and privation, perhaps because she always had rich relatives she could call upon for help (such as, for instance, when she needed an abortion).[10] It was a callousness and sense of entitlement that she carried with her for the rest of her life, and it permeates her ideology.

I grew up with emigrants from Russia, people who hated Russia as much as she did. But while I see similarities in temperament—these weren't always the nicest people in the world—the Russian-born émigrés I knew were shaped by suffering that Rand had never experienced. They were not talented or lucky. They were not screenwriters who had the good fortune to become friends with Cecil B. DeMille; they were common working people. If they were "entrepreneurs" (tailors or shoemakers) it was because their English language skills were inadequate for higher-paying jobs.

Atlas Shrugged was as foreign to their experience, and to mine, as the writings of Eldridge Cleaver—an author who, unlike Rand, was on assigned reading lists at the City College of New York. The only capitalists I ever saw were overworked storekeepers, snarling gypsy-cab drivers, and smack dealers on 135th Street. She saw a free, unregulated market as the defining institution of a free society. To me, a free, unregulated market was Benny the Goniff selling fruit from a stall in front of a butcher shop on Kingsbridge Road, screaming, "*Whoaaaaa!* We got melons here!" in a high-pitched Yiddish accent, sneaking rotten fruit into the bag and counting out ten when a dozen were ordered.

Benny's spirit drifted downtown to Wall Street. In place of Benny the Goniff as my archetypical capitalist was a new cast of characters: respected financial services firms cheating their customers in the back offices, promoters and gangsters pushing stocks, and hedge fund managers gaming the bond market as adeptly as Abbadabba Berman used to manipulate the pari-mutuel totals at racetracks for Dutch Schultz's numbers racket. In a previous era, without the benefit of education, they would have been pushcart peddlers or muffler salesmen or bookies. Instead of red-faced Benny in his stained undershirt there was the esteemed electronic-trading advocate Bernie Madoff in his monogrammed underwear. Both blended together in my perceptions, small-timer and big wheel.

Rand hovered under the radar after her fame petered out in the 1960s. She was no longer of any consequence. The horror that commentators and magazine writers expressed toward Rand softened into a kind of haughty condescension. The serious critics of Rand were few and, perhaps justifiably, marginalized. Why bother with a woman of such limited appeal? As I perused pro- and anti-Rand literature, I was struck by how few books were written by non-libertarians and non-Objectivists intent on critically analyzing her philosophy. One of the first, and probably the best, was by a noted psychoanalyst, Dr. Albert Ellis. Among his many books was a slim volume from 1968, updated in 2006, dissecting Objectivism in detail. It was a candle in the dark vastness, but it was largely ignored.[11] Ellis died in 2007, and Rand's most famous enemy on the right, Bill Buckley, passed a year later. It was as if Rand, though dead for more than twenty-five years, had outlived all of her major adversaries.

The media, while noting her surge in popularity after 2008, continued to treat her like a freak. *The New Yorker* ran a gently condescending Talk of the Town piece in April 2009 about a monthly gathering of Rand acolytes in Manhattan, portraying them as amusing eccentrics.[12] It was as if contempt was too obvious to express when the subject was Ayn Rand, much as it would be if the article had been about a gathering of neo-Nazis or flat-earth theorists. To most of her natural enemies, especially on the left, Rand was not worth the trouble. She was ignored when not ridiculed, her Objectivism dismissed as a kind of souped-up libertarianism, when it was addressed at all.

But out there in the Heartland, and in the world of right-wing media and talk radio, Rand was being taken very seriously. Her Objectivism seemed to thrive in the deprivation and fear of the post-financial-crisis recession. Her revival was slow but steady, and achieved apotheosis at the midpoint of the reviled Barack Obama's first term in office. In the fall of 2010, a Zogby poll conducted for the Ayn Rand Institute found that 29 percent of 2,100 adult respondents had read *Atlas Shrugged,* and half of them said the novel had affected their thinking on political or ethical issues.

The poll was the punch line of an elaborate, cruel joke: The failure of the markets to correct abuses—a glaring and oft-repeated weakness of capitalism—reinforced the influence of the heroine of capitalism.

To many of the new generation of Ayn Rand followers, Objectivism was not an ideology or philosophy, but a weapon to be used to advance their preexisting agendas. On his Fox News show, Glenn Beck had regularly condemned Wall Street and especially Goldman Sachs, sketching out elaborate conspiracy theories on his blackboard. Yet he simultaneously promoted the books and theories of a woman who cherished Wall Street. Nowhere on that blackboard did he ever disclose that the cochairperson of the Ayn Rand Institute was an associate general counsel of Goldman Sachs.[13] With Beck, John Stossel, and other Fox commentators advancing her ideology and invoking her name, Rand was a symbol of the new thinking that was required to beat Obama and restore business to its rightful place of supremacy.

Cutting taxes and resuming the march of deregulation—to the extent that it was ever interrupted—was not enough. Business now was to be the *moral* leader of America.

Rand would lead the way to a new nation, a better nation, one that paid homage to its "job-creating" businesspeople and denigrated its government. Early in 2009, sales of *Atlas Shrugged* tripled over the year before.[14] During the years that followed, even Rand's obscure early works and essay anthologies, dull and pedantic as they often were, sold amazingly well. Among the hottest sellers was her tribute to self-indulgence, *The Virtue of Selfishness.* This collection of dense essays, published in 1964, is one of the most popular books on philosophy and ethics in the English language. That's right. I don't mean one of the most popular books at the Ayn Rand Bookstore in Irvine, California. I mean *the English language.*

In 1999, when Rand was far less popular than she is today, a reader survey by Random House put *The Virtue of Selfishness* at the top of the list of the best nonfiction books published since 1900. Number three was *Objectivism: The Philosophy of Ayn Rand,* published in 1991 by Rand's "intellectual heir" and longtime associate Leonard Peikoff (pronounced "pea-cough"), cofounder of the Ayn Rand Institute. In a concurrent survey, readers voted *Atlas Shrugged* the very best novel published since 1900. That kind of survey can be easily rigged, but it was not far off the mark. Amazon.com sales rankings, even before they were boosted by an *Atlas Shrugged* movie released in 2011, have demonstrated that Rand's appeal is truly widespread. *Virtue* consistently ranks among the best-selling books at Amazon on the subject of "ethics and morality," well ahead of conventional tomes like *Profiles in Courage* by John F. Kennedy.

Rand once caused an immense ruckus by calling Kennedy's New Frontier "fascist." Now, a half-century later, Rand is winning against the people who viewed her as a crackpot when she said that. It is her posthumous act of revenge against Bennett Cerf, the Random House publisher who refused to publish her rant on the "Fascist New Deal," in which she compared Kennedy to Adolf Hitler.[15] *Virtue* also usually ranks high in Amazon sales rankings of books on epistemology, the theory of knowledge.

Since Rand never wrote a comprehensive outline of her philosophy, *Atlas Shrugged* is the basic text for Rand followers. A total of 600,000 copies of the book were sold in 2009, an all-time record. In that year, the ARI gave away, free of charge, 347,000 copies of the book to high schools in the United States and Canada. In April 2011 the book hit number four in the Amazon rankings when a movie version of the novel was released. When *GQ* magazine called Rand "2009's most influential author," it wasn't hyperbole. The free-market thinkers Friedrich Hayek and Ludwig von Mises surged in popularity, too, but neither could match Rand in sheer longevity, appeal to the young, and accessibility of her writings to a broad national audience. *The Economist* found a relationship between sales of *Atlas Shrugged* and hiccups in the economy and bailout announcements.[16]

The Tea Party movement was directly inspired by Rand, and in a manner far more fundamental than the "Who is John Galt?" and "Ayn Rand Was Right" signs proliferating at rallies. The first Tea Party rallies were inspired by a self-described Ayn Rander[17] named Rick Santelli, and Rand is as much a part of the Tea Party movement's soul as Ronald Reagan, Glenn Beck, and Jesus Christ. Author and essayist David Frum observed in early 2010 that the Tea Party was trying "to reinvent the GOP as the 'party of Ayn Rand.' "[18]

By embracing Rand's vision of laissez-faire, no-government capitalism, the Tea Party was the latest variation on a long-running theme in American politics, described by Thomas Frank in his 2004 book *What's the Matter with Kansas?* At the time, voters were persuaded to pull the lever for candidates dedicated to the agenda of multinational corporations because they seemed like ordinary folks who despised Hollywood. Today, the pro-business agenda requires no camouflage. After the worst economic calamity since the Great Depression, in 2010 voters regularly acted against their economic self-interests, voting into office politicians who openly favored big business and Wall Street over the people in their communities being foreclosed-upon, evicted, and thrown out on the street. Capitalism was a heroic force, to be defended from Obama.

The difference from 2004 was Rand. She made it not only emotionally satisfying but deeply *moral* to take positions that sided with the super-rich. There was little serious pushback from critics of Rand, only sporadic attempts to assert their own values or the morality of their position.

It was a missed opportunity of historic dimensions. The financial crisis could have been the beginning of a new era in business, an era of reform and invigorated regulation. Instead, it petered out into passivity and inaction, as voters elected candidates who were acolytes of Ayn Rand or fellow travelers on the far right. They seized control of the House of Representatives, doomed meaningful Wall Street reform, and threatened funding of regulatory agencies and rollback of the feeble reforms that were enacted.

The new stars of the Republican Party were either Rand followers or otherwise channeling her views. Ron Johnson, when he ran for the Senate in Wisconsin in 2010, beat Democratic incumbent Russ Feingold on a platform that was saturated with Ayn Rand doctrine. Johnson said that his "foundational book" was *Atlas Shrugged,* stoutly defending Rand when the subject was broached in a televised debate with incumbent Feingold. Mike Lee, the far-right Tea Party candidate elected to the Senate from Utah, adhered to Rand's ideology and counted her books as among his favorites.[19] Rand Paul (not named after Ayn Rand, despite the rumor), spoke out against Title II of the Civil Rights Act of 1964, which requires public accommodations to serve everyone, regardless of race, color, or creed. He later backtracked, but it was a magical moment for Rand followers. For the first time in decades, a candidate of a major party had endorsed Ayn Rand's view that the government had no right to tell businessmen not to discriminate. Even the undercurrent of violence that could be found in some of Sharron Angle's statements when she ran for the U.S. Senate in Nevada, her "Second Amendment" insinuations of armed rebellion, had precedent in the killings, bombings, gassings, and piracy that form an essential part of *Atlas Shrugged.*

In 2011, a Rand acolyte named Paul Ryan, a Republican from Wisconsin, became chairman of the House Budget Committee. Ryan once said, at a gathering in honor of Rand, that "the reason I got involved in public service, by and large, if I had to credit one thinker, one person, it would be Ayn Rand."[20] Ryan said that Obama's economic policies sounded like "something right out of an Ayn Rand novel." It would have surprised no one who understood Rand's ideology when Ryan defied conventional politics and targeted Medicare in April 2011. Medicare was on the Rand hit list before the program even existed.

Ryan's push to overhaul Medicare aroused stiff opposition, but rarely was the case for keeping Medicare—not the pragmatic but the moral case—ever asserted. Moral arguments were a Randian preserve. In a *Chicago Tribune* opinion piece in May 2011, in the midst of denunciations of his Medicare plan, Ryan stood fast, and salted his argument with Rand-flavored rhetoric. His plan, he said, would let "seniors act as value-conscious consumers in a transparent and competitive market."[21] To Rand the market was supreme, and consumers existed not as individuals with little bargaining power, but as a mighty economic force requiring no protection from government. Ryan's plan was an incremental step toward a goal long favored by Objectivists—abolition of Medicare.

Rand had become the Tom Joad of the right. One could almost hear her saying: "Wherever there's a fight where rich people can get richer, I'll be there. Wherever there's a regulator beating up on a banker, I'll be there."

Rand was there in 2010 and 2011, and she is with us today.

Rand is there as Wall Street seeks to dismantle the few restraints that were imposed after the financial crisis.

Rand is there as the right tries to eliminate Obama's health care plan, uses the debt limit to extract immense spending cuts, and seeks to turn back the clock to the days before the New Deal and Great Society.

Rand is there with every effort to threaten Congress with gridlock to advance the right's agenda.

Rand is with us, as pugnacious as ever, on the thirtieth anniversary of her death. March 6, 2012 falls in the midst of the most ideologically polarized presidential campaign since Richard Nixon crushed George McGovern in 1972. She and her followers are primed and ready. But what about the rest of us?

You may have guessed that I am not a fan of Ayn Rand, but if you're expecting an anti-Rand polemic you're likely to be disappointed. In researching this book, I came away with respect for the dedication and sincerity of her followers, and an appreciation of Rand's ability to tap into the emotions of the American people and influence the national dialogue.

It's easy to lampoon Rand and her acolytes as a fringe cult. Her inner circle probably met the definition of a cult in the past,[22] and some of those traits linger on in the highest echelons of the Rand movement. But dismissing Rand and her followers as cultists ignores the strength of her appeal for nearly seven decades—not to crackpots but to intelligent, educated, even brilliant people. Alan Greenspan in the early 1950s, when he fell under the sway of Rand, was one of the rising stars of economics. What is it about her that people like Greenspan find so alluring?

In writing this book I was acutely aware of my own ideological baggage: a long-held belief that capitalism needs to be controlled. I this baggage into the world of Ayn Rand as if I was boarding an old Trailways bus. It weighed heavily upon me as I resumed the journey that I interrupted when I was a teenager.

I would need to read her books and essays. I would need to meet her acolytes. It was my solemn and distasteful journalistic duty. I expected that I would hate it.

I had underestimated Ayn Rand.

CHAPTER ONE

The Believers

They knew it, those Objectivists. One of them said to me, "I hope we have an impact on you." He knew.

That remark was made to me at one of the monthly meetings of Ayn Rand followers in Manhattan. I was becoming a regular participant. Oddly, I was liking it and growing fond of the people who attended. Even odder was that I was enjoying her novels and becoming vaguely simpatico to her beliefs, even though they were contrary to everything I had been taught and experienced since infancy. Her novels were compelling and persuasive in ways that I couldn't quite put my finger on. The publisher Bennett Cerf had a similar reaction to Rand as a person. He said in his memoirs that "I found myself liking her, though I had not expected to."[1]

Atlas Shrugged was on my coffee table, gathering dust, for several weeks before I picked it up. I had a copy of one of its innumerable softcover editions, with a foreword by her aide, heir, and sidekick Leonard Peikoff. Eventually I forced myself to read it. Initially, I was in agreement with my teenage self that this book wasn't very good.

I was repelled by Rand's leaden phraseology and too-cute way of naming her characters. The villains have names like "Balph" and "Slagenhop." A public official who advocates mooching is named "Wesley Mouch." It was Dickensian without being witty. They are physically repulsive and they spout inanities; clay pigeons tossed in the air so Rand could blast them with a shotgun.

For example: "A very young girl in white evening gown asked timidly, 'What is the essence of life, Mr. Eubank?' 'Suffering,' said Balph Eubank, 'defeat and suffering.'" Eubank favors a law limiting the sale of any book to ten thousand copies. But what if it's a good story? "'Plot is a primitive vulgarity in literature,' said Balph Eubank, contemptuously."[2]

Some of my notes as I read the book: "Implausible." "Anti-American." "Defense needs/establishment absent." (Odd for a book published at the height of the Cold War.) "Characters live in moral vacuum." "Contempt for poor."

But then, as the pages flipped by, my resistance eroded. I began to admire her skill at pacing such an immense work of fiction. The Hollywood screenwriter in her was becoming evident. I felt ashamed. It was as if I was savoring *Mein Kampf,* chortling along with *der Führer* as he expounded wittily on the disease-carrying vermin that were my ancestral burden. I carried around this massive book in a tote bag, keeping its title hidden as I walked the collectivist streets of Greenwich Village, avoiding the eyes of passersby.

It became plain to me that her appeal is more than just political. Her novels serve collectively as the Big Book of Objectivism, a self-help manual as well as a work of fiction and ideological hornbook. Embedded in her work is a singular view of the psychology of human relationships, sans family. She never had children and didn't provide much insight into the parent-child relationship, but she certainly had strong opinions on how to deal with moochers, sorry SOBs, and louses that might be found within one's family. The basic message is that one jettisons them without a second thought. And as for adultery: What of it? What's good enough for Hank Rearden is surely good enough for any follower of his exploits as a thin, sexy steel manufacturer, long-suffering breadwinner for an ungrateful family and Dagny's main squeeze.

Racy sex scenes, steamy romantic triangles, and an unconventional view of nuptial relations are the sugar that *Atlas Shrugged* and *The Fountainhead* spread on the sour grapefruit of philosophical exposition. Neither is an homage to family values, to say the least. In both novels, all of the major characters are isolated, existential figures, sort of what you'd find in a film noir. Not an Ozzie nor a Harriet nor a Ward Cleaver was to be found in Ayn Rand's fantasy world. Few children, fewer behaving like children. No Wally, no Beaver. June Cleaver would have been a hard-charging exec or the inventor of an ore-refining process. The Fred Rutherfords and other second-handers and collectivists in the Cleaver family circle would have been treated with the kind of cold contempt that only a Rand character could dish out.

Atlas and *Fountainhead* made it easy to love individualism and no-government capitalism because it was a world of healthy, young heroes and repulsive villains. There were no inconvenient elderly defecating upon themselves in nursing homes. No paraplegic war veterans without means of support. No refugees from far-off lands with unmarketable skills. No KKK rallies. No exploitation of the poor. No rat-infested slums. No racial minorities. Poverty and unemployment are a distant, alien presence. The only member of the underclass Dagny encounters is a railroad hobo who turns out to be an Objectivist with a lead on Galt. There is nobody and nothing to interrupt the monotonous picture, nothing to upset the stereotypes, no migrant workers toiling for pennies. Rand, acting as God, made those people invisible while she whitened the hearts of American business. The only societal problem in the world of *Atlas Shrugged* is that government is mean to business and unfair to the wealthy.

The two inanely skewed Rand opuses were the intellectual backstory of the group meetings that I attended. The members were polite and tolerant if one was not up to speed on Rand's works, just as they were reasonably courteous to the occasional collectivist who happened by, but it was hard to follow the discussions without having a working knowledge of her novels and nomenclature. "Checking premises" was one common catchphrase. Rand liked to say that people who disagreed with her were utilizing incorrect premises in their thought processes.

I was introduced to these meetings by my initial tour guide to Objectivism, a man who was literally a tour guide. His name was Frederick Cookinham, and in his spare time he gave walking tours of "Ayn Rand's New York."[3] He is the author of a rambling but intriguing self-published volume of Ayn Rand-inspired thought, *The Age of Rand: Imagining an Objectivist Future World*. Despite the title, it spends more time mulling Rand's philosophy than imagining the future. It's a thoughtful book, at times amusing, a quality not often found in Objectivist literature. It takes a skeptical attitude toward the keepers of the Objectivist flame at the Ayn Rand Institute, and is far from hero-worshiping when it comes to Rand herself. For example, he points out that though Rand opposed racism, "there remain so many references in her writings to the 'pest holes of Asia' and 'naked savages' who want foreign aid from the United States, that her assumption is clear, despite her actually defining a 'savage' as someone who believes in magic."

Fred was disturbed by Rand's opinion of Mahatma Gandhi, as contained in a 1948 letter from Rand to right-wing writer Isabel Paterson one week after Gandhi was killed.[4] She called his assassination "an almost cruel piece of historical irony" and said that it was almost as if a higher intelligence in the universe had carried out a "nice sardonic gesture." Rand said, "Here was a man who spent his life fighting to get the British out of India in the name of peace, brotherly love and non-violence. He got what he asked for."

Fred was nonplussed. "What is she saying here?" Seemed pretty obvious to me: Gandhi was an altruist and got the fate that he deserved. It was a good example of the cold-bloodedness that she so often displayed. Fred doesn't resolve his dilemma, and points out, somewhat dubiously, that Rand and Gandhi are actually "allies," at least in a limited sense, as both believed that the ends justify the means. Personally I can't conceive of two individuals with less in common, even if Gandhi did display individuality of an almost Roarkish dimension.

It was clear from reading his book, and from joining him on his walking tour, that Fred was an independent thinker, certainly no cultist.[5] I met him for lunch at an Au Bon Pain sandwich-and-coffee joint in Lower Manhattan, not far from where Rand was famously photographed with Federal Hall in the background, wearing a solid-gold dollar-sign brooch.

Fred was in his mid-fifties, had a salt-and-pepper beard and a disconcerting resemblance to Richard Dreyfuss. He worked as a proofreader for a law firm when not giving tours, and sang in a light-opera company in his spare time. Like most people I met who sipped from the cup of Rand, Fred first stumbled upon her books at an early age. He was eleven when he found *Anthem*, one of Rand's early novellas, and *Atlas Shrugged* in his brother's bookcase. He eagerly consumed the shorter book, which was the story of a tyrannical society in which collectivism runs rampant, a harsher version of the fantasy world of *Atlas Shrugged*, in which people are referred to by numbers and the word "I" is eliminated. *Atlas* was far too big for him to read immediately, but the book intrigued him, and he began reading it when he was thirteen. He plowed right through it.

At the State University of New York in Cortland, he told me over our sandwiches, "the first thing I did was join the Libertarian Party." At the time, libertarians were a freewheeling, quasi-anarchist group of people, and not yet quite so neatly folded into the conservative movement as they are today. At one point Daniel Ellsberg of Pentagon Papers fame gave a speech on campus. Fred got his autograph on an issue of *Reason* magazine that featured an interview with Ellsberg. Fred recalled that Ellsberg told him that *Reason*'s libertarian views were close to his own. That was understandable because libertarianism, especially in its early days, had a serious appeal to the left as well as the right. Libertarians opposed encroachments on one's freedom in the style of the New Left, and received some notoriety for advocating legalization of marijuana. (Rand did, too, though it was hardly a central plank in her platform.)

I ran by him the name of a *Reason* writer I once knew, but Fred hadn't heard of him. "I don't keep up on the news," Fred told me. Instead, he spent his off hours reading books. Indeed, Fred was a quiet sort, studious and well-informed on historical minutiae. He was a regular at the bimonthly meetings of the American Revolution Roundtable.

Fred felt sufficiently simpatico to Rand's philosophy during her lifetime that he attended her funeral in 1982, braving the cold of the northern Westchester cemetery to see her buried beside her long-suffering husband, a kindhearted, alcoholic former actor named Frank O'Connor. Fred met Rand only once—"barely," he said—just to get her autograph. It was 1978, and Leonard Peikoff had just given a lecture on the "Basic Principles of Objectivism" at the Hotel Pennsylvania. Rand was in attendance, as she often was when a member of her inner circle was speaking. Fred found that Rand was just as she was described in the press. "Irascible," he said. "Short fuse." He found it amusing.

I asked what Rand meant to him, and Fred was, unsurprisingly, philosophical. "Because I was so young, there wasn't very much there for Rand to compete against," he told me. "I often wondered how I would have turned out if I hadn't happened to pick up that book or had happened to pick up some other book."

Rand's influence on Fred was a bit of a surprise to me: She actually made him less anti-union and less of a cold warrior. He was from a conservative, Republican household in Upstate New York. Very "white bread, mayonnaise," Middle American. His father had a management position at a road construction company, and negotiated with a muscle-flexing Teamsters Union then run by Jimmy Hoffa. Unsurprisingly, the elder Cookinham took a dim view of unions. "It was Rand who got me out of that mentality, and got me more sympathetic to unions. She made the point that as people have a right to form companies, so they also have a right to form unions."

Fred was right. Rand was opposed to the Taft–Hartley Act, a postwar measure that weakened unions and enabled states to enact "right to work" laws that prohibited companies from firing workers who wouldn't join unions. In a 1949 letter, she objected to "government's 'right to curb a union'—or to curb anyone's economic activities."[6]

"People don't expect that," said Fred. "A lot of libertarians and Objectivists I don't think get this. They have a kind of instinctive fear and hatred of unions." It is instinctive, apparently, for many on the right to feel that companies can bind together in their own rational self-interest—Rand opposed antitrust laws—but that the same actions are bad when carried out by their employees.

Rand, he said, also kept him from falling into the paranoid "Buckleyite" Cold War worldview, by not subscribing to conspiracy theories and the anti-Communist hysteria of the times. He pointed to one of her essays, "Extremism, Or the Art of Smearing," which appeared in her anthology *Capitalism: The Unknown Ideal,* as an example. "That, by the way, is the only place in any of her writings in which she mentioned Joe McCarthy, and then only parenthetically, just to say 'I am not a supporter of Joe McCarthy,'" he noted. Fred's argument had a kernel of truth, except that the purpose of the essay was to attack *critics* of McCarthyism, not to knock McCarthy or the paranoia he engendered.*

Fred was actively involved in the Libertarian Party in New York through the mid-1990s. He worked in the thankless trenches of politics, passing out leaflets on the inhospitable sidewalks of New York. Over time he became disillusioned. Libertarians in New York forever occupy a tiny

* Rand did say in the "Extremism, Or the Art of Smearing" essay (first published in 1964) that she was "not an admirer of Senator McCarthy." However, other accounts portray her as a supporter of McCarthy. See Heller, *Ayn Rand and the World She Made,* pp. 246–47. In the "Extremism" essay she has no particular bone to pick with McCarthyism—she says that it was never "proven" that McCarthy had engaged in trumped-up charges against people. The purpose of the essay, in fact, was to denounce use of terms like "McCarthyism" and "extremist," which she viewed as smears applied to people who were merely anti-Communist. Hence the "smearing" title of her essay, which attacks smearing of the right, not by the right.

substratum of the local political scene, with little impact on the electorate or the political dialogue. "I saw a lack of seriousness of purpose," he told me. Fred had a similarly negative opinion of the Tea Party, which he dismissed as "amateur stuff," with even less of a future than the Libertarian Party. "A flash in the pan," was his verdict. "A media creation."

Fred clued me in to the regularly scheduled meetings of New York City Objectivists, which were held the last Sunday of every month. The regular venue was the Midtown Restaurant, a coffee shop on East 55th Street that was as bland and generic as its name. Sitting at tables pushed together near the front were about twenty mostly middle-aged men and women, some of whom were Rand followers since the 1960s, when her deputy Nathaniel Branden gave lectures at the McAlpin Hotel and other venues in Manhattan, usually on or around 34th Street. Rand lived nearby, in the dowdy Murray Hill neighborhood on the east side of Manhattan, during the last three decades of her life. The offices of the Nathaniel Branden Institute, an early version of the Ayn Rand Institute, were in close proximity.

Murray Hill was the ground zero of Objectivism for Rand's last three decades in New York. Rand lived the life of a modest retiree or reasonably successful freelance writer, not a dowager. Her last home was in a nondescript apartment building at 120 East 34th Street, and she previously lived in a sprawling postwar residential monstrosity at 36 East 36th Street. Some of her closest followers, including Nathaniel and Barbara Branden (ranking second and third in the Objectivist hierarchy), lived nearby. I was surprised we weren't meeting somewhere in Murray Hill or near Wall Street, given their historical links to Objectivism and abundance of inexpensive eateries.

This was the same regular Objectivist gathering that was profiled in *The New Yorker* a year earlier. Expecting hard-eyed right-wing fanatics, I was surprised that these were mellow, low-key individuals. The atmosphere was academic, intellectual, about what one would find at a Mensa meeting. There was the same thrown-together quality. A former tennis pro here, a hedge fund manager there.

The Ayn Rand group meetings were an ad hoc successor to the Collective, which was the self-consciously ironic name that Rand and her acolytes gave to weekly gatherings at Rand's apartment in the 1950s and 1960s. The Collective is probably best known for being a kind of Objectivist Jordan River, at which Alan Greenspan was baptized in the faith. The direct Rand connection to Manhattan had eroded ever since the Comintern of the movement, the ARI, set up shop in the more congenially right-wing environs of Orange County, California, a few years after Rand's death.

The meetings had a structure. First the members of the group introduced themselves for the benefit of newcomers, and then there was general discussion as people dug into their late lunches. (Separate checks were given despite the size of the group, as was suitable for people who rejected collectivism in all its forms.) I noticed that introductions tended to dominate the meetings, as members used the opportunity to expound on the events of the day, discuss books they'd read, and announce upcoming events in the Objectivist community.

The August 2010 meeting was one day after the Glenn Beck Restoring Honor rally, and I expected the Randers to feel gratified and enthusiastic. Beck was a big fan of Rand. He mentioned her favorably on a number of occasions, and his attacks on churches promoting social justice could have easily emerged from Rand herself. But nobody talked about the rally initially. These were talkers, intellectuals, not rally-goers. Presiding was Benny Pollak, who was originally from Chile and worked for a Wall Street bank. He also was a founding member of the New York City Skeptics, which cast a gimlet eye at pseudoscience, quackery, and the like. I'd long been attracted to the skepticism movement, and it never occurred to me that there might be synergy between skepticism and Objectivism. The commonality was distaste for mysticism, which Rand mentioned frequently and with her customary contempt.

I sat between Fred and Don Hauptman, a cheery brown-bearded fellow. Don contributed occasional articles on Rand-related subjects to *The*

New Individualist, an Objectivist newsletter, and once spent $50,000 at Christie's to buy the original galley proofs from an interview Rand gave to *Playboy* in 1964. "I'm comfortable," he explained to me. Opposite me sat Sandi, a young paralegal at an immigration law firm who had just read *Atlas Shrugged* a second time, "and I don't think there's anything in it I disagree with." A few seats over was Iris Bell, who had done some graphic design work for Rand, and was included in an oral history that was about to be published by the ARI. She and her husband, Paul, who first encountered Objectivism listening to a Nathaniel Branden radio broadcast in 1960, were the most senior Objectivists at the meeting. Their views, seasoned by years of study, were granted a certain deference.

Except for the Rand preoccupation of almost everyone in attendance, these were the kind of people one might find at any ordinary Manhattan dinner party, though the atmosphere was considerably more sober. The same could have been said about the Collective, I imagine, except for the added element of Rand herself dominating the proceedings. Most of the Collective members were friends and relatives of Barbara Branden, and many were Canadians like the Brandens. Winnipeg-born Leonard Peikoff was Barbara's cousin. Her best friend Joan Mitchell was briefly married to Greenspan, and brought the future Fed chairman into the fold. The demographics of both old and new Ayn Rand salons were uniformly Caucasian and largely Jewish. (Two of the Objectivists in attendance at the Midtown Restaurant had flirted with Orthodox Judaism before being rescued by Objectivism.) One difference was age: The latter-day Collectivists were considerably older than the twentysomethings who used to crowd around Rand.

It was plain to see that these were ordinary, apparently well-adjusted, somewhat brighter-than-average people who were secure and happy in their Objectivism. Adherence to Objectivism provided these people with a clear ideology and sense of purpose. The monthly meetings were a sanctuary from the collectivist horrors of modern American life, sometimes recounted in gruesome detail (such as one member's unpleasant encounter with ruffian union members on the subway).

The introductions melded into meandering conversations on various subjects. Andy George, a musician who was inspired to the Rand cause by Rush, a rock band whose members were Rand buffs, brought to the attention of the group an "unbelievable environmentalist program" he saw on the Planet Green cable TV channel called *No Impact Man*. It was a documentary about a New York family that for one year avoided all products that impacted negatively on the environment. Andy described an Internet post he had written excoriating this harmless little experiment as an example of hypocritical altruism at its worst. One low point, Andy said, comes when the subject of the documentary "is admonished by an overfed small-time Greenwich Village organic farmer whom [he] admires. He's quietly scolded for not being altruistic enough, like a scene between Ellsworth M. Toohey and Peter Keating"—two despised characters in *The Fountainhead*.

The group was generally optimistic about the future of Objectivism. Paul Bell pointed out that he was pleasantly surprised to learn that a late-night radio host, Doug McIntyre of "Red Eye Radio," had read all of Rand's books, and had subscribed to an Objectivist newsletter during her lifetime.

Benny, while acknowledging that Rand was ubiquitous, wondered whether people were interested in her philosophy or saw her only as a "flag-bearer for capitalism." It was a good question. Many people quoted Rand, to praise or discredit her, but how many actually were acquainted with her views?

Fred agreed that it was hard to get people to talk about the aspects of her doctrine that did not involve economics. "Not so many people are prepared to talk about epistemology, for example," he said. That troubled Benny, because in the national dialogue involving capitalism and the role of government, "there's never a discussion of what's right. Is it moral?"

Income taxes, for instance. "They're immoral." Benny had a point: The national dialogue over taxes and spending rarely crossed over into a discussion of morality. Was it right to tax the rich at a higher rate than the poor? Was it wrong not to do so?

There was a murmur of agreement, and someone pointed out that many people nowadays are like Gail Wynand in *The Fountainhead*—"a practical guy who's not in touch at all with the abstract aspect of what he's doing"—thereby leaving himself open to being manipulated by the diabolical Ellsworth Toohey. (In the book, Toohey is a powerful architecture critic for Wynand's newspaper, and uses the column to smear Howard Roark and as a platform to advance the evils of altruism and collectivism. By the end of the book he turns his venom on Wynand and destroys his newspaper.)

After a time the conversation drifted to how the old immigrant self-help societies and Underwriters Laboratories (UL), a private safety-certification lab, exemplified how government doesn't need to be involved in ensuring the health and safety of the public. To the group, the solution seemed blindingly obvious. "Why not have a UL for cosmetics?" one group member suggested.

I didn't know much about UL, but I had fair knowledge of the Independent Bukarester Sick Aid Association, to which my father's family once belonged. It was founded in the early part of the twentieth century by Jewish immigrants from Bucharest, Romania. The group provided members with rudimentary health and burial benefits, not as a political statement but because these were poor people who had no access to health care. Rich people didn't need health and burial societies because they could afford doctors and cemetery plots. By the 1970s it lingered on as a burial society, having long before purchased plots at cemeteries in Queens and Long Island for use by its aging members. But the "sick aid" part of the association's mandate was long supplanted by private insurance and Medicare.

I'm sure that if I'd suggested back then that "the society," as they called it, might solve the nation's health care crisis, I'd have been considered meshugah.[7]

Such was the reality of the old immigrant aid societies. They were formed out of necessity, when America had no social safety net for the poor and elderly, and they disbanded because the government did, eventually, provide medical benefits for senior citizens. They were relics of a bygone era. The Rand group, however, was hot on the idea. "When government doesn't want people to know about alternatives to government, they don't teach it in the schools," Fred pointed out. Someone else piped up that he took the Tenement Museum tour on the Lower East Side and that it was completely politicized, with progress in society credited only to the "regulators and government, and not the inventors and industrialists."

Eventually the group got around to discussing Glenn Beck's Restoring Honor rally. The warmth and fuzziness that I expected were absent. Beck's embrace of Rand wasn't mentioned by anyone.

The group was worried. The problem was fundamental, and seemed to be a real sticking point. "Glenn Beck keeps bringing up religion and mystical stuff," said one. "Nobody wants to question their premises at all," chimed in Judi, a technology project manager at a Wall Street firm and part-time actress. Larry, a construction manager from Long Island, pointed out that Beck once said that what people need to do is "not follow reason but turn to God. And that's very destructive."

Larry was referring to one of Objectivism's principal tenets, one of the characteristics that sets it apart from other right-wing credos. Objectivism is ardently atheistic, lumping in all religions with faith healers, mystics, and voodoo-doll-pin-stickers. Rand felt that religion was antithetical to reason, and couldn't stomach the altruistic doctrines of the major religions, especially Christianity.

It was plain that Beck's embrace of religion presented Ayn Rand acolytes with a serious dilemma. His support sold books and kept the Rand name in the public eye to an extent that nobody else could approach. In early 2010 he devoted an entire program to *Atlas Shrugged*, featuring Yaron Brook, Israeli-born executive director of the Ayn Rand Institute. All the ARI's PR efforts, and even the movie version of *Atlas Shrugged*, could not come close to the publicity that Beck lavished on Rand.

I was hearing some of the same expressions of concern about Beck as one might encounter at a progressive political gathering. Judi wondered if Beck was "pushing people in the direction of rationality or in the direction of fear, uncertainty, and doubt. Therefore 'follow me, I can guide you.'" Rationality is one of the nonnegotiable components of Rand's belief system (irrational as much of her views might seem to non-acolytes).

"Glenn Beck scares me," said an older lady, a longtime follower of the movement. "If he came to power he would become a demagogue."

I sensed a kind of stirring here, a recognition of fundamental incompatibility that couldn't easily be overcome. My feeling was confirmed when Larry recounted how he formed a Tea Party group on Long Island in early 2009, just as the movement was beginning. In doing so, he said, he put aside his Objectivist ideology. "I had no one to discuss it with," he said. "I didn't know what to say to these people." He found that the Tea Party rank and file was upset with Obama, but that was about it. There was no philosophical content to their dissatisfaction. "I really wasn't sure. Were they really looking for individual rights and freedom, or were they looking for the resurrection of the Republican Party?" The more he talked to Tea Party people, the more his doubts grew.

"The religious people—I think a lot of them may be Objectivists at heart," said Benny, "but they still have to toe the Republican party line."

Paul Bell stood up to speak. "Rand says that change comes about between elections, not during the election itself, that it's what happens on the ground, between the elections," he said. "Yesterday I gave over three hours of my life to watch the entire Restoring Honor rally, to watch the entire proceedings, because I wanted to understand what was going on over there." Paul said that he might have found an event like that frightening a year or two before, but no longer. "I happen to like Glenn Beck on balance. There's a lot of things to dislike about him, not the least of which is his overt turn recently toward return to God. But Beck does appeal to a lot of people." Paul spoke admiringly of Sarah Palin. He liked her speech at the rally. "This is someone to take seriously. This is not a lightweight." Whether you like her or not, "that's where some help is coming as far as fighting off the push toward almost total collectivism."

"But don't you find her incredibly anti-intellectual, though?" asked Judi.

"No," Paul said firmly.

"Anti-education?"

"No," said Paul. "Is she the world's leading intellectual or authority on the body politic? The answer there is obvious. But is she essentially a strong person of character who is unintimidated by what's going on?"

Paul's preliminary assessment of the rally was that Beck "had the right diagnosis but not necessarily the right cure." The problem, he said, was "that so many people feel the need for religion now," which he attributed to "a growing sense of amorality in the culture."

"As far as why I no longer feared what happened yesterday—listen up folks," Paul said. The cluttering of dishes and side talk stopped.

"Those people right now are our only hope. It's them that are going to save the country. There's more of them than there are of us."

"Who are them?" someone asked.

"The people who believe in God."

The group was momentarily stunned. It was like a Hassidic Jewish sect in Williamsburg hearing that the only hope for redemption could be found in the Baptist church down the street.

Paul continued, "It's a religious awakening as a stand-in for philosophical morality." There were murmurs of agreement. "The most urgent thing right now is to get rid of the cretins, in both political parties, who are hell-bent on destroying the country."

"The country?" an older lady interjected. "The world."

CHAPTER TWO

The Pre-Objectivist Objectivist

Iris Bell was the closest to Rand of any of the Midtown Restaurant Objectivists, so I was anxious to meet her. She wasn't a member of the Collective like Greenspan, but Rand had been a focus of her life for more than five decades. I also got a sense that she was an independent sort, and would be able to give me a rounded perspective.

Iris was willing (or at least not unwilling) to be interviewed, but she put me off for some time. She was busy with various things, among them her monthly duties as organizer of the Junto, the libertarian-Objectivist group founded and sponsored by the options trader and author Victor Niederhoffer. I was having the same experience with Yaron Brook, whose PR guy Kurt Kramer had been deflecting my fervent e-mail and telephone entreaties like the overprotective mother of a delicate Southern belle. I had higher hopes for Iris, however, as she had just been burned in an interview for a sanitized ARI oral history of Rand, and this was her opportunity to set the record straight.

Iris was cherished by the Midtown Restaurant Objectivists because she was a living link to Rand. The personal connection, and the seniority and Rand knowledge of some of its members, made the meetings a valuable source of Randian insights. I noticed that the older members of the group, including Iris, tended to separate the character of Rand and the people around her from her Objectivist ideology, which they supported wholeheartedly. This added to their credibility, and made attending the meetings more valuable for my purposes as a semi-detached observer.

Iris was at or near seventy but the years had been kind to her, and you could see that she had been quite a looker when she knew Rand forty-plus years ago. She was a graphic designer, and in Rand's day had designed the cover of the newsletter that Rand and Nathaniel Branden jointly published before their stormy breakup. She made a brief appearance in Anne Heller's Rand biography.

The impression I got from attending a few meetings was that Iris was no fan of the ARI or its leaders, and was annoyed by the stranglehold of that institution on Rand's legacy. She took pains to point out to me, when we chatted once after a meeting, that Rand's published diaries and journals had been expurgated by the ARI. In her 2009 Rand biography, Jennifer Burns calls the omissions "significant and problematic."[1]

Iris had her own experience with Objectivist censorship. She was one of the former Rand associates interviewed for *100 Voices*, an anthology of interviews that was published by the Ayn Rand Oral History Project, a branch of the ARI, late in 2010.[2] Iris spoke bluntly during her interview with the ARI writer. There was "a level of dishonesty that I thought should be on the record," she said at one of the Midtown Restaurant meetings. She wanted to be sure that years from now, "what I experienced, what I actually saw, conversations I had with people," would be preserved for posterity. She gave the ARI writer four hours of interviews in 1999, and she recalled that they were "completely negative."

But when she saw an advance copy of *100 Voices*, she was annoyed to find that her interview had been not just abridged but expurgated. "They had managed to find all these positive things I said," which had "nothing to do with the whole feel of the conversation I had with them." Iris said she was in touch with a number of other people quoted in the book, and the same thing was done to them.

I met Iris at her apartment building in Manhattan near the United Nations, a mile or so north of where Rand spent her final years. We walked to the food court in the Citigroup building on 53rd Street, where there was a reasonably quiet public space, albeit with a few homeless people lounging in the vicinity.

Iris was quite happy to tell me about her parents and her upbringing, which were a source of considerable pride. She was born Iris Furstenberg in Chicago, the granddaughter of Eastern European Jewish immigrants. Her parents were methodical, intellectual people who applied reason to their everyday activities, and their rationality is one of Iris's most vivid childhood memories. They met in 1938 and, after deciding to be married, spent the next two years "putting into words their life view, their life plan." That kind of systematic intellectualizing would be unusual today and it was certainly atypical for a working-class Chicago couple in the 1930s. Even though no one in the family had read Ayn Rand, who had yet to make her mark, "I grew up as an Objectivist," Iris told me. Her parents felt that "you should put as much into words as possible to really know what you're doing, to compare things and be sure that you're consistent." That's why, after they began reading Rand, "All of us said, 'Objectivism, this is us.' "

Her parents' objective, well-reasoned criteria for their lives to come was set forth in their life plan. They would have children "for the experience of watching them become themselves." Their children would grow up to become their own selves, not to complete their parents' lives or do what they wished they had done. It was refreshingly counter-stereotypical. Listening to Iris, I felt as if I was transported into a Randian version of Clifford Odets's *Awake and Sing*, with the Marxist grandfather morphing into an Objectivist.

The Furstenbergs were not well educated, but they knew how to use the library. They got hold of every book they could find on childrearing, studying how children were raised to personhood in every culture available at the Chicago Public Library. "They wanted to know what they were doing," Iris pointed out. The result was a rational upbringing. No manipulating mamas in the Furstenberg family circle. No guilt tripping, no nagging. When Iris went on her first date, her mother told Iris to call her at 10:30 p.m. Iris asked why. Her mother said that she wasn't sure why but that all her friends did that with their daughters. Iris pointed out that if she wanted to have sex she could do it at any time of day, and that if she was in an auto accident the police would call, so she didn't know why it was necessary to call. "She said, 'You're right,'" Iris recalled.

Her parents were the children of shopkeepers, and were enthusiastic defenders of free enterprise from detractors such as her mother's brother, who was a more typical Odets character—a Communist postal worker. (An image of a rabble-rousing Newman from *Seinfeld* flitted through my head.) Randian ideology fit well into this harmonious picture of domesticated capitalism, and Rand books entered the household when Iris was eighteen and attending art school in downtown Chicago. She was a studious sort—once reminding her high school teacher when she forgot to assign homework—and was so driven and serious that two of her classmates said that she reminded them of a character from an Ayn Rand novel. They had just read *Atlas Shrugged* and *The Fountainhead*. At their suggestion she read the novels in their published order.

"I got maybe a dozen pages into *The Fountainhead* when I realized that this was the world I grew up in," Iris recalled. "I wondered if the author—who I assumed was male, I had no idea—would know what kind of life her characters would have." After all, Iris had lived such a life. But after more reading she realized that "she knew more than I did."

Iris's initiation into organized Rand-dom was swift. She mailed in a card that was included in her copy of *Atlas,* and soon received a mailing from the Nathaniel Branden Institute, Rand's personal evangelical society, announcing that the NBI was about to begin a lecture series in Chicago. Iris signed up for the first lecture, which would be by Branden in the flesh.

She then got a call from the NBI representative in Chicago, a young man named Ed Nash, who invited her to a reception for Branden at Nash's sleek bachelor pad on Rush Street.

It was a heady experience for young Iris, moving rapidly from casual Rand reader to invitee to an NBI reception. There was a definite glamour surrounding Nash, who was a political activist and rising star in the very hot field of direct marketing. Iris attended, but was not swept off her feet. Branden presided regally over the gathering, which sounded to me a lot like the Midtown Restaurant meetings, but with cuter people. Apparently Nash had utilized his direct-marketing skills to effectuate a kind of mixer for young, Objectivist-oriented people. Iris did not particularly like Branden, considering him to be pompous, a quality that burns its way through photos taken of him decades ago.

The party didn't make much of an impression on Iris but she apparently had an effect on Nash, who began a patient effort to woo her. She was engaged at the time to an amiable young man she'd met at art school. "A diamond in the rough," she called him. He was from a "cowboy family" in Texas, possessed solid American values, but he had an irredeemable flaw. He hadn't read Rand, which was bad enough, and "the deeper I got into Objectivism the more upset he became." She commiserated with Nash, who was, not surprisingly, sympathetic to her boyfriend woes. She ended the relationship and began dating Nash.

Well, "dating" may be something of an understatement, as they were married two weeks later. It was a very small wedding at city hall. "We wanted only perfect people, and I don't know what we thought was wrong with our mutual friends," she recalled. "No one was good enough to be invited to our wedding." The same issue arose with her wedding dress, which was black and sleeveless, as it was the only one to which neither of them had any objections. "Now I look at it as 'Why should he have any say in what I'm wearing?' We were very mixed up. It was not a good idea."

The marriage foundered after a couple of years. As was customary at the time in unions between Objectivists, Nash went to New York to consult Nathaniel and Barbara Branden, and perhaps others in the Objectivist hierarchy, about the trouble with the marriage and the possibility of divorce. "People said to me afterward it was as if he was getting permission," said Iris. "He telephoned me from New York and said something like 'Are we in love?'" She responded in the negative, and that was the end of it. It was 1964 or 1965. "It was an Objectivist mess," she said. "A lot of people in that period were kind of marrying the first Objectivists they met."

By now I began to understand why so much of what Iris said didn't make the cut for *100 Voices*. My clarity on that point was further enhanced by her anecdotes of life in the Rand orbit of the 1960s.

Iris and Nash were often in New York during their period of connubial non-bliss. During their first trip east they met one of Nash's friends, a novelist and former member of Rand's inner circle, just before Iris was about to meet Rand for the first time at a holiday party. The novelist said, "I know you're meeting Rand at a party tomorrow. You should know about me." She took Iris into the bedroom and showed her a letter that she had received from the NBI. Iris didn't recall who at the NBI signed the letter, or its specific details. "She had done something wrong. I read the thing twice and I couldn't make sense of it." Iris said. "She had done something that was not considered right, whatever it was. She could continue to come to lectures, but wasn't allowed to talk to any of the inner circle people." It was Iris's first contact with one of the features of life in Objectivism, both during Rand's lifetime and, more infrequently, up to the present day—the Objectivist Excommunication.

She recalled her introduction to that Randian institution in a bemused fashion. Her new acquaintance was now an unperson. "In theory," she said laconically, "I shouldn't be in her house and talking to her, because she had been thrown out of Objectivism." The purpose of showing her the letter was to determine if Iris still wanted to remain in her home, because "if I'm an official Objectivist and I see that letter, and I see that she's been thrown out of the inner circle, I shouldn't have anything to do with her."

There were a lot of expulsions at the time, a lot of "trials." She said, "I don't know if they were monthly, weekly, three times a week. There were a lot of people thrown out; everybody was frightened about them." Still, when Iris was shown the letter she "just shrugged it off." She thought it was strange, but did not change her opinion of Rand.

The weirdness continued at her first encounter with Rand a few days later. This time she was more profoundly impressed, and not favorably. Nash introduced Iris as his new bride, and told Rand that she had helped design ads for the NBI. Rand said, "Tell me how much you like the ads." Iris felt that "here's my chance to tell her something she didn't know." So she began to tell Rand about how she designed the ads. "I said, 'You figure out what is the most important thing for people to know, and you make that largest.'"

Iris noticed that Rand's eyes widened in anger. She didn't know what she said that teed her off. Ed Nash said, "Oh, excuse me," and pulled her away. "I think I could have lived my life and never guessed what made her angry," said Iris. "Ed said, I said 'you.' It was as if I was telling her how she should design an ad. I should have said 'one.'" Ayn Rand did not like to be told what to do, even when she wasn't being told what to do.

Iris viewed the whole thing as a minor eccentricity, something that she and her parents wouldn't do. "I did hope that this would be an extension of the world I'd grown up in. It became clear that it wasn't," Iris said.

Some months later, Iris attended a meeting at Rand's apartment with Rand, Branden, and Nash. Rand's husband Frank O'Connor was also present but sitting far off to the side. The subject was a lecture series that Nash had proposed for Rand, which included a planned appearance at McCormick Place in Chicago. There was "interminable conversation" about travel arrangements, airplane (which Rand hated) versus train, including "if they flew should they [Rand and Branden] fly on the same plane, and what it would mean to Objectivism if the plane went down and they both were on it."

Iris interjected that she had just read an article that said that it was far more dangerous to be in an automobile in a city than to be in an airplane. Bad move. Rand didn't like plane travel, period. The remark was out of order. "Ed Nash and Nathaniel both screamed out my name, which meant 'shut up,' and Rand went on as if I hadn't said a word. I thought, 'In my home, my mother would have said, 'Hey, Iris just gave us a fact. We can't pretend like we didn't hear it.'" But facts weren't always Rand's priority, on subjects far more consequential than whether to take a train or plane to Chicago. The incident stood out in Iris's mind as an example of how Rand's behavior differed from what she saw in her own family, the pre-Objectivist Objectivists, for whom objective facts were supreme, even if it meant not demanding that your teenage daughter call her worried mother at 10:30 p.m. "Rand was willing to wipe out reality," said Iris. Still, Iris didn't make a fuss. It wasn't like her to take people to task when they didn't live up to Objectivist principles, even when they called themselves Objectivists, or were Ayn Rand herself. "I just know that about the person. I can continue to be friends with them or pull away from them"—even Rand, though she didn't.

Iris moved to New York in the mid-1960s, after separating from Nash. She was welcomed back to the fold, her split with Nash having no impact on her standing with the Rand crowd, and she continued to design NBI ads and the cover of Rand's newsletter. Iris was impressed that Rand refused her offer to design the newsletter gratis, preferring to pay for the work. She got to know Objectivist luminaries like Peikoff, whom she remembered as this "strange little kid hanging around." She also ran into Greenspan and sat next to him at a dinner party, where they had a pleasant chat about the joys of listening to music on airplanes. There was a social scene in the Objectivist community back then, with anniversary and holiday parties and even an Objectivist softball team. Rand was at the center, remote, not anyone's idea of a smothering Jewish mother (unless you were Branden, and that was not exactly a mother-son relationship).

Iris met Rand often and was always a bit starstruck. She remembered once having coffee and cake at Rand's apartment. It was still vividly lodged in her memory after half a century; she even recalled the brand (Chock Full O'Nuts). Iris really liked it and offered to refill the cup. Rand, ever the gracious host, said she'd get the coffee. Iris remembers thinking, "This is Ayn Rand! And I'm going to ask her to walk all the way into the kitchen to get the coffee and come back!" But that was fine, Rand was happy to get the coffee. Rand was mercurial like that. She could be sweet and generous just as she was capable of being abrupt and nasty. The nasty side didn't emerge at all in *100 Voices* and other ARI propaganda.

As depicted in the authorized treatments of her life, Rand "never got angry, or when she did get angry it was always justified." Iris said that even though Rand never screamed, at times "she projected such rage that people would run out of the room or lecture hall," she said. "And I never thought what she did was justified." A student might ask a question about Kant, and Rand would react as if the student was Kant in the flesh and was "trying to take over the lecture. It was truly horrible." That happened all the time at NBI lectures, Iris recalled.

In social situations, similarly, Rand would give vent to her dark side. Once, Iris was at a party when Patrecia Scott, a Rand acolyte who would later marry Branden, came late because she had just been to see the hit Broadway play *Man of La Mancha*. Iris recalled: "She was just so thrilled to tell everyone about this beautiful experience she had. She described the sets and the costumes and the music. When she got done, Rand started questioning her. 'What is the purpose of art?' 'Does this fit?' I felt like she was cutting Patrecia into little pieces until there was nothing left of her. Patrecia, who came in saying 'I had just had this wonderful experience seeing this beautiful play,' ended up saying, I don't remember the words but the idea was, it's a bad play. This man has an unattainable dream. It's evil. I watched this person going from pure joy to being destroyed."

Iris opened a window into the Rand world of decades ago, when Rand was still alive and her movement was little more than a cult. But what about the members of today's Objectivist inner circle? Who are they? *What* are they?

The best way to find out was to meet those who matter most to any organized group of people, be they Objectivists, Republicans, Democrats, or alumni organizations: the ones who give them money.

CHAPTER THREE

The Winners

When Rick Santelli ranted about aid to "losers" being kicked out of their homes, he raised an implied question: Who are the "winners"? One reasonable conjecture is that the winners are people who are just like the prosperous commodities traders who were cheering him on. They are wealthy people who have no social conscience and believe that having one is undesirable. They believe (and have ample evidence to believe) that they are on the right side of history in their proud and assertive lack of compassion for those less fortunate than themselves. They are tired of being made to feel guilty that they are rich and have no social conscience.

I was among them, surrounded by winners. They were 150 strong, carefully attired, optimistic people. Trends were going their way. It was a good day, a happy day, and they were gathering this evening to share the joy of being part of the cutting edge, and to provide money for the purpose of advancing their way of life—and, above all, their way of thinking.

The Wayne-Falkland was unavailable, so the Ayn Rand Institute's "Atlas Shrugged Revolution" fund-raiser had to settle for the St. Regis, a mansion-like beaux arts hotel at Fifth Avenue and 55th Street. It was built at the turn of the century, and it was intimidating. The closer I came to it, the more it made me uncomfortable. Shouldn't I be coming in through the service entrance? It was that kind of place. It was a splendid substitute for the Wayne-Falkland; probably the most elegant hotel in the city, oozing with money—as well it should, for this was a convention of the guiltless rich.

It was mid-September 2010, and the Rand-inspired Tea Party movement was, by all the polls and all appearances, threatening to sweep the November elections. The Republican establishment had already surrendered. The Democrats were sullen, facing the Tea Party onslaught with the gumption of South Vietnamese troops scattering before NVA tanks in 1975. Against them was a display of raw power, bare-knuckled right-wing populist energy. From the standpoint of the people gathered here, what was needed was harnessing, intellectual regimentation. Here at the St. Regis is where the money, the discipline, and, above all, the properly checked premises would flow, to stockpile ideological fuel that would be needed to take America back from the statists, altruists, and socialists.

I should mention that the Wayne-Falkland was not available for this event because it is fictional. That is the impossibly splendiferous New York hotel in *Atlas Shrugged* where all the major characters stay when they are in the city. Fred Cookinham explained in his walking tour that it was probably based on the Waldorf-Astoria because of its proximity to the Taggart railroad terminal, which was probably modeled on Grand Central. However, the Waldorf lacked the sheer opulence of the St. Regis. This was a hotel with twenty-four-hour butler service, if one so required. It was popular with diplomats and, in bygone days, Alfred Hitchcock.

The pre-dinner reception was in the Louis XIV Room and the dinner was in the Versailles Room. Louis XIV was an eighteenth-century French monarch known as the Sun King. His Palace of Versailles symbolized the greatness and grandeur that only ancestral money can bring.

Rand did not like Louis XIV. She explained in an August 1962 *Los Angeles Times* column that he was "an archetypical despot: a pretentious mediocrity with grandiose ambitions." That was bad enough, I suppose, but what really rankled her was that Louis's chief advisor, Jean-Baptiste Colbert, "one of the early modern statists," inaugurated "countless government controls and minute regulations that choked the business community."[1] Holding the fund-raiser in rooms inspired by those heathens may have been the biggest symbolic affront to Rand since 1976, when Norman Thomas High School was erected a few yards from her last home in New York City.[2]

The people in attendance were sublimely unaware of any of this as they nibbled at the upscale hors d'oeuvres. This was no place for ham-handed treat-grabbing; elegant eating was underway. No toasted corn muffins were to be seen. No matzo ball soup. The Midtown Restaurant, just a few blocks to the east, could not compete with the satiny St. Regis. My monthly-meeting Objectivists, cerebral and noticeably downscale (except perhaps for the free-spending Don Hauptman), would have been out of place, socially and demographically, at this $1,500-a-plate event which I was unenthusiastically permitted to attend by the ARI. I assume that my presence at this dinner was somewhere within the rational self-interest of the ARI, perhaps by giving me a better appreciation of the group's base of financial support and exposing me to the scintillating speeches on tap for the evening. It was certainly in my rational self-interest to attend, and would have been even if I wasn't writing this book, as it was the finest feed I've ever had at a banquet.

My badge indicated that I was assigned to the Brown Table. At first I thought the tables were color coded, as at summer camp, but then I saw that my table was hosted by Jim Brown, principal and partner of Brandes Asset Management, which had contributed $25,000 to the cause this evening. Sitting two places to my left was Cameron, a young Internet entrepreneur who does not read the news. Not just newspapers, but news of any kind. "You need to for your job, I don't need to for mine," he told me with conviction. I must confess that it was momentarily hard for me to think of any counterargument to persuade this fellow to read the news (or to read anything, for that matter). I guess I'd never checked my premises on that point. Why read the news? Why read?

Nevertheless, this appeared to be the media table. Seated across from me was Andrew Napolitano, the Fox News commentator known by his former New Jersey Superior Court title of "Judge." Next to Cameron was Kurt Kramer, the Ayn Rand Institute's tall and thin PR aide, an *Atlas Shrugged* character were it not for his wispy blond goatee, serving as a conspicuous repudiation of Rand's lifelong disdain for facial hair.

I reluctantly turned away from my pan-roasted filet mignon, its perfectly cooked internal redness offset by olive oil crushed potatoes with chives and garlic, festooned with red onion marmalade. Yaron Brook was at the microphone, speaking about his emigration from Israel, a country that in his childhood was gripped in the yoke of its founders' fetid socialism. They were disturbing memories, a background to overcome, but he succeeded.

Brook was lean and prematurely gray, with a triangular face and rimless glasses. He spoke in a punchy style, projecting forcefully as the experienced speaker that he was, his voice booming over the PA system, his accent flavored more by Boston than Tel Aviv, and with a slight Elmer Fuddish inflection, his Rs sounding like Ws at times. His was the classic immigrant's dream—America as the land of opportunity. Being an Objectivist, he didn't put it quite that way. America is a land of individual freedom, he said, and "what those rights really mean is we have the right to be left alone from the coercion of others, but primarily from the coercion of government leaders," he said. "The Founders understood that the greatest violators of rights were always government."

Brook was the chief spokesman, the writer of columns, the appearer on cable TV, functioning this evening as master of ceremonies. He was successor to Leonard Peikoff, now pushing eighty, once Rand's most youthful protégé. Grinning wide-mouthed from pictures of the Collective. He was "more or less retired" I was told by Kramer in an e-mail rebuffing my interview request, though I could see that Peikoff was at work on a book and maintained a Web site from which he issued regular podcasts. I had a copy of his book *The Ominous Parallels*, which was published in 1982 and carried an enthusiastic endorsement and foreword from Rand herself.* *Ominous* draws parallels between the United States and the pre-Nazi Weimar Republic. It is a dense, self-consciously serious book, with one chapter titled "Kant Versus America." "Contrary to the Marxist theory, big business has been one of the least influential groups in American history" Peikoff argues, repeating a theme that occasionally leaches through the soil of Randian literature.[3]

As in all things Peikoffian, he was echoing the distant voice of his master. Rand had argued that America's business elite is actually not an elite at all but a persecuted minority, quivering under the collectivist lash, unjustly scapegoated, and just a step away from the gas chamber or Gulag. "Every movement that seeks to enslave a country, every dictatorship or potential dictatorship, needs some minority group as a scapegoat which it can blame for the nation's troubles and use as a justification of its own demands for dictatorial powers," Rand asserted in a 1962 lecture. "In Soviet Russia, the scapegoat was the bourgeoisie; in Nazi Germany, it was the Jewish people; in America, it is the businessman."[4] These and other oddball Rand comments were rarely quoted by Objectivist luminaries in their speeches, essays, and TV appearances.

Apocalyptic extremism was not directly articulated in Brook's talk, even as he lamented how "this country has deteriorated dramatically in all those respects which made me want to come, the freedom of individuals, the role of the government" in our lives. "We all know that things are not getting better," he said. "Things are getting worse. This country is—whether we like it or not—this country's bankrupt."

There was a ray of hope, not that any of the assembled financiers and their spouses should rest on their laurels for one minute. "Soon there's

* The book also carried an enthusiastic endorsement from Leonard Peikoff himself. Its subtitle calls it "a brilliant study."

going to be a substantial Republican victory in November. I'm all for that," he said to appreciative murmuring in the crowd. "I vote Republican." But the central problem, he said, was not a lack of Republican power but distorted thinking—"a hatred of business." To make matters even more forbidding, the minds of young people were being gradually destroyed. A cancer was afoot at the universities. "The better a university is, the more anticapitalist, the more antibusiness it is, the more anti-reason it is, the more anti-everything that made this country great, those universities become," Brook pointed out to the impressed and hushed crowd.

I was trying to get my arms around Harvard Business School, the Yale School of Management, and Wharton as "antibusiness" when Brook transitioned from the crisis in education to decry the constant and historical failure of public stimulus. "We do it over and over and over again. We learn nothing." Whether the Obama stimulus package was large enough to be considered stimulus was open to debate, but this was not an evening for quibbling. It was an evening for intensive networking, and quaffing, and absorbing stirring speeches.

"Ayn Rand understood that the fundamental mover, the fundamental shaper of society, the fundamental shaper of history, is philosophy—ideas. If there's one thing that's unique about the Ayn Rand Institute is that we take ideas seriously," he said. "Yes we do public policy. We're very involved in education. But in all those we bring a philosophical angle, a philosophical approach that asks fundamental questions about what is going on. We talk about economics, but we don't talk about it just as pure economics. We talk about it as fundamental ideas, ideas of what do you do in terms of morality and self-interest or in terms of self-sacrifice.

"Only we take a philosophical approach," he said. And he was right. Only Randers ever talk about the moral basis for what they believe, which is that capitalism—unimpeded, no-government capitalism—is the only moral system. He and Benny Pollak recognized what the rest of the nation had overlooked—that all the arguments over social programs, Medicare, and taxation boil down to opposing concepts of morality, different definitions of right and wrong.

I expected the audience to hiss when Brook uttered the Randian expletive "self-sacrifice," but too many were ensconced in still-unfinished *moelleux aux chocolat* with coconut sorbet and berry chutney. We placed our forks down to digest the fundamental challenge, which Brook characterized as poised between reason—"using our minds"—and faith, whether it be "faith from the left or faith from the right. It doesn't matter." Such is the real conflict of ideals. "Conservatives, libertarians, they don't have those ideas, and many of them don't want those ideas. They don't think this is a philosophical gap."

Note that Brook lumped in libertarians with conservatives. It's hard to say which were more deeply despised by Rand. To her, libertarians were flaky nobodies, and she viewed conservatives the way Stokely Carmichael viewed the NAACP, as sleepy establishmentarians satisfied with crumbs from massa's table. "Conservatism: An Obituary" was one of her essays for the *Capitalism* anthology, and Brook hewed to the party line by writing a eulogy for neocons on the ARI Web site.

In his St. Regis talk he enunciated a theme that might surprise Rand-bashers on the left: What the world faced was not a struggle between capitalism and socialism, or big and little government, but between reason and faith. It was a dichotomy that Rand had been flogging since her earliest days, and I saw its appeal to intellectuals on the right—though not the great masses of ordinary, nonintellectual, non-wealthy Americans for whom faith in God was a permanent and indelible feature of life.

Brook's own history was an intriguing journey through the shoals of faith, as he was born in a country predicated on religion that adopted sectarian socialism during its first three decades. A few years earlier, he was quoted in the *Jerusalem Post* setting forth his own ideas on Israel, a mélange of right-wing hard-line views and a rejection of the religious basis for Israel's existence. Rand herself was strongly pro-Israel, not as a fulfillment of Biblical prophecies but as an outpost of Western civilization in a savage Middle East. Brook, continuing along those general lines, believed that Israel needed to crush Hamas, and that West Bank settlements were important for Israel's security and should not be dismantled. Settlers like him, not surprisingly, but the feeling is not mutual. He told the *Post* that "their whole basis for agreeing with me is corrupt and wrong." He said that "the logic of 'God promised this and gave me this' is one that can only lead to bloodshed and war." He opposed government confiscation of private Arab land for settlements.[5]

Religion is portrayed in Rand's novels as the enemy of objectivity. Her novels present a world without Catholics, Protestants, Muslims, or Jews. They are as devoid of ethnicity as TV shows in the 1950s. The homogenized American hue of her novels' characters was evident in a brief documentary on *Atlas Shrugged* that Brook played for the St. Regis audience. Characters from the novel were played by actors—all thin, white, and unhyphenated. A representative sampling of "real Americans" of various colors was shown praising the book's virtues as we sipped our Cakebread Chardonnay. There was respectful applause. It was brief, only a few minutes, but conveyed the same general message as *Ayn Rand: A Sense of Life*, an ARI-sanctioned propaganda film that, despite its overt hagiography and gaping omissions, was nominated for an Academy Award in 1998.

After the film and after others came to the mike, Brook returned to mention one of the ARI's major initiatives. The staggering numbers in the Zogby poll showed that Rand was pushing hard into the American consciousness, but not hard enough. A major effort was afoot to influence the minds of America when they are most open to new ideas. The Objectivist movement was no longer going to wait around for some random kid to drop into the library or hear about *Atlas* and *Fountainhead* by word of mouth. Young readers were getting a good dose of Rand whether they liked it or not.

"Every English teacher in the United States gets an offer from us. If they will teach Ayn Rand's books, we will deliver as many copies as they need for free. When we initially started this program we had a few thousand of the books sent out," he said.

"Today we're shipping three hundred and fifty-thousand copies of the books a year."

The applause was as thunderous as the contradiction was awe-inspiring.

Ayn Rand didn't believe in the use of force, and she didn't believe in government-run schools. She viewed government power as a "gun." Yet here we had hundreds of thousands of students, many if not most in schools funded by "gun"-wielding governments, being forced at "gun"-point to read the books of a person who would have kicked those kids out of those very schools and shut them down.

The Rand novels, Brook argued, meet a classroom need by the simple fact of not being boring. That was debatable. And if popular authors are to be taught to high school kids, why Rand? Just because the well-heeled people in this room can afford to put those books in thousands of classrooms? It seemed to me that they met a classroom need by the simple fact of being free of charge at a time of budget cutbacks.

Brook provided a prompt answer to that unasked but obvious question: because it was necessary. "Because we view the challenge this country faces as fundamentally a philosophical challenge, we view education as a fundamental challenge that we face." It was a bit circular but I caught the drift.

The contradictions multiplied upon themselves as Brook turned over the microphone to Tara Smith, a professor of philosophy at the University of Texas at Austin, identified in the program as the "BB&T Chair for the Study of Objectivism and Anthem Foundation fellow." She was, in other words, the Alan Greenspan of academia—an Objectivist (a credo that opposes state-funded education) working for a state-funded college, teaching the principles of the philosophy that would abolish the institution where she shared the blessings of Objectivism with her students. Rand said in *Atlas Shrugged:* "Contradictions do not exist. Whenever you think that you are facing a contradiction, check your premises. You will find that one of them is wrong." What premise was wrong in this instance? I could only think of one: Objectivism is free of contradictions.

The ARI, Smith said, is as much interested in the humanities as in economics and business. "This is unusual," she said. The humanities are typically dismissed as esoteric, self-indulgent. "What we think depends on how we think," she said. "And that's where the humanities are really critical."

It's all about the ability to rationally interpret the events around one. "The real problem we have today, both inside and outside academia, is the number of well-meaning people who think they are being rational and objective in reaching their conclusions," the professor went on.

"Perhaps you've had the experience that I've had in the last few years. A lot of the really charged political debates about deficits or health care or what have you. I wonder if you've had the experience of leaving the conversation and wondering, 'How could he think that?' 'How are they thinking?' 'What are they not thinking about?' 'What are the practical implications of not thinking through because they don't know how to think?' "

Objectivism, she said, is the answer to these asked but not very obvious questions, for it teaches objective thinking. "Lasting, deep cultural change is going to take some deep changes in the way people think," she said.*

There was no problem on that front with this audience, whose minds were already thinking objectively. The applause was wildly enthusiastic. Smith had skillfully reiterated the point of the evening, which was as much about thought-process-improvement as it was about the need to sit down and write checks. The media frequently applies "astroturfing" labels to right-wing groups, citing hidden corporate agendas. But there was no sub-

* Smith missed an opportunity to change the way I think. She declined to be interviewed for this book.

terfuge here. The corporate sponsorship was openly proclaimed, the objective of the evening was as stated: to change the way Americans deploy their brain cells.

It was as ambitious a program of mind-reprogramming as one could find outside of North Korea and science-fiction movies. Americans are said to be resistant to indoctrination and heavy-handed ideology. Yet here we had a gathering of apparently reasonable, intelligent Americans, applauding their hands raw about the prospect of young people being force-fed the works of an ideologue far outside of the American mainstream.

Brook returned to the front of the pleasantly satiated audience. In sales, this would be called the "closing."

"The conflict we are engaged in is not a simplistic one," he said in his booming voice. "It's not an economic struggle, a political struggle, a class struggle. This is a deeply philosophical struggle. This is a fundamental struggle about how people think. It's about what people conceive as right and wrong."

Point made. Repetitive, but effective. I sensed true joy among the people around me. Like any skilled orator, Brook had captured precisely the fears, hopes, and aspirations of his audience, articulated them and made them appear both reasonable and achievable. What's wrong with changing the way the American people think? The evening was not conducive to asking, "Is it anybody's business? Is it a reasonable objective?" The answer would be "Hell yes, if you can plant enough op-eds, make enough TV appearances, indoctrinate enough far-right politicians and Tea Partiers, and ship enough books to enough teachers to ram down the throats of enough pupils."

After the speeches, as the assembled Objectivists congregated and chatted, there was a general feeling of satisfaction, not of impending combat. Yes, the road ahead would be hard, but they were making progress; their cause was advancing. Yet I sensed a feeling of almost permanent alienation. That was an undercurrent in the speeches, especially Brook's. His ambition, the thought-improvement of America, was lofty because the need was great, yet the objective seemed far in the distance, like Mount Fuji as viewed from Tokyo.

Would anything ever satisfy these people other than a total elimination of all social programs, all of Medicare, all of Social Security, all government-funded education? All regulations restraining business? All federal, state, and local agencies that do anything but shoot guns and put people on trial? That was Ayn Rand's objective. Her vision of a utopian America was of a country whose economic and social system is forever free of the stain of government, down to the last park ranger and road salter.

It would be a radical capitalist paradise that is as much a fevered dream as the socialist paradise envisioned by Marx. At no time since the dawn of mankind has Rand's vision of a completely government-free capitalist society ever taken root. It didn't happen in Dickensian England; nor in the era of the robber barons; nor in the cow towns of the Western frontier, where the only regulator was a six-shooter (except perhaps in Billy the Kid's New Mexico, where a vigilante group was called "The Regulators"). Even the most remote Old West settlements had one-room schoolhouses and post offices. During the wild and free days of no-holds-barred Western expansion, an entire people were forced into very un-Objectivist reservations by the government gun (literally) and kept on the federal dole. Every reader of Dickens knows that in addition to Victorian England's prisons there were workhouses, paid for by Scrooge's taxes. Rand acknowledged in 1963 that "a fully free, capitalist system has not yet existed anywhere."[6]

That was the theory, harsh and uncompromising. And then there was the reality, for which compromises could be made—when Rand was personally involved.

Throughout her life, Rand stridently opposed any government program to provide assistance to seniors and the poor, and she was dead set against Medicare from its first stirrings during the Kennedy administration. Writing in the January 1963 edition of *The Objectivist Newsletter*, Rand derided "humanitarian" (her scare quotes) projects that, as she saw it, were to be "imposed by political means, that is, by *force*, on an unlimited number of human beings.

"'Medicare' is an example of such a project," she said. "'Isn't it desirable that the aged should have medical care in times of illness?' its advocates clamor. Considered out of context, the answer would be: yes, it is desirable. Who would have a reason to say no? And it is at this point that the mental processes of a collectivized brain are cut off; the rest is fog."

The "fog," she said, "hides such facts as the enslavement and, therefore, the destruction of medical science, the regimentation and disintegration of all medical practice, and the sacrifice of the professional integrity, the freedom, the careers, the ambitions, the achievements, the happiness, the *lives* of the very men who are to provide that 'desirable' goal—the doctors."

At the time, Medicare was mired in Congress, held up by impassioned opposition from organized medicine and the right. It was finally enacted in 1965, and Rand's successors have continued her opposition to Medicare. In a statement on changes to Medicare in 2008, Yaron Brook summarized the Objectivist position on government-paid medical care for the aged, which is that there shouldn't be any. "If the government guarantees health care to people, costs have to skyrocket. When someone else is footing the bill for health-care costs, consumers demand medical services without having to consider their real price." Brook went on to advocate "returning to a truly free system where each individual is responsible for his own health-care costs," which would "unleash the power of capitalism in the medical industry, leading ultimately to high quality, affordable medical care for Americans. Let's start looking at ways to phase out government interference in medicine."[7]

Nothing really surprising here—except when you consider that Ayn Rand enrolled in Medicare.

Late in her life, as her husband Frank O'Connor fell deeper into dementia, Rand realized that, best-selling author though she was, she did not have the financial resources to cope with the afflictions of old age. Rand had lung cancer, and Frank was suffering from a disease that was labor-intensive and ruinously expensive to treat. In *100 Voices,* her former social worker Evva Pryor described how Rand applied for Medicare and Social Security, two government programs that would be among the first to be crushed beneath the tank treads of Objectivism. Rand had paid in to Social Security all of her life, so she felt that there was no contradiction. But Medicare? The program whose existence she had opposed from the very beginning? The one that was enslaving medical science?

Pryor and Rand would have discussions. Pryor recalled that "the initial agreement was on greed. *She had to see that there was such a thing as greed in this world.* Doctors could cost an awful lot more money than books earn, and she could be totally wiped out by medical bills if she didn't watch it [emphasis added]." Rand "didn't feel an individual should take help"—but she did. When Rand's economic interests were at stake, the poor, enslaved doctors became greedy money-grubbers—with "greedy" used in the conventional, non-Randian sense, to connote something grasping, selfish (in the non-Randian sense), and harmful to others.

The deed was done. "Whether she agreed or not is not the issue, she saw the necessity for both her and Frank."[8] Reality had intruded upon her ideological pipedreams.

You have to read the *Capitalism* anthology, especially an essay by Alan Greenspan entitled "The Assault on Integrity," to realize how remarkable this passage truly is. In his essay, reflecting official Rand doctrine, Greenspan said, "It is precisely the 'greed' of the businessman or, more appropriately, his profit-seeking, which is the unexcelled protector of the consumer." The error of "collectivists," he asserts, is that they refuse to recognize that "it is in the self-interest of every businessman to have a reputation for honest dealings and a quality product."[9]

So how come Rand wasn't willing to let the greed of doctors be her unexcelled protector? And what about the millions of people in this country who depend on Medicare? Is it permissible for them to not rely upon greed to protect them? Can they carve out an exception to Objectivist ideology, just as Rand did?

If Rand had been a mother, would her children have attended public schools and public colleges like the University of Texas? Would her grandchildren have been taught by Tara Smith the principles of a philosophy that opposed government funding for public colleges like the University of Texas?*

Some might call this hypocrisy, but that is not a particularly useful assessment, accurate though it may be. A more polite way of referring to this is that it is a contradiction, which Rand said did not exist. Or perhaps it is simply that Objectivism has no practical purpose except to promote the economic interests of the people bankrolling it, the rationally self-interested people surrounding me at the St. Regis, regardless of its potential to bring ruin to everyone else—including its founder.

Contradictions, and ideology, fade away when one's own personal interests are at stake. Only the very wealthy, a category that did not include Rand in her golden years, can afford Objectivist ideological purity. With compensation from the ARI that exceeded $439,000 in 2009,† plus whatever he derives as managing director of a private equity firm, Brook may be able to afford philosophical consistency and not enroll in Medicare and Social Security when he retires.[11] Not many other people would have that luxury.

I didn't know about the rest of the people in the room. My hunch was that none of them would hesitate to apply for Medicare if their trust funds, golden parachutes, or executive retirement health care plans fail to provide adequate coverage. For now, it was not an issue and was unlikely ever to be an issue.

* State funding is not a theoretical issue for the University of Texas. In 2011, bills in the state legislature called for cutting the UT budget by as much as 20 percent.[10]

† Including a $180K bonus that he didn't get in 2010, according to the ARI's IRS filings.

Their view of the public interest had been shaped by Ayn Rand, who taught that there is no such thing as the public interest. She wrote that "there is no such entity as 'the public,' since the public is merely a number of individuals," so that "any claimed implied conflict of 'the public interest' with private interests means that some men are to be sacrificed to the interests and the wishes of others."[12] It was a sublimely enticing argument for wealthy businessmen who had no interest whatever in the public interest. Rand made their callousness seem supremely moral. Sure the public can go to hell. There is no public! Yet the taxpayers of America paid Rand's and Frank O'Connor's medical expenses solely because they were eligible members of *the public*, and because of a moral principle: that caring for seniors is in the *public interest*. It is the right thing to do.

Heaped on top of that irony was another: the altruism of the government, even a degree of self-sacrifice, in paying the medical bills of a woman who opposed Medicare and devoted her life to fighting the system of government that created programs like that. It was a kind of pre-bailout bailout. The government bailed out Objectivism in the person of its founder, just as it would bail out Wall Street in 2008, rescuing large firms that would do nothing if smaller firms, and ordinary citizens of course, were ever to founder because of their own poor choices.

In this room beneath the chandeliers named after the palace of a sovereign Rand despised, the remains of our sumptuous dinner being cleared away by silent, uniformed waiters, the inherent paradox that this posed did not exist.

CHAPTER FOUR

The Banker

In Objectivism, atheism is a kind of ethical elevator music, always in the background, not requiring acknowledgment. Rand's heroes stand alone against the world, not wanting help from any living being, not wasting their time praying to a nonexistent deity. Rand rejected religion and all the bad stuff that comes with it, all the baggage that makes it uncomfortable to live a suitably selfish, greed-driven life. She called the objectionable aspects of religion, the barriers to guilt-free monetary accumulation, "mysticism." Others call it "ethics" and "morality."

In Rand's works there are no "God is dead" histrionics, no Madalyn Murray O'Hair-style stridency. Here's a typical reference to atheism in *The Fountainhead:*

> PETER KEATING: "Why did you decide to become an architect?"
>
> HOWARD ROARK: "I didn't know it then. But it's because I never believed in God."
>
> PETER KEATING: "Come on, talk sense."
>
> HOWARD ROARK: "Because I love this earth. That's all I love. I don't like the shape of things on this earth. I want to change them."[1]

Atheism is not proudly shouted from the rooftops but mumbled, even whispered. Take this passage from *Atlas Shrugged,* in which John Galt says:

> They claim that they perceive a mode of being superior to your existence on this earth. The mystics of spirit call it "another dimension," which consists of denying dimensions. The mystics of muscle call it "the future," which consists of denying the present. To exist is to possess identity. What identity are they able to give to their superior realm? They keep telling you what it is *not,* but never tell you what it *is.* All their identifications consist of negating: God is that which no human mind can know, they say—and proceed to demand that you consider it knowledge—God is non-man, heaven is non-earth, soul is non-body, virtue is non-profit, A is non-A, perception is non-sensory, knowledge is non-reason. Their definitions are not acts of defining, but of wiping out.[2]

This passage is cited on the Ayn Rand Institute's Web site as an answer to the questions: "Is Objectivism atheistic?" and "What is the Objectivist attitude toward religion?" Also cited is an excerpt from a 1964 interview with *Playboy* magazine.

The interviewer's question was: "Has no religion, in your estimation, ever offered anything of constructive value to human life?"[3]

Rand's response: "Qua religion, no—in the sense of blind belief, belief unsupported by, or contrary to, the facts of reality and the conclusions of reason. Faith, as such, is extremely detrimental to human life: it is the negation of reason. But you must remember that religion is an early form of philosophy, that the first attempts to explain the universe, to give a coherent frame of reference to man's life and a code of moral values, were made by religion, before men graduated or developed enough to have philosophy."

Both questions could have been addressed simply, without reference to characters in novels or wordy quotations: "Yes, Objectivism is atheistic" and "No, Ayn Rand found no value in religion."

Or the ARI could have pulled out this quote from Rand in 1928: Religion, she said, is "the great poison of mankind." Or this quote from 1934: "I want to fight religion as the root of all human lying and the only excuse for suffering." Or this, also from 1934: Religion is "the first enemy of the ability to think."[4]

Following Rand in this as in all things, observant Objectivists have been militant atheists down through the years, from the Brandens and their friends and relatives in the Collective to her followers today.

I had religion in the back of my mind as I stopped by a hotel in Midtown Manhattan to meet John Allison, corporate America's leading Objectivist. I've never been terribly religious, and reading Rand's novels, essays, and journal entries made me even more alienated from religion. I was meeting Allison two days before Yom Kippur, the Day of Atonement, a fast day and the most solemn Jewish holiday. I had no plans to observe it, and I conveniently blamed that on Rand's influence. My rational, fact-based nonparticipation gnawed at me. I was aware of being in the midst of the Days of Awe, the period between the Jewish New Year and Yom Kippur. It is said that God has books in which he writes the names of those who will live and those who will die in the year ahead, sort of the way corporations decide at year end whom to let go. I always found that vaguely intimidating, certainly an implied threat that I didn't much care for. Orthodox Jews engage in various rituals during that time. A few years ago I participated in one, twirling money around my head three times and saying a prayer. I dropped it after deciding it was less likely to extend my life than putting in more hours at the gym.

Despite having abandoned the great poison of mankind, some lingering doubts—Rand would have called them superstitions—remained. I hoped that I could square away some of them while meeting Allison. He is generally referred to in the media by his full name of John A. Allison IV, but in person was not quite so stuffy. He has a practiced common touch, found among CEOs who are good at their jobs and experienced at talking with people like me.

We met in the lobby of his hotel, which was situated reasonably close to the Taggart Terminal (Grand Central to you). He looked the part of an Objectivist hero, being thin and reasonably tall. An anthropologist would have a field day researching body types among followers of Ayn Rand. As of this writing I have yet to meet a short, obese Objectivist.

Allison was a modern-day counterpart to Midas Mulligan, the financier Rand enshrined in *Atlas Shrugged* as the founder of what became Galt's Gulch, the Objectivist paradise in the Rocky Mountains. He was both an accomplished businessman and an Objectivist thinker. I'm sure that Rand would have cherished his company. She seemed to respect the genuinely accomplished more than the sycophants who surrounded her.

In December 2008, at the age of sixty, Allison stepped down as CEO of BB&T Corporation, a bank holding company in North Carolina that emerged from the financial crisis relatively unscathed despite being aggressive in some respects, but none of the ones that damaged or ruined other banks.

BB&T was originally a stodgy, down-home bank. The initials stood for Branch Banking & Trust. But Allison had the Midas touch (if I may inject a business-press cliché). He joined what was then a sleepy Dixie bank in 1971, straight out of the University of North Carolina. After working his way up through the ranks, he became CEO in 1989. He began orchestrating a series of mergers, which turned BB&T from a prosperous local bank to a major regional presence with $136.5 billion in assets, versus $4.5 billion when he took over, and $275 million when he originally joined the bank. This made him the Horatio Alger of banking (albeit a Horatio Alger who was pressured to accept federal bailout money in 2008, even though he didn't need it).

Horatio Alger was the embodiment of the Protestant Work Ethic, the

Calvinist blend of faith and capitalism that had no place in the bold new world of Objectivism. Allison also fit the definition of an Organization Man, having spent his entire career at the same large company. Rand despised the species of corporate drone that was documented in William H. Whyte's seminal 1956 book. Whyte described a kind of corporate collectivist who sheds his individuality to devote himself to large companies, seeking security in the organizational womb. In a 1958 column, Rand dismissed the "miserable little socialized, self-abnegating mediocrities described by Mr. Whyte."[5] John Allison, Organization Man, seemed dedicated to shattering this stereotype.

"Are you an Objectivist?" Allison asked me as we began our conversation. I wanted to delve into his belief system, and here he was, asking me about mine.

No problem. He had every right to ask because, after all, whether one is an Objectivist—actually Rand preferred that her acolytes call themselves "students of Objectivism"—fundamentally influences how one sees the world. I took this not as a challenge but as an expression of curiosity, just to know whether we could communicate in the same language. I replied that I was not, but that I had read both *Fountainhead* and *Atlas*. The answer seemed to satisfy him. Had I not read those novels—well, what could we have talked about? It would have been like a Venusian attempting a dialogue with a Catholic bishop.

I felt as if I was back in college, talking with a faculty advisor. Which sort of made sense, as he was a college professor. He certainly had devoted himself to pondering moral issues, and I had begun to see the edge that that gave to Randians. They were already ahead of the game just by giving thought to moral questions. Whether their take on morality was correct or not was beside the point. Their arsenals were well stocked with intellectual ammunition.

To Allison, Objectivism was an all-encompassing philosophy, one that had steered his entire life just as concretely as others might be guided by their early religious teachings, except that there were no "mystical" and perhaps off-putting references to the Almighty as one finds among the religious. As seemed to be the case whenever I talked with Objectivists, I felt as if I was being subtly if unintentionally pressured to convert, to be baptized, to come to Christ in the form of the dead Jewish lady.

Just as observant Christians read their Bible and observant Jews study their Talmud since their youth, those who flock to the grand old lady of radical capitalism ordinarily commence their self-education as adolescents or shortly thereafter. Allison started his Rand readings when he was twenty and studying business and economics at UNC. He was in a bookstore and the title caught his eye: *Capitalism: The Unknown Ideal.* He was the first Objectivist I'd met who was not initially swept into the fold by her novels. The *Capitalism* anthology, published in 1967, was heavy-duty, applied Objectivism, with all the charm and wit of an Army training manual.

"The title captivated me," said Allison. He read and enjoyed it. He thought Greenspan's essays for the anthology, which were off-the-charts radical, were "excellent," but also "ironic" because of Greenspan's later posts in government and at the helm of the Federal Reserve. I wasn't sure "ironic," while accurate as far as it went, was necessarily the most apt word to use to describe Greenspan's essays, which advocated a return to the gold standard, repeal of antitrust laws, and the wholesale slaughter of every form of regulation. I also found it hard to reconcile this cordial, scholarly—he was now a "distinguished professor of practice" at Wake Forest University—gentleman with the holder of such extreme views. It's a disconnect I often experienced in the presence of ardent Objectivists.

After polishing off the *Capitalism* anthology, Allison moved on to the novels and other Rand writings. The net effect on his thinking, he told me, was to provide a kind of structure to his belief system, and to enhance his understanding of its rectitude. "Rand gave me a sense, after reading all of her materials, of what I'd call a sense of moral certainty," he said. "She has a very systematic approach, starting with metaphysics to epistemology to ethics to politics to esthetics." He then told me, in well-practiced fashion, how influential Objectivism was in guiding his life and the operation of his bank "because of its thoroughness, structure, and integration."

None of this seemed particularly convincing to me, but we did find common ground on one thing—the tough-love (without the love) approach to personal relations that resonated through all of Rand's books, especially *Atlas Shrugged.* "It's very powerful," he agreed. "That's justice." One can quibble about individuality, especially when brought to extremes, and certainly argue over the merits of no-government capitalism, but who can argue with justice? Allison told me that the Rand view of family relationships was helpful to him in his personal relationships, and "made me clearer about the kind of people I wanted to be around." His wife read *Atlas Shrugged* after they met, which "helped us get closer together."

This is an aspect of Rand's appeal that is not always appreciated by nonbelievers. In addition to her strident ruminations on capitalism and her advocacy of turning government back to the Stone Age, she was a kind of proto-Dr. Phil. "Rand is fundamentally a defender that you ought to make logical decisions based on the facts to begin with," Allison told me, as we sat in a combination cocktail lounge-lobby. (His logical decision was not to order anything to drink, and neither did I.) "Reality," he continued, saying that word with conviction. "To use your mind as your means of survival, success, and happiness. That you should act in your rational self-interest, what I would call properly understood, not taking advantage of other people nor self-sacrificing, that we really are traders, we trade value for value, we get better together . . . and life is really about creating win-win relationships."

Well, who can argue with win-win relationships and using your mind? It's certainly more appealing than dumping every social safety-net program on the face of the earth. As a matter of fact, one could embrace any economic system and find this kind of thinking perfectly appealing. Surely there's nothing wrong with rational self-interest, and self-sacrifice is, arguably, not a particularly good thing if you view it the way Rand stacked the deck.

"That's a very powerful moral code to successful relationships," he went on. He seemed to be using the word "powerful" a lot in this conversation but I had to agree with him, at least insofar as the fictional characters in *Atlas Shrugged* are concerned. Even when cheating on each other, they ooze Rand's version of morality. Rand's adulterous spouses don't have a roll in the hay; they realize each other's uppermost values, which certainly seems less dirty. The objections in Albert Ellis's book, in which he ripped holes in these very concepts with the thoroughness of a malfunctioning Weed Eater, receded into the distance as I listened to Allison's gentle drawl.

As a matter of fact, Allison made pretty much all of Rand's noneconomic arguments make sense. His reasoning was . . . well, I guess "powerful" is the word, but only if one didn't think about it too carefully. One Objectivist concept that I had trouble grasping was the view that there is no such thing as a conflict of interest. If you perceive a conflict of interest, she said in *Atlas* through one of her characters, you need to "check your premises."

Rand took that point one step further in *The Virtue of Selfishness,* saying that "there are no conflicts of interest among rational men even in the issue of love. Like any other value, love is not a static quantity to be divided, but an unlimited response to be earned."[6] In *Atlas,* Rand's jilted heroes take that position whenever Dagny dumps them. In *Fountainhead,* Howard Roark has a similar attitude when the foxy spoiled rich girl Dominique Francon enters into a loveless marriage with newspaper magnate Gail Wynand even though she is hot for Roark. He doesn't mind, not even when Dominique goes out of her way to keep Roark from getting work during the Great Depression. (Her reasons are rational and Objectivist, but still come across as a bit kinky.)

"Are there zero conflicts? I don't know," said Allison, "but I think there are many less conflicts than people imagine. Do you really want a woman to marry you who really loves someone else? Of course not. And I think that's the essence of her argument, that when we really think through things carefully, there aren't that many conflicts with other people. And I found that in my career. Now there may be people you don't want to have relationships with, but I think her broader context is that there are huge opportunities for successful relationships that are good for both of us, and one task in life is to figure out how to do that where it's to your benefit to do it."

That sounds awfully elegant, but it seems that Rand's own life contradicts this beguiling bit of doctrine. In the 1950s she was a walking conflict of interest, as she bedded Nathaniel Branden despite the pained objections of her listless husband and Barbara Branden. The reality was that it was brute force—Rand's economic power over her husband and the much younger Branden, and Branden's psychological hold over his wife—that permitted this conflict of interest to play out for many years.

In romantic love, Rand writes, there are no losers in a romantic triangle when a woman chooses one of the two men. "The 'loser' cannot have what the 'winner' has earned." Ellis called this "incredibly false," observing that people's interests "obviously often clash."[7] Ellis was no spiritualist in his opposition to Objectivism, by the way, but rather a skeptic and atheist who was the father of Rational Emotive Behavior Therapy, which is based on the rigorous application of rational thought. Yet Ellis ferociously objected to Objectivism, which is also based on, ostensibly at least, rationality.

Throughout Ellis's book he complains about Rand's "anti-empiricism." Translated into plain English, this means "she doesn't know what she's talking about." An ordinary mortal might have acknowledged that a conflict of interest existed after Rand's breakup with Branden in 1968, when he dumped her for a much younger woman. But there's no evidence that she did. Instead she went into denial, publicly smearing him.

I mentioned to Allison that while I agreed with some of what Rand said, such as opposing the Vietnam War, I found that she drifted off into conclusions that were unsupportable much of the time. On romantic love, for instance, Rand said that "a man who is convinced of his own uselessness will be drawn to a woman he despises—because she will reflect his own secret self, she will release him from that objective reality that he is a fraud." But a therapist of Ellis's experience saw through that for the rubbish that it was, pointing out that men convinced of their worthlessness more likely will be drawn to women they respect, to compensate for their own feelings of inadequacy.[8]

Allison had an easy (if predictable) answer to my dilemma. "One of the things she kept pointing out, which I found very helpful to my life, is that you really have to check your premises. You ought to ask yourself why you believe what you believe," he said. In the past when he'd disagreed with her, he found that it was because he held beliefs that "didn't make a lot of sense."

That may be so if one had no first-hand knowledge of what Rand was talking about. But what if it was *Rand* who wasn't making sense? What if *her* premises were wrong? I noticed that Rand often expounded on things that were well beyond her area of expertise, such as psychology. It was said that Rand was a debater par excellence. She certainly knew what to say to members of the studio audience who confronted her on the Phil Donahue show in 1979. But she declined to debate Ellis, and there's no record of her ever going toe-to-toe with any prominent person who opposed her belief system.

Despite all my lingering misgivings, I had to admit that her writings on U.S. foreign policy had a certain logic to them. Allison, pleased with this point of agreement, described to me how Ayn Rand totally reversed his view of the Vietnam War in the 1960s. Before he understood Objectivism, he said, "I thought that the United States was really pursuing its self-interests in the Vietnam War. But when I started really analyzing and reflecting on it, I was really just defending America for the decision we had made." He came to realize that it wasn't in U.S. interests to become involved in Vietnam. "That doesn't mean that I agreed with the antiwar demonstrators," he said. "I really didn't. But I agreed with Rand it was the wrong place to defend America, if that was our principle." In a Randian sense, he shifted his premise from "being on the American side" to "what's in our national self-interest?"

I mentioned to Allison that Rand used the very same logic to argue against U.S. involvement in World War II. He looked at me blankly. I had touched a raw nerve. In this day and age, with the Greatest Generation idolized as it dies out, the fading memories of that war are among the few remaining untouchable subjects of American history. "Don't know enough about it to comment," he said.

How could that be? Allison was a serious student of Objectivism, and Rand's outspoken opposition to U.S. involvement in World War II was a significant chapter of her life. So was her support of antiwar presidential candidate Wendell Willkie, whom she disavowed after he joined the Roosevelt Administration. I pressed the point, and Allison told me that what he recalled was that she argued that "the Germans and Russians would have killed each other off, and we would have been better off. Which is possible."

I expressed some doubt about that, but Allison was unfazed. "That goes back to this premise that we've all been told that being in World War II was a good thing," he said. "I'm not sure we shouldn't have gotten in World War II but I think her argument is a very—you know, would these bad guys have killed each other off?

"And the answer is, they might have," he said, guffawing at the prospect.

Allison was noncommittal on Rand's stance. "It's hard to know if it's true or not," he said. "We helped the Russians a lot, and set ourselves up for a lot of cost and risk after World War II." But wait a moment, I said. Didn't Germany declare war on the United States after Pearl Harbor?

"She would argue that we helped set up Pearl Harbor by how we treated the Japanese," he replied.

Allison was right: That's just what she would have argued. In a book review that appeared in the December 1962 edition of *The Objectivist Newsletter*, Barbara Branden quoted with approval an author who said that Roosevelt "knowingly invited" the attacks on Hawaii and the Philippines. The book, called *The Roosevelt Myth* by John T. Flynn, was praised by Branden as a "ruthlessly factual presentation of the events of the New Deal period." Nothing appeared in the newsletter without Rand's approval as co-editor and publisher. Barbara Branden's then-husband Nathaniel was the other co-editor.

Something about this discussion disturbed me. I was enjoying it—I almost always liked chatting with Objectivists, for some reason—but it bugged me a little. Here I was, a few days before Yom Kippur, discussing whether there was something fundamentally fouled up about the war that kept Nazi Germany from turning more of my relatives into soap. There was something—well, I guess the word that comes to mind is *amoral*—about the stance he was taking.

It seemed to me that of all the wars in American history, none were more justified on humanitarian reasons alone than that one. To Objectivists, however, any arguments predicated on humanity, benevolence, and other forms of altruism are not only nonstarters, but inherently evil. My concerns, they would argue, were purely "tribal" and not "objective."

What I was touching on in my talk with Allison was not Rand the anti-empiricist, but Rand the crosser of red lines. World War II was one. The civil rights laws, which she opposed, were another. Rand needed to cross those red lines, she needed to slaughter those sacred cows, if her belief system was to have any claim to intellectual honesty. The problem for her followers was that she had them handcuffed. They needed to follow her across those same red lines lest they forfeit their own claim to intellectual honesty.

Would the Tea Party John Galt sign-holders, raised on a diet of John Wayne movies and *Band of Brothers,* ever accept the position that World War II was, maybe, optional? That perhaps we should have just sat that one out? That perhaps their grandfathers were wounded at Anzio for no particular reason in the philosophical scheme of things? In a 1974 article referring to American participation in wars of the twentieth century, including World War II, and the "disabled, the crippled the mangled of those wars' battlefields," Rand said that "no one has ever told them why they had to fight nor what their sacrifices accomplished."[9] That passage brings to mind a scene in the 1946 movie *The Best Years of Our Lives,* in which an armless veteran assaults a man for saying just that kind of thing. It was a scene, and a movie, that pleased audiences greatly but which Rand despised.*

Rand's propensity for red-line crossing can be found in abundance in the selections of her private writings published in ARI-sanctioned collections over the years. In an October 1941 letter[10] to DeWitt Emery, head of the National Small Business Men's Association, she spoke of her admiration for Henry Ford—the auto magnate, publisher of the racist *Dearborn Independent* and the stridently bigoted *The International Jew,* disseminator of the *Protocols of the Elders of Zion* hoax, and serial Jew-baiter. Ford today is one of the most widely loathed figures in the history of American industry. But Rand loved Ford. She pushed to meet him like an awestruck bobby-soxer panting after Frank Sinatra, long after Ford's anti-Semitic reputation was firmly established, forgetting that as a Jew she might not be his type.

She gushed: "I am a natural-born hero worshipper, but I find damn few heroes to worship—and he's one of my last few, because he is a symbol

* See Harriman, *Journals of Ayn Rand,* pp. 367–69, for a depiction of Rand's intense hatred of this movie, which she felt was degrading to capitalism. According to Rand, the drugstore fight scene depicted the man who was beaten up as being not just anti-Communist but "anti-Semitic and anti-Negro as well," implying that "these two attitudes [hating Commies and minorities] go hand in hand." In fact, the scene does not portray the character as denigrating Jews or blacks. I wonder if Rand even saw this movie. In her later years she wrote reviews of books and movies she didn't see. See Walker, *The Ayn Rand Cult,* p. 224.

of the capitalism system at its best." She begged for an audience with this capitalist hero, who only a few years before was the proud recipient of the Grand Cross of the German Eagle from Nazi Germany.

She was definitely a hero-worshiper, and her choice of heroes seemed ideologically inconsistent. I ordered up Rand's FBI file in a Freedom of Information Act request, and found a syrupy letter that she wrote in January 1966 to J. Edgar Hoover, one of the most heavy-handed government bureaucrats in U.S. history. If Rand was true to her philosophy she'd have wanted to keep her distance from this man. Instead she tried to cozy up to him. Hoover was quoted by *The Saturday Evening Post* that he "disavows the ultraconservative political label, terms himself an 'objectivist.'" Rand seized upon that to ask if that meant "that you agreed with my philosophy of Objectivism." Whatever his response, "I should like very much to meet you—to discuss a personal-political problem."

Hoover scribbled on the bottom of her letter, "I have never said I was an 'objectivist,' whatever that is." One of Hoover's aides recommended in a memo "that the Director not take time from his busy schedule to see captioned individual." In a response to Rand, Hoover duly cited his busy schedule in declining to schedule a meeting, and said that he "never stated that I am an objectivist." Rand's letter and Hoover's response were, unsurpisingly, omitted from the ARI-sanctioned *Letters of Ayn Rand*. The nature of that "personal-political problem" has been lost to history.[11] Rand had made two previous attempts to see Hoover, in 1947 and 1957, both without success.[12]

While Allison's view of geopolitics was interesting, I was far more interested in getting a sense of how this accomplished businessman utilized Randian precepts in running his business. I had interviewed many CEOs over the years, and knew that top-level executives could be very concrete on such things when they so desired.

"This sounds obvious," Allison said, "but when you're absolutely clear about your values, you have more success."

It wasn't obvious to me at all, actually. Allison had this explanation: "Rand is an advocate of purpose, that people need to be purpose directed, that human action is purpose directed, organizations have to be purposeful—that is a very powerful leadership." It might be, if, as he said, it didn't sound a bit simplistic, as was what he said about making "logical decisions based on the facts." Few people outside of mental institutions would claim to make logical decisions contrary to the facts.

"Now I don't think a lot of businesspeople would technically argue with that," he conceded, "but a lot of their decisions aren't made based logically on the facts. And if you hold that as a value, as a principle: 'We're going to self-discipline ourselves, we're going to make logical decisions based on the facts,' you're much less likely to *evade,*" he said, putting emphasis on that last word, "you're much less likely to make decisions over emotional things—you want your bank to be bigger than the other guy's bank—those kinds of emotional things."

Another pillar of Rand's philosophy was self-esteem, he said, "and how you earn self-esteem from how you live your life. That if you have a clear set of principles, you live consistent with the principles, you act with integrity, you're honest—all those things are not duties, but means to success and happiness. Then you're much more likely to have a company that acts on principle, has integrity, is honest," not because you feel this is something you "should" do, but because you view it as a path to success.

It wasn't clear to me how any of this was unique to Objectivism. What corporate executive, even the most crooked, doesn't view himself as honest? I've known CEOs I wouldn't let borrow a pencil who thought their lives were beacons of integrity. I'm sure that Enron's Jeff Skilling, as he mops floors or does whatever cons do at Englewood Federal Correctional Institution, spends his waking hours troubled by how an honest guy like him wound up in the pen.

Yet there was one aspect of Rand's philosophy, as outlined in *The Fountainhead,* that did make sense to me and I eagerly raised this point with Allison: her advocacy of individuality in the workplace, her dislike of corporate groupthink and overreliance on committees. Individuality is one of the pillars of Objectivism, and Howard Roark is its standard-bearer. In *Fountainhead,* Roark receives an invitation from the leaders of a western city to design a "March of the Centuries" fair. Roark, who is desperate for work in the middle of the Great Depression, is hired as part of a team of eight architects. Roark agrees to take the job—on the condition that the other seven architects aren't hired. He insists on working alone, knowing full well that his stubbornness will cause him to lose the job. "I don't work with collectives. I don't consult, I don't co-operate, I don't collaborate," he says.[13]

That was one of the passages in *Fountainhead* that appealed to me the most. What's more, here was a Rand hero, one of the towering figures of her body of work, who *doesn't like money.* "Does he like money?" Ellsworth Toohey asks Peter Keating. "No," answers Keating, a longtime friend of Roark's who presumably wasn't engaged in this exchange for the purpose of passing on misinformation to the reader.[14]

Keep in mind that *The Fountainhead* is one of the two basic texts of Objectivism, the Palestinian Talmud of the Objectivist liturgy even if *Atlas Shrugged* stands taller as the more-authoritative, more-quoted Babylonian Talmud. I was anxious to hear Allison's views on what these and similar passages in *The Fountainhead* teach us about modern corporate management. Did he run his bank that way, without committees and collaboration?

No, he didn't.

"I really like the characters in *Atlas Shrugged* better than *The Fountainhead* because I think they were more developed," said Allison. As CEO of the bank, he wanted employees to think for themselves, but teamwork was still essential. "In an organizational context, we are 'in it together,' and we have to have a team."

"Where teamwork gets misinterpreted," he said, "is where it becomes that somehow we're going to groupthink this out."

But Roark was no team player, groupthink or no groupthink. That was the entire point of the book—the individual over the collective. And what is a team if not a collective? A team player wouldn't have turned down a chance to work with a great team of architects. A team player wouldn't have blown up Cortlandt Homes, come to think of it. Would Roark have been satisfied if some member of the city administration had come to him and said, "We're in it together"?

What I was seeing here is a perennial issue for Ayn Rand followers—the need to finesse aspects of her teachings that make no sense, or seem superficially coherent but crumble upon even cursory examination.* Much as one might dislike committees, they are needed for the operation of large organizations. Yet Rand, in *Fountainhead,* is adamantly opposed to any kind of group decision making.

Allison proceeded to describe to me how meetings at BB&T were structured so as to not be "popularity contests" and to bring out the best thinking of the people at the bank. All good stuff, and there's no dispute that BB&T was a well-managed bank while Allison was there, avoiding many of the pitfalls that troubled banks in general during the decade. But I was hard-pressed to figure out what any of this had to do with Rand—or how it was consistent with the extreme individualism espoused in *Fountainhead.* In fact, it seemed arguable that applying Rand's individual-over-collective principle might put a company out of business, especially if greed were factored in.

Allison suggested that I take a look at *Atlas Shrugged,* "which is a little more mature." But that didn't resolve this contradiction, because *Atlas* is

* Sympathetic treatments of Ayn Rand, and Objectivist propaganda generally, tend to ignore *The Fountainhead*'s anti-teamwork message. A good example is *Ayn Rand and Business* (New York: Texere, 2001), by Donna Greiner and Theodore Kinni. It discusses Howard Roark at length while skirting his strong aversion to working with others—one of the bedrock principles of modern American management.

aimed in a different ideological direction—not at individuality but capitalism, which is barely mentioned in *Fountainhead.* Even the expletives are different. Instead of the dastardly "second-handers" of *Fountainhead,* Rand hoots at "looters" running amok in *Atlas Shrugged.*

Allison later sent me a pamphlet that is distributed to all bank employees, setting forth the "BB&T Philosophy." It's saturated with Objectivism, though Rand's name is never mentioned. The "attributes of an outstanding BB&T employee" are defined as purpose, rationality, and self-esteem. It's certainly hard to argue with any of those traits. Does anyone want shiftless, irrational, self-hating curs in their cubicles? The only discordant note is a passage toward the beginning containing obligatory language on "making the communities in which we work better places to be," which is a genuflect toward standard small-town altruism. This being a bank, I'm sure they don't mean it, so I guess it doesn't matter.

A good corporate manager is a compromiser, a conciliator, a negotiator, and Allison appeared to be all those things. Could there be compromise and conciliation between Objectivism and the followers of Jehovah? As Rand's stature grows in the American right, atheism is going to be a sticking point with the all-important Christian wing of the Republican Party and the Tea Party movement. All these God-fearing people mustn't be dissed, not if Rand is to have any traction with them. As Paul Bell pointed out at the Objectivist group meeting some weeks earlier, the "people who believe in God" are necessary to eradicate the plague of collectivism sweeping the nation.

Allison pointed out to me that there are people who call themselves "Christian Objectivists." To me, that seemed as much an oxymoron as those obnoxious "Hebrew Christians" who hand out pamphlets on street corners. People have told Allison on many occasions that they agree with Rand on everything but religion. But in the Objectivist canon, rationality is incompatible with faith. You can use loaves and fishes to make sardine sandwiches, but you can't use five of them to feed the multitude.

Allison has walked down this path before. He told me that he had a "very religious upbringing." And now? He groped for the mildest way to express his atheism. "I would call myself now primarily an advocate of reason. I'm not antireligious as much as I'm nonreligious." It "evolved over a period of time."

I could hear the hisses and boos at Tea Party rallies. A godless right-wing North Carolina banker? Multiple stereotypes were being smashed on the floor before my eyes, right here in a nice hotel on Lexington Avenue.

I confided to Allison that my own faith had been undermined by reading Rand. Why go to the synagogue on the High Holidays? Why pray? What's the point?

He was sympathetic. I felt a bond forming over this issue. "Here's what Rand said. These are very powerful arguments," said Allison, now acting as my spiritual advisor as well as my guidance counselor. "First she said that anybody who asserts the existence of God has to prove it. And she said that religious people want to avoid it in an area where they would never accept that argument in any other part of their lives. 'Prove the existence of God and I'll believe it' is what she said. Of course, nobody has proved the existence of God. And related to that she rejected faith as a means of knowledge.

"And she did it for a very good reason, I think," he continued. "She said if you look at what happens in wars, if my faith is different from your faith, and neither one of us can prove it, we say we both got it from some magical means, there's no way to settle the dispute without going to war. She said faith is very dangerous because it's not subject to proof."

It was hard to argue with Allison on that point. In fact, he won me over. Two days later I slept late on Yom Kippur and ate a hearty breakfast. I felt relieved. But I didn't feel good about it.

CHAPTER FIVE

The Apostates

John Allison had a valid point when he said that faith is dangerous because it is not subject to proof. One could say that about any religion or cult. As a matter of fact, one could say that about Objectivism. Political and philosophical movements don't have fervent believers or hated apostates. They don't tar opponents as evil. They don't excommunicate dissidents. They don't vilify people who have personal entanglements with the leader of the movement. Objectivism does.

The most famous Rand excommunicatees were Nathaniel and Barbara Branden, Rand's most prominent deputies. Both are still with us, and both talked with me, Barbara considerably longer than Nathaniel, who for many years was second only to Rand herself in the Objectivist hierarchy.

Nathaniel, born Nathan Blumenthal in Ontario, was a student at UCLA when he wrote a fan letter to Rand and was invited to visit her at the Rand ranch in the San Fernando Valley. Branden's fiancée Barbara (née Weidman), also Canadian, joined Nathaniel in a close relationship with Rand. When they moved to New York in the early 1950s to study at New York University, Rand moved to the city as well. The so-called "Collective" formed around them, and in its early years largely consisted of Barbara's relatives and friends from Canada. Among them were her cousin Leonard Peikoff and a friend of Barbara's who had just married a gawky young economist named Alan Greenspan.

There's no point in rehashing what happened next in any great detail, titillating as it may be. Today we would call it an inappropriate sexual relationship. Rand and Branden began an affair in 1955 after getting the agonized "permission" of both spouses. They broke it off in 1968 when Branden fell for a younger woman, also not his wife. Barbara Branden told the whole grimy story in her 1986 book *The Passion of Ayn Rand*. A Showtime movie adapted from the book followed in 1999, starring Helen Mirren as Rand, Julie Delpy as Barbara, Eric Stoltz as Nathaniel, and Peter Fonda playing Frank O'Connor. Seeing Helen Mirren, as Rand, engaged in sexual intercourse must be one of the more lurid moments in TV-movie history, and the film's critical reception was mixed. A *New York Times* reviewer said that "even the estimable Helen Mirren cannot make a compelling protagonist of loopy old Ayn Rand."[1] Whatever the film's artistic merits, it and the book did a fine job of trashing what was left of Rand's reputation.

Excommunications were already a feature of Objectivist life by the time Iris Bell joined the Rand circle in the early 1960s. After her split from the Brandens, Rand became progressively more paranoid and neurotic. Loyalists quit one after the other in disgust at her obnoxious behavior—such as hounding Collective members about their views of art—or were removed from her presence for minor slights. Of the dwindling number of Collective members who remained loyal and unpurged at the time of her death, the most prominent were Peikoff and Alan Greenspan.

The excommunications and purges continued long after her death. The most recent bloodletting took place late in 2010, and involved an Ayn Rand Institute board member named John McCaskey.[2] Like the earlier rumbles in Objectivism, the McCaskey dirty linen was aired only in Randian circles. Even the Branden break received nary a mention in the media at the time it happened. McCaskey, an Objectivist academic on the ARI board, was privately critical of a book for which Peikoff had penned an introduction. Peikoff dashed off an e-mail to a Goldman Sachs attorney who served as the ARI board cochairperson. He said, "When a great book sponsored by the Institute and championed by me—I hope you still know who I am and what my intellectual status is in Objectivism—is denounced by a member of the Board of the Institute which I founded someone has to go and will go. It is your prerogative to decide whom." Peikoff has never been accused of being humble.

Although McCaskey had raised money for the ARI, it was of no consequence. He had offended Leonard Peikoff. The e-mail went on: "As Ayn would have put it, that raises him one rung in Hell, but it does not convert Objectivism into pragmatism." McCaskey promptly resigned, calling Peikoff's remarks "insultingly unjust."[3]

If this seems almost like a family quarrel, it's because it was exactly that. As is common in cults, what surrounded the Spiritual Leader was a kind of insular, extended, dysfunctional family. The photographs of Ayn Rand's inner circle of the 1950s and 1960s have a sepia-toned character, an innocence, the young gathering to listen to the old, to talk. They reminded me of photos of family gatherings from that era, sans kids. When I mentioned this to Barbara Branden, she agreed. "We were united by common values, and we were sort of alone in a hostile universe," she said. "And we did have a sense of family, caring for each other and wanting to spend time together, yes."

It was very much a family, replete with the kind of breakups and alienation that happen in families, with relatives sometimes not talking for years. Barbara hasn't talked to her cousin Leonard Peikoff since 1968. In a documentary about Peikoff, a direct-to-DVD release called *Leonard Peikoff: In His Own Words,* Peikoff talks about being introduced to Rand by a cousin. He doesn't say that the cousin was Barbara Branden. Neither Barbara nor Nathaniel Branden is mentioned by name in that stirringly narcissistic self-celebration. That's because they were unpersons after the split with Rand.

In the Rand cult of the 1950s and 1960s, if you were on the outs with this family, you were *evil.* "That's a word that Objectivists toss around with gay abandon," Barbara said. You were denounced, sometimes publicly. You were shunned. You were not a person.

The Branden excommunication, or the "Break" as it is known to Objectivists, was the most momentous division within Rand's world during her lifetime, kind of a Grand Inquisition with adultery thrown in. Barbara is past eighty now, and she had once been as close to Ayn Rand as a daughter to a mother—albeit a mother who was sleeping with her daughter's husband. I didn't reach out to Barbara to rake over that well-worn scandal, but we did discuss the film. She wasn't happy with the emphasis on sex in the movie, but she had no control over that. She did think that Peter Fonda's portrayal of Frank O'Connor—Rand's hapless, gentle, cuckolded husband—was a moving performance, one that she said unerringly captured the tortured soul of the man who had the misfortune to be married to Ayn Rand.

The film version of *The Passion of Ayn Rand* wasn't exactly *Citizen Kane,* but it was much better than the critically skewered *Atlas Shrugged* movie that was released in April 2011, and Barbara's book has stood the test of time. It was initially denounced as fiction by Peikoff (even though he said he never read it). But even Peikoff was forced to eventually admit, in the ARI documentary *Sense of Life,* that its central revelation—that Rand had been sleeping with her young deputy, Nathaniel Branden—was true. It began by mutual consent, but ultimately degenerated into sexual harassment. When Branden wanted to end the affair, Rand would not take no for an answer. She did more than break up with him; she sought to destroy him. She trashed both Brandens, especially Nathaniel, at length in an Objectivist newsletter.[4] But except for die-hard Objectivists, most people who have given the matter any serious thought have sided with the Brandens.

I had a brief telephone chat with a frail-sounding Nathaniel Branden, now in his eighties. Unlike his ex-wife, who was quite happy to talk, interviewing him was like pulling teeth. He begged off after about fifteen minutes. I'm not sure whether he cut short the interview out of fatigue or annoyance with my questions (my suspicion is a bit of both).

Despite a curse that Rand placed on his head like a Gypsy queen in a bad movie, Branden has done quite well for himself in the post-Rand era. Since his split with Rand his career veered away from Objectivism toward pop psychology, and he has authored numerous books on self-esteem, in addition to his tell-all memoir *My Years with Ayn Rand*. Generally speaking he has not asserted his Randian seniority, though he has occasionally appeared on panels. "I've had a lot of health problems. I've sort of withdrawn from the world," he said. He didn't seem to be following the nation's political struggles, but did have an opinion on the Tea Party movement. It wasn't very positive. "Their whole approach is not intellectual," he said. "I have no quarrel with the Tea Parties but I don't know what they're going to accomplish in the long run."

In a conventional political, philosophical, or social movement, old warriors like the Brandens would be considered a valuable resource, and their spat with Rand would be viewed as ancient history. But Objectivism is anything but conventional. The ARI, still dominated by Peikoff, continues to view the Brandens as unspeakable traitors, even though Rand's accusations against them were false and both remain stout defenders of Objectivism and Rand's works. "All [Peikoff] knows is that Ayn broke with me, and that's all he has to know. I'm evil. I'm really the devil incarnate," Barbara said laconically. In *Sense of Life,* the ARI-sanctioned propaganda film, the Brandens are referred to only briefly and disparagingly, and without giving their side of the story. That was not a fluke or oversight. The filmmaker's access to the ARI archives was conditioned on not interviewing the Brandens and largely omitting them from the film.[5] Neither of the Brandens was interviewed for *100 Voices,* the ARI oral history published late in 2010. Included were edited transcripts of interviews with every other person who had any kind of contact with Rand, from her sister in Russia to the actor Robert Stack, whose TV performances she enjoyed. But there was nothing from two of the most pivotal figures in Objectivist history.

It's really quite extraordinary that such a rich source of Rand lore is ignored by the ARI elders—and good news, I suppose, for people who don't like Objectivism. The Brandens hold a position that can be claimed by few people alive today: They had been in the Objectivist movement from the very beginning. Until the Break with Rand, Nathaniel and Barbara Branden were her top aides; after them came Peikoff and Greenspan, at about the same level of Randian status. Barbara and Nathaniel were entrusted by Rand to write a sycophantic volume called *Who Is Ayn Rand?* in 1962. As chief speaker at the NBI, Branden was the Elmer Gantry of Objectivism. Both Nathaniel and Barbara were involved in publishing Objectivist newsletters with Rand. Nathaniel contributed to the Rand anthologies and wrote copiously for her newsletters, making him the most prominent author of Randian doctrine other than Rand herself.

Given her history, I was anxious to get Barbara Branden's perspective on the Rand revival. To an outsider, it would seem that Rand was never more popular than she is today, even more so than she was at the height of her post-*Atlas* fame in the late 1950s and early 1960s. Barbara agreed. Back then, she said, Objectivism was shunned. "It was a period during which Ayn's ideas were so brand new, they were condemned everywhere, really everywhere," she said. But now, night has turned into day. "It's quite remarkable what's going on, that Ayn's having a greater influence, specifically politically, than she's ever had before. It's an immense influence. It's everywhere," she said. What makes this especially stunning, she said, is that "for years she was as much ignored as it was possible to ignore her. It's no longer true. She can't be ignored."

During Barbara's nearly two decades in the Rand inner circle, Rand was little more than a pariah. "You know," she said, "at the time *Atlas Shrugged* came out, the real disappointment to Ayn was that although the sales after the beginning picked up and did well and the fan mail reached the ceiling, nevertheless, there were no public voices of significant people defending her. That was very painful to her. Today, there's all sorts of public voices everywhere." She happily reeled off for me the names of the Fox commentators who were constantly evoking Rand, sounding more like a fresh convert to the cause than someone who had been excommunicated by the grand old lady of radical capitalism.

To Barbara, the reason for the Rand resurgence is simple: The state of the nation is a mess. People are looking for solutions, "and people are finding that Ayn Rand has a consistent alternative." That was not the case when *Atlas* was first published in the midst of the postwar prosperity. Unions were much stronger than they are today, and even during the Eisenhower Administration there was greater respect for traditional, liberal, New Deal values than there is today, when the radical right is attacking all of the cherished progressive icons, from public radio to Planned Parenthood to Medicare.

Rand "was tremendously isolated" during the 1950s, Barbara said, "and she was for many years. Not now." Barbara recounted the new Rand Era with total satisfaction, consistent with the view of many acolytes that Rand was a flawed human being but created an essentially sound philosophy.

Barbara began to see the Rand revival gathering strength during the George W. Bush administration. "It's when I think people became utterly disillusioned politically," she said, "and realized that the direction of this country is pretty bad and were turning against liberalism and seeing that it wasn't working." Then the election of Barack Obama—"the worst disaster ever to hit this country"—helped Rand on her rise. "There, in my view, the disaster of liberalism was naked in a way it had never been before."

One might not agree with her negative view of liberalism, but in one sense her assessment seemed quite canny. Obama had indeed been outspoken in his progressivism, so I guess there had to be a backlash. And there was. Its name was Rand. Obama came into office at the time of the worst economic disaster since the Great Depression, for which he was blamed, no matter how many times he correctly pointed out that it didn't begin on his watch. It didn't matter how forcefully Obama portrayed himself as an agent of change; after January 20, 2009, he became the status quo. And as Barbara pointed out to me, "People could not avoid seeing that something was wrong with the status quo. Desperately wrong."

I'm sure Barbara spoke for her old mentor when she said that the 2008 financial crisis showed "people that they need an alternative to what's happening at present. What's going on now has led us into a depression, and we're not going to get out of it by doing the same thing we've always been doing." While the media and studies of the crisis, including the Financial Crisis Inquiry Commission, focused on the actions of the banks and the failures of regulators, Objectivism gained from—and promoted—a revisionist history of the crisis, which laid the blame directly on the lap of government. When I gently pointed out to Barbara the standard view that perhaps the crisis was a product of out-of-control capitalism, she responded, as Rand would have, "We haven't seen out-of-control capitalism in about a hundred and fifty years."

Now, this might sound like the typical right-libertarian view of the crisis, which it is, but it was not coming from a typical libertarian right-winger. It was coming from a pioneer of Objectivism, someone who was present at the creation of the credo that has become so prominent since 2008. As a matter of fact, this was the woman who convinced Alan Greenspan, back in the fifties, that the government should not be in the business of chartering banks. This was briefly alluded to in Nathaniel Branden's memoir, but was omitted entirely from *The Passion of Ayn Rand*.[6]

"It was at a party, if I remember correctly, and somehow, I don't remember how the subject came up, but the two of us were talking and somehow it came up, and I spoke my piece and apparently it made sense to him," said Barbara. "I was very proud of myself but I'm not an economist." But Greenspan was—an economic consultant of increasing influence among some of the top industrial companies of America. "I probably couldn't have said one sentence more on the subject than I did say" to Greenspan, she recalled, given her limited knowledge of banking.

There is no reference to that conversation, and only a fleeting reference to his old comrades the Brandens, in Greenspan's voluminous 2007 memoir, *The Age of Turbulence*. He portrays his devotion to Rand as a youthful fling, like an early infatuation with Deep Purple. In an epilogue for the paperback edition, written in the midst of the financial crisis, Greenspan gives his version of the nightmare that was then unfolding. It was classic Greenspan—lengthy, convoluted, but with a bottom line that hewed closely to Rand. No new regulation of the financial markets was necessary. "If material well being is our goal," he said, "I see no alternative to global market capitalism."[7]

Barbara seemed as loyal to Rand's philosophy as ever, but her view of the modern-day Objectivist leadership was harsh. She called the Ayn Rand Institute a hotbed of "Objectivist fundamentalists" and felt that their strict view of Objectivism had harmed the cause. "They're doing some good things, they're spreading her books, but I think that they're doing more harm than good because of their fanaticism and their dogmatism."

That raised a question that I needed to explore: Does Objectivism have to be fanatical and dogmatic? Is there such a thing as a "moderate Objectivism," willing to change with the times and modulate its views?

In Judaism there is the reform branch. Christianity has Unitarians. Can there be such a thing for the followers of the grand old lady of radical capitalism?

Is there a place for a First Reformed Church of Rand?

CHAPTER SIX

The Secessionist

Of all the various squabbles, excommunications, walkouts, and general unpleasantness that have beset the Ayn Rand movement over the years, beginning with the Branden Break and continuing through the recent McCaskey kerfuffle, the one that keeps reverberating took place about twenty years ago. It was a division within the ranks of the Randians that was as significant and permanent as the Break, except for being G-rated.

Most intra-Objectivist squabbles are of little concern to outsiders, but this one is noteworthy because it involves the relationship between Randians and their much larger group of stepchildren, the libertarians. If it is ever resolved, Objectivism will become even stronger than it is today, and its opponents will be even more off-balance than they already are.

To the outside world, libertarians and Objectivists are roughly the same. In fact, they are not just separate movements but bitter rivals, with most of the bitterness coming from the Objectivist side. If you want to annoy an orthodox Objectivist, call him a libertarian. That's just what Greenspan did in his memoirs, when he said, "Rand wrote [*The Fountainhead*] to illustrate a philosophy she had come to, one that emphasized reason, individualism and enlightened self-interest. Later she named it objectivism; today she would be called a libertarian."[1] She might be, but it would be wrong, as a veteran Objectivist like Greenspan knew perfectly well. This seems like a blatant attempt by Greenspan to disguise the extremist character of Rand's radical, no-government, atheistic, and, to a great many people, shockingly amoral belief system.

Libertarians and Objectivists have a lot in common, but from the beginning the libertarians annoyed the hell out of Rand. At its dawn in the early 1970s, the libertarian movement was widely viewed as a quirky right-wing variation of the New Left, sharing its anarchic, antiestablishment spirit. Rand dismissed it out of hand.[2] "I disapprove of, disagree with and have no connection with, the latest aberration of some conservatives, the so-called 'hippies of the right' who attempt to snare the younger or more careless ones of my readers by claiming simultaneously to be followers of my philosophy and advocates of anarchism," she wrote in her newsletter in 1971.[3]

It was a failure of imagination and a major political blunder, in hindsight, because libertarianism matured over the years to become the influential political movement that it is today. I doubt very much that Rand would have cared that she was losing friends and failing to influence people. It was not in her nature to pander to people she viewed as unworthy. To this day, the Ayn Rand Institute keeps the faith with Rand's libertarian-bashing, carrying on its Web site a page of excerpts from Rand's lectures in which she bad-mouthed libertarians. It includes a quotation from 1972, in which she said she would "rather vote for Bob Hope, the Marx Brothers, or Jerry Lewis." There's also a passage from 1973, in which she called the Libertarian Party a "cheap attempt at publicity" that would not succeed, and said that libertarians were her "enemies" and were "plagiarizing my ideas."[4]

That kind of overheated language was typical of Rand. She did not hesitate to lash out at her brethren on the right, repeatedly expressing revulsion at, for instance, anti-intellectualism among Republicans and conservatives. In a 1974 newsletter article, Rand expressed outrage about a proposal to impose government controls on the press, condemning "the *smell* of the conservatives' style: the stale odor of rancorous anti-intellectuality, concrete-bound stubbornness, shifting murk, evasion, appeasement, compromise—and, ultimately, nothing but a festering hostility."[5]

Rand, determined to maintain ideological purity, would never have backed off from her opposition to the libertarians. This attitude persisted long after her death. In 1989, the editor of ARI's *The Intellectual Activist* newsletter, Peter Schwartz, argued that libertarianism was "evil" and spoke out against "trafficking with Libertarians." The reason for Schwartz's ire was that an Objectivist activist named David Kelley, a friend of Peikoff's, had tried to open a dialogue with libertarians and had failed to denounce *The Passion of Ayn Rand.*[6] Schwartz maintained that "the 'benefits' of speaking to Libertarian groups are as nonexistent as the 'benefits' of exhibiting books at an Iranian fair." Schwartz described libertarians as a "movement that embraces the advocates of child-molesting, the proponents of unilateral U.S. disarmament, the LSD-taking and bomb-throwing members of the New Left, the communist guerrillas in Central America and the baby-killing followers of Yassir Arafat. These views have all been accepted under the Libertarian umbrella (and remain accepted under it by everyone who still calls himself a Libertarian)."[7]

Kelley was drummed out of the Objectivist movement for that transgression. Colleges were warned by the ARI not to invite him as a speaker. "This is the behavior of religious zealots," Kelley later wrote.[8] But unlike previous ruptures in Objectivism, in which the dissidents quietly slinked off, Kelley published a rebuttal of the attacks against him and founded a competing group called the Institute for Objectivist Studies, which morphed into the Objectivist Center, now known as the Atlas Society.

If Objectivism is a religion, the Kelley expulsion falls into place as a natural part of the evolution of the creed. All major religions have internal schisms. Kelley's principal difference with the ARI is that he believes in Objectivism as an open system, capable of evolving and open to new ideas, while the ARI views Objectivism as a closed system, an all-encompassing credo that was handed down as a complete entity by Rand, with Murray Hill serving as a kind of Objectivist Mount Sinai. Like Moses descending down the mountain to give the Law to the ungrateful children of Israel, Rand descended down the elevator of 36 East 36th Street (and later her apartment building on 34th Street) to give Objectivist Law to the unwelcoming and unworthy peoples of the world.

Libertarians, being live-and-let-live types, don't seem to care that Rand thought that they were pond scum, that Kelley was purged for talking to them, and that Rand objected violently to their adopting her views. She is idolized like a rejecting but flawless mother-figure, and remains one of the founding ideological parents of libertarianism.

Actually, Rand wound up on the wrong side of history. Libertarians may have seemed flaky and derivative in the early 1970s, but they did not turn out to be the flash-in-the-pan cretins that Rand, and later Schwartz, thought they were. The Objectivist movement, bad-mouthing notwithstanding, is slowly recognizing that fact. In recent years, especially since the rise of the Tea Party, the Objectivist-libertarian gulf has eroded. While it used to be a Grand Canyon of recriminations and name-calling (at least by Rand and her followers), it has gradually narrowed to a mere roadside ditch that can be easily leaped. This is a significant development that hasn't gotten much attention outside of Objectivist circles, and has the potential to extend Rand's influence.

The Tea Party has helped bring Objectivists and libertarians together. Yaron Brook cannily latched on to the importance of the movement, giving the keynote address at one of the largest Tea Party rallies, held in Boston on July 4, 2009. The energy of the gathering, and dozens of others across the country, presented an opportunity that was not to be missed. Rather than repeat Rand's mistake and turn up their noses at the God-fearing, libertarian-leaning crowds waiving their unauthorized "Who is John Galt?" posters, the keepers of the Rand flame at the ARI decided to join them rather than take on the impossible task of beating them.

The ARI created a page catering to the Tea Party masses on its Web site, carefully sanitized to make no mention of atheism.[9] It hosted an "Intellectual Ammunition Strategy Workshop," attended free of charge by 250 Tea Party organizers, a day before the 9/12 Tea Party in Washington, D.C., in September 2009. "The goal of these gatherings is to get Congress and the Obama administration [to] hear our voices," said an online flyer advertising the capacity-crowd workshop. "However mostly they have heard only emotionalism, mixed messages, and vaguely partisan bromides. To make the Tea Party movement an effective weapon in the war of ideas for individual liberty, the attendees must argue coherently and consistently for positive goals."[10]

What's considerably more interesting than this standard Objectivist rhetoric is the cosponsor of the workshop: the Competitive Enterprise Institute, a libertarian think tank.

The libertarian-Objectivist relationship came full circle in early 2010, when Yaron Brook gave a speech at the Oxford Libertarian Society.[11] Twenty-one years earlier, Kelley was drummed out of the ARI and denounced because, among other things, he appeared before the libertarian "Laissez Faire Supper Club."

It seemed that a radically new concept was sweeping Ayn Rand's America: accommodation. That impression was reinforced when I read chitchat on Internet message boards that the ARI had actually moved to reconcile with David Kelley! That would be like a reunification of Roman Catholicism with the Eastern Orthodox church. For years, Kelley's exclusion from the Objectivist movement was the epitome of much of what was wrong with Objectivism from the far-right harmony perspective—its Soviet-style lack of tolerance, its rigidity, its leaders' tendency to make harsh moral judgments about people wavering from the party line. If there ever is to be a kumbaya on the far right, if both wings of Objectivism are to unite, then to link arms with their comrades in the libertarian movement and the Tea Party, they could form a Radical Capitalist United Front capable of sweeping all before them. Democrats and liberals may scoff at this as an alliance of "wingnuts," but progressives have always failed to judge the strength of right-wing populism and the ideological muscle of Ayn Rand. The 2010 midterm elections proved that.

I reached out to David Kelley, to see if this report was true. Meanwhile, I mulled the implications.

I could see the ARI dominating such an alliance. The Atlas Society is much smaller than the ARI, judging from their IRS financial filings.[12] Their IRS returns are public information thanks to regulations that require disclosure of finances for tax-exempt, nonprofit 501(c)(3) charitable organizations. Yes, both are *nonprofit* groups, in contrast to the old Nathaniel Branden Institute, which was a profit-making operation. In the irony-resistant Objectivist world there is evidently no contradiction between these groups' ideology and their nonprofit status. Apparently the ARI's Tea Party evangelism and political agitation—the St. Regis fund-raiser was as political an event as I've ever attended—didn't fall afoul of the prohibitions against political activity by 501(c)(3) organizations, which rake in tax-deductible donations from donors. IRS rules prohibit nonprofits from favoring "groups of candidates."[13] I guess you have to hand out campaign buttons to get the IRS interested in such things, though there were inklings in mid-2011 that this blasé attitude may be changing. The IRS was starting to take a hard look at nonprofit groups with a political agenda. Their tax-exempt status was not only an indirect taxpayer subsidy for political activity—quite an irony, considering the Objectivist stance toward taxation—but also shielded the identity of financial backers.[14]

Both the ARI and Atlas Society seemed to be doing quite well despite the hard times that had befallen nonprofits in general. That's not surprising, given that both were feel-good groups serving the interests of rich people, and rich people can afford to splurge on their own self-interests in any economic climate. In 2009, the last year for which I could get comparable figures, the Atlas Society's contributions and grants of $1.1 million were a fraction of the $6.5 million that was taken in by the ARI in the same year, and Kelley drew a far smaller salary of $67,496, compared with Brook's $439,000. Viewed as a proportion of annual contributions, Brook's compensation package, even subtracting his $180,000 bonus, was considerably more generous than Kelley's. In 2010, the ARI's income increased dramatically to $11.8 million, in a vivid illustration of the growing popularity of radical capitalism.[15] Comparable figures for the Atlas Society (which still files with the IRS as the "Objectivist Center" for some reason) weren't available.

In theory at least, a reunification or alliance between the two rival organizations, combining ideological rigor with a more open attitude, would improve the chances of Rand becoming more palatable to the non-Objectivist world. It also might appeal to the rank and file.

I was picking up indications that the ARI's dogmatic approach turned off not a few ordinary Randians. That was true for some of the people I met in New York Objectivist circles, including Victor Niederhoffer, the trader and Junto organizer. Victor and his wife, Susan, were both close to the Atlas Society and less enamored of the ARI, which Susan described to me as "too doctrinaire." I hadn't raised the subject of the Atlas Society with John Allison, but he struck me as an ecumenical sort despite his fairly hard-line approach to Objectivism. When I spoke with Barbara Branden, she understandably viewed the Atlas Society far more favorably than the ARI, telling me that Atlas "does good work. They're open to other ideas. They're open to debate."

"The ARI," she said, "considers Ayn Rand next to a goddess. Not next to—she's a goddess. Perfect. But Kelley's group feels that she was a human being and made mistakes, both in her personal life and in her ideas. They agree with her to a considerable extent but they're not fanatics."

When I finally spoke with David Kelley, he was cautious. "Maybe we should put our cards on the table. I don't read the financial press very much, but from a quick look at some of the things you've written I have a pretty strong impression that you write from a different perspective from Objectivism," he said, diplomatically understating the case. "So I'm happy to speak with you, but there's a certain degree of caution here because we're interested in promoting Ayn Rand and providing information about her."

This was no malcontent intent on blowing the whistle on Objectivism. His concerns notwithstanding, he did talk to me, albeit cautiously. To try to break the ice, I told him about how in the 1990s the free market was considered the enemy by members of the Mafia trying to exploit microcap stocks. In fact, I explicitly made that point in my 2003 book *Born to Steal*. Kelley was only partly mollified. "The Mafia is not a free market," he sniffed (which was actually my point . . .). We chatted a little about Poughkeepsie, New York, where he used to live and which was my mother's hometown. No ice broken there, either.

After a while he relaxed a little and told me about his childhood in Shaker Heights, an affluent Cleveland suburb, where he was the son of a politically active lawyer. He read *The Fountainhead* in high school. It pointed the way toward the kind of person he wanted to be (and became, judging from his individualistic stance toward the Objectivist establishment). Kelley was born in 1949, so he came of age during the great conformist movement known as the counterculture.

I asked him to relate his early Rand readings to the mores of the time. "Maybe I can put it this way," he responded, "a little bit of a philosophical simplification. The kind of values that were taught through families, churches, newspapers, were still kind of a mix of 'make your own way in the world' and 'be part of a team, the American Team.' Be nice to people. It was a mix of what philosophically would be egoism and altruism." Also a touch of Organization Man, too, I guess. All healthy values, at least to non-Objectivists, but a mishmash.

Kelley was not from a particularly religious family, and he was an atheist from early in life, which eased his eventual transition into Objectivism. "Rand clarified so many things, had thought so much further down roads that I was beginning to explore in my high school level way." Her rejection of altruism didn't bother him. "I could see that she was not against benevolence or against friendship or love." The idea of self-sacrifice never made sense to him, and neither did the "glorification of what for want of a better word I would call 'niceness,' the emphasis on niceness in WASP society." But it was clear that Rand was in favor of positive relationships, what she described as the "trader principle": offering "value for value" and "not expecting people to give you anything unless you have something to offer, and vice versa," he said.

I was hearing that slice of Objectivist dogma frequently from Allison and the other Objectivists I encountered. They'd quote Rand as idealizing the "trader" as "a man who earns what he gets and does not give or take the undeserved." She contended that "a trader does not expect to be paid for his defaults, only for his achievements."[16] As a philosophical position it had a certain elegance. It sure sounded kind of . . . well I guess the word is *nice*. But I had a lot of trouble with that concept, for her idealized image of the trader struck me as entirely fictitious. Perhaps she shouldn't have said "trader." She could have made up something, like "give-and-taker," to describe this nonexistent species of human.

Her description of "traders" had nothing in common with the real-life traders most people encounter during their lives, whether they are the corner grocer, the other side of a stock trade, or Walmart. I doubt that many actual traders view themselves as Rand described them, as that would indicate a degree of self-delusion that would hamper them in the performance of their duties. They don't give a damn if their gains are "undeserved." They buy low and sell high, and are compensated on their ability to do that. That doesn't make them bad people. It's simply their job. If they traded only "value for value" in "win-win" situations they'd get fired. "Fair trade" is an advertising slogan, not a business practice. As Albert Ellis pointed out, "All over the world in various kinds of economies, a trader generally is mainly interested in taking what he does not (according to Ms. Rand's standards) deserve. One siren call of capitalists is 'caveat emptor' or 'let the buyer beware.' "*

Such contradictions between reality and rhetoric didn't bother Kelley as a young acolyte. He was sold. Adopting Rand's philosophy presented not a philosophical but a practical problem because of the emphasis on conformity in his suburban habitat. Adopting Randian ideas was like wearing white socks with a tuxedo. Kelley found that the counterculture swapped its own brand of uniformity for the adult variety. "That was even more conformist," Kelley said. "That was picking out the altruistic, collectivist side. It was celebrated as individualism" but it wasn't. He reacted strongly against that, more strongly against the rigid conformity of his peers than of his parents' generation. At the same time, Rand's influence on his political thinking alienated him from his parents, who were Roosevelt Democrats. "We had quite a few arguments over the dinner table. My dad had very strong political interests."

Walter C. Kelley was an old-fashioned progressive, a municipal lawyer

* Ellis also observed: "A trader does not treat people as independent equals, but usually tries to fool them, even enslave them to his wishes. He prefers to deal with them by means of trickery or forced and coercive exchange without competition trying to get them to do his bidding, whether they like it or not. He does expect to be paid for his defaults as well as his achievements. And, in most cases, he tries to blame others for his failures not to mention to rationalize, when he does fail, and pretend that he has not. Rand's picture of the capitalist producer and trader is ideal; and it is an ideal that is so far removed from social and biological reality that it probably never will be realized. Worse, she deludes herself that her ideal is reality, that people are the way she pictures them. No wonder she is so horribly disillusioned with people's actual behavior!"[17]

in Cleveland who was mayor of Shaker Heights in the 1970s. During that time he gained a national reputation for liberal policies, getting a pat on the back from *The New York Times* for promoting "benign steering" that encouraged racial integration.[18] Kelley said his disputes with his father, though sometimes heated, were intellectual, not emotional. "Politics is not all of life," he pointed out. Still, one can only imagine what a dyed-in-the-wool liberal like Walter Kelley must have thought of his son's flirtation with the radical right.

Shaker Heights had a large Jewish population and was a bit more progressive than most Midwestern suburbs. Undeterred by his liberal environs and lamentable family background, Kelley doggedly tracked down right-thinking teenagers to exchange ideas, and continued his Objectivist studies by subscribing to Rand's newsletter *The Objectivist.* He studied philosophy at Brown University, a decision that he says was partially influenced by his fascination with Rand. She was rarely taught in colleges, and Brown was no exception. "My teachers were not interested in Rand. They knew of her and they actually discouraged people from taking [her philosophy] as a serious topic." It didn't hurt his academic career, even though he did hear about people saying behind his back, "How can Kelley be interested in that nut?"

Kelley was in the class of 1971, so he was in college at the height of the Vietnam War upheavals. Kelley recalled that some of his classmates were "seriously fellow travelers" who wanted the Vietcong to win. "They had revolution envy," he said. Kelley was on the periphery of a student group that opposed the takeover of a building by radical students, but that was about the extent of his political involvement on campus. He traveled up to Boston for a couple of Rand's annual appearances at the Ford Hall Forum, but never spoke with her, though "she did autograph my copy of *The Fountainhead.*"

After graduate study at Princeton University, Kelley took a teaching post at Vassar College in 1975, and he became acquainted with the small group of people who knew Rand personally. He met her on a couple of occasions during group meetings at her apartment on 34th Street. The gatherings were "not particularly intimate," he said. Rand impressed Kelley as "warm and hospitable, interested in ideas. She'd really engage with you. If she was talking with you, you'd know that she was talking with you, she'd focus on it." But Kelley took pains to point out that he was in no way a member of her inner circle.

One might have gathered otherwise from the prominent role that Kelley played at the funerals of both Rand and her husband, Frank O'Connor. Kelley read a Kipling poem at Frank's funeral in 1979. That, however, was at the request of his friend and mentor Leonard Peikoff, and not a sign of any particular intimacy with Rand. "Leonard didn't feel he could do it, so he asked me," Kelley explained. He read a poem at Rand's funeral in 1982, "as a service to someone I admired and learned so much from." That again was Peikoff, who later excommunicated him from Objectivism. But for the time being he was a member of the small fraternity of Rand insiders that coalesced after her death.

Kelley worked with Peikoff on his fire-breathing book *The Ominous Parallels,* and they began collaborating on an Ayn Rand reader. But then everything fell apart when Barbara Branden's book received a rave review in an obscure newsletter called *On Principle*. The problem was that Kelley was on the editorial advisory board of the newsletter. Peikoff was ready for a book burning, while Kelley thought that "the book and some of the revelations in it were kind of overdue and ought to be dealt with openly." He refused to leave the editorial board despite pressure from Peikoff. Then the libertarian supper club lecture was used against him, and it escalated into the kind of infighting that so frequently plagues Mediterranean families, co-op boards, garden clubs, and fringe political movements.[19]

It all seems petty now, but it was a major cataclysm among Objectivists at the time. What makes it seem even pettier is that the Ayn Rand Institute now actively forms alliances with libertarians. "Under Yaron Brook, for the past five years, they've changed completely," Kelley said. "They're engaged in projects with a number of organizations, American Enterprise Institute, the Atlas Economic Research Foundation"—no connection to the Atlas Society—"and yes, it is ironic that they've changed position."

Speaking of changed positions, had Rand's successors at the ARI changed their minds about Kelley and his group? Were they moving toward a merger, perhaps? I was intrigued by the Internet chatter about a meeting between Kelley and Brook sometime in the recent past.

So he told me about it, a bit grudgingly. It turns out the meeting took place in 2007, and was the first time the two sides had met since the rift. "We met to take stock, to see where we stood," said Kelley. "In one way it was a cordial meeting, but the lines were still drawn pretty sharply, not so much on the libertarian issue because they essentially had adopted our policy, but on the open versus closed view of Objectivism as a philosophy, which they still maintained." Kelley found that Brook had not opened up the ARI very much, and "not at all on the key issues of Objectivism."

Such as the continued existence of the Atlas Society.

"When we met, he said in so many words that he wanted us out of the way. He wanted the ARI to be the only Objectivist spokesman. That's not exactly opening up," Kelley said with the standard Objectivist lack of emotion.

No, it's definitely not opening up. Nor did it seem an especially American position. After all, isn't diversity of opinion an American point of view? Not to a religion, I suppose. There was no suggestion of force, he said, but there was "an effort to convince our board members to switch sides and kill us by starvation of funds."

Brook, he said, had approached several of the Atlas Society's board members to try to convince them to quit, including one board member, John Aglialoro, who was at the meeting. Aglialoro was CEO of Cybex

International, the gym-equipment manufacturer, who for some years was involved in production of a movie version of *Atlas Shrugged*. It was finally released to universal derision in April 2011.

Since board members are also the top contributors to the Atlas Society, Brook's assault on Kelley's group sounded a lot like "force" to me.

I asked Kelley to give me a rundown of the people participating in the meeting. There was Kelley and Brook, Kelley's deputy Ed Hudgins, and Aglialoro, among others. Kelley was running through the participants at the meeting in an even tone when a name whipped on by me almost without my noticing. It sounded a lot like—did he say John Allison?

Yes, he did. I was dumbstruck. *My* John Allison? My guidance counselor? The down-home North Carolina banker? "He and Yaron were making the pitch," said Kelley. Based on my conversation with Allison, it was hard for me to visualize this cerebral executive trying to muscle an entire organization out of existence. But according to Kelley he had, and, to make the entire affair seem less menacing than ludicrous, it didn't work.*

So there went my ARI–Atlas Society merger fantasy circling the drain. For Objectivists, libertarians, and advocates of no-government capitalism, it's a bad thing. It means continued disunity in the Rand camp. But it's not so great for opponents of Objectivism, either. The existence of two groups—one Orthodox and one Reform—means that there are two separate paths for proselytizing newcomers, from two groups pursuing the same radical capitalist agenda. I guess it's one of those "lose-lose" situations.

As for the issue that has bothered many people on the right over the

* I asked Allison about the ARI–Atlas meeting sometime later, and he more or less corroborated Kelley's account. He called it a "fairly friendly meeting." Brook "was searching for some kind of reconciliation, but there were philosophical issues that David Kelley holds that Yaron believes are inconsistent with Rand's philosophy. Unless David took a different view of those issues, it would be difficult to reintegrate the effort." As for the approach to donors to stop sending money to the Atlas Society, Allison said "I understand how David would interpret it that way," and put it in the context of ARI competing with Atlas for donor funds. "I think the approach would have been, ARI would have said, 'Look, if you support Objectivism, we believe that what David Kelley's doing is actually hurting Objectivism, because he's got a distortion of Rand's philosophy, and therefore instead of giving to David, you ought to give to us.'"

years, the Objectivist rejection of religion, none of this infighting counts for very much. Kelley agreed that there has been some pushback from Tea Party activists and other right-leaning people regarding the Objectivist devotion to atheism. But it doesn't matter. That is one issue that unites all true-blue Objectivists, be they ARI hard-liners, Atlas Society open-model thinkers, or Midtown Restaurant loyalists. Whether they struggled with the issue or not, all eventually fall in line, or cannot call themselves followers of the lady with the pageboy haircut.

"Atheism has been one of the 'nuts' people encounter when they get involved in Objectivism," Kelley conceded, "one of the hard things. It's a point of resistance for a lot of people."

One can certainly accept Objectivism without the atheism. But that's a bit like drinking decaffeinated coffee in the morning and expecting to get a buzz. A God-fearing Objectivist may not be dragged into an alley and beaten up, but he won't ever be truly part of the movement. "It's not that we're antireligion, per se, or anti-God," said Kelley. "We're in favor of reason so therefore against faith." It's not opposition to religious doctrine, he said, but how one functions. Or as Yaron Brook and Tara Smith would put it, how one thinks.

Whatever else may transpire between Objectivist factions, whether they're open, closed, or ajar, it doesn't matter. "There's no difference where we stand," Kelley told me. "We're atheists." And that's that. No ifs, ands, or buts.

Amen.

CHAPTER SEVEN

The Cool Objectivist

By this point I was seeing why Objectivism was so widely viewed as a religion or cult, whose core values were militant atheism, hyper-individualism, worship of capitalism, and repudiation of Judeo-Christian concepts of morality. It was exclusivist and intolerant; it was prone to rigidity and vilified ideological opponents. While the Atlas Society was a bit more flexible, it was small and weak compared to the more doctrinaire Ayn Rand Institute.

Thanks to the Tea Party, the thoughts of Ayn Rand were now being communicated to millions of Americans who otherwise would be indifferent or even hostile to her message. Yet her ideological adversaries, especially on the left, were still not taking her seriously. The chattering classes viewed her as little more than a nuisance. In 2010 the *Wonkette* blog ran a series of cartoons entitled "Ayn Rand's Adventures in Wonderland," a satirical depiction of Rand in contemporary America, starring a serial-vomiting, racist Rand. That cartoon series, and personal attacks in liberal-leaning blogs, was about as much as one saw in critiques of Rand, outside of conservative and libertarian circles.

If ridicule was all the mainstream of America could offer to counter Rand, it would not be enough. Rand would win the ideological struggle. Where was the appetite to debate the ideological basis of regulation-free, government-free, conscience-free, conventional-ethics-free, compassion-free capitalism?

I found a ray of hope during the St. Regis fund-raiser. One of the speakers, a money management executive named Barry Colvin, spoke about the formation of a New York chapter of the ARI. I was cheered by one of its upcoming events: a series of debates with living, breathing, non-Objectivists. Liberals! The first of three debates was set for the day after Valentine's Day, 2011.

Over the years, Yaron Brook had engaged in a number of debates on subjects ranging from immigration (for) to foreign aid (against). But those debates were tepid affairs, with Brook facing off against the likes of an anti-immigrant Minuteman. Not since the heyday of the Nathaniel Branden Institute had any leading Objectivist debated anyone of stature from the political mainstream.

That debate took place in May 1967, a year before the great unraveling of the Branden–Rand professional and romantic partnership. The venue was the grand ballroom of the New Yorker Hotel, a handsome Art Deco structure on, as usual, 34th Street. Branden and Dr. Albert Ellis slugged it out, before a raucous audience of 1,100 people. It was supposed to be a debate on the virtues of Ellis's Rational Emotive Behavior Therapy versus Objectivist Psychology. Ellis had previously found some value in Objectivism, and he conceded that *The Fountainhead's* individualistic outlook "influenced me somewhat as I developed my method" of psychotherapy.[1] Rand refused to debate him, but Branden agreed.

The debate degenerated into a free-for-all, and so permanently embittered Ellis that he wrote a book in 1968 entitled *Is Objectivism a Religion?*, which was reprinted in an expanded edition published shortly before his death. "In spite of sticking rigorously to the conditions of the debate," Ellis wrote, "the objectivists who were present, and Branden in particular, became incensed, vitriolic, and accused me of skullduggery on several counts."[2] What provoked Branden and his fellow Randers (who, according to Ellis, had packed the audience), was that he had the gall to critique Objectivism!

Quoting a letter sent to him after the debate by Branden, Ellis recalled in his book that the Rand protégé accused him of "a vitriolic, irrelevant and gratuitous attack on the lack of believability (to you) of Ayn Rand's fictional heroes—thus causing Miss Rand, who was one of my guests that evening, to be insulted in a context where she had no means to protest or answer you." The letter was published in full in the December 1967 issue of *The Objectivist* newsletter.[3]

According to Ellis, what outraged Branden and Rand was that he had critiqued Howard Roark and John Galt as "impossible humans—or, rather, super-humans." That is hardly an off-the-wall accusation or a personal attack on Rand, but she, her lover, and the Rand acolytes in attendance were infuriated.

"In the midst of my saying this," Ellis recounted, "Ayn Rand, who was sitting near the front of the audience, became terribly disturbed and jumped up, exclaiming, 'I'm not going to listen to this debate!'" She then tried to leave the packed ballroom, and Branden "then angrily jumped up himself and shouted into the microphone that he did not think it was ethical or honorable for me to attack a person who by the rules of the occasion was not free to speak for herself." Citing Ellis's "behavior," Branden declined to release an audio recording of the debate, as doing so required mutual permission.

Ellis, putting on his therapist hat, suggests in his book that if "Ayn Rand were truly in good mental health (not to mention as 'heroic' as many of the objectivists like to think of themselves as being), she would surely not take my accusations too seriously, and would merely convince herself, calmly and collectedly, that her heroes are not really 'utterly impossible humans,' would smilingly think of me as being at least slightly addled, and would listen to the rest of my accusations with equanimity."[4] One of the

Objectivists in the audience, Robert Flanzer, told me that the audience was also riled by a comment by Ellis that even Hitler was not an unequivocally bad human being—a remark that Branden seized upon and used joyously. Flanzer, a dentist and longtime Rand follower, didn't remember much about the debate except that and Rand's attempted walkout. He agreed that it was quite a bare-knuckles affair.

I was struck by the quasi-religious character of the hostility expressed by Objectivists during and after the debate. When Rand got out of her seat and refused to listen to Ellis, she was functioning less as the leader of a philosophical movement than as an ayatollah, a Trotskyite leader, or an ultra-Orthodox rabbi might behave were his core beliefs challenged. That did not bode well for any debates the Objectivists might be thinking of launching forty-four years later.

I didn't have a chance to buttonhole Barry Colvin during the St. Regis fund-raiser, but I caught up with him a few weeks later. He was in his early forties, thin though not especially tall, and had a wispy blond beard. In fact he slightly resembled the ARI flack Kurt Kramer, except for being more willing to return my calls. We arranged to meet at the Yale Club, just across Vanderbilt Avenue from Grand Central/Taggart Terminal. As we settled into comfortable leather chairs in the lobby, he explained to me that even though he was not a member, he often met people at the Yale Club because it was not especially stringent at checking IDs. He had formerly been a member of the Army-Navy Club in Washington, D.C., despite his lack of service credentials, which was far less expensive than the Yale Club but provided reciprocal access.

This was a clever fellow, with an impish and irreverent quality. I immediately found myself liking him—a common affliction when I encountered Objectivists. It helped that he seemed to have an open-minded attitude toward Objectivism, as reflected in his eagerness to organize debates.

The program for the fund-raiser described Colvin in humdrum terms as vice chairman of a somewhat obscure money management operation called Balyasny Asset Management. The firm, which had about $2.5 billion under management, was part of a Wall Street institution that over the years has become a refuge of unrestrained capitalism—about as close as one can find to a Galt's Gulch in today's world.

Balyasny ran hedge funds. Those are private partnerships structured for the wealthy, and during the financial crisis they became noted for their ability to forecast and exploit the coming ruination in mortgage-backed securities. This made them subject to criticism, especially when a hedge fund manager, John Paulson, was found to have collaborated with Goldman Sachs in designing a financial product, pegged to the performance of subprime mortgages, that was sold to institutional investors. Paulson was "short"—wagering against the mortgage market. There was a huge furor when word of that emerged, and the Securities and Exchange Commission sued Goldman, which settled the charges by paying a $550 million penalty. (As is customary, Goldman neither admitted nor denied wrongdoing.) Paulson, however, had no particular legal obligation in such a situation, and was not penalized. I interviewed Paulson for *Portfolio* magazine early in 2009. Though we didn't discuss Rand, it was plain from his single-minded, lifelong devotion to making a bundle that he would have warmed the cockles of her heart, and probably vice versa.

Hedge funds had no direct role in the financial collapse. But their very existence influenced the culture of Wall Street in one significant area—compensation. Hedge funds generally retain 20 percent of the profits of their underlying portfolios as an incentive fee, which is as lucrative an arrangement as one can find anywhere in the financial world. In return they offer investors a wider assortment of investment strategies than are available from ordinary mutual funds or money management companies. The incentive-fee pay model was so ridiculously generous that it contaminated the soil, encouraging banks to offer their traders and bankers enormous bucks, so as to discourage brain drain to hedge funds.

The salient feature of the hedge fund pay model is that it is totally selfish. There is no real downside to making reckless bets. Hedge funds are supposed to recoup losses before paying fund managers, but they are more likely to go out of business and start up anew than to operate without paying their managers for the indefinite future. At banks, similarly, getting a piece of the take extends only to gains. There are no givebacks if trades turn sour. Thus bankers have an incentive to take risks with their employers' money but no disincentives to deter them from losing money. Were it not for the fee-happy culture that infected Wall Street in the 1990s and 2000s, in which bankers could strike it rich by making risky bets on mortgage-backed securities—heedless of the risks—the financial crisis might never have happened.

That me-first pay structure, putting the interests of individual traders and bankers ahead of their employers—and the financial system endangered by their recklessness—was conspicuously Randian. It is official Rand doctrine that a businessman who puts the interests of shareholders over his own personal money-grubbing is just a despised altruist at heart. Leonard Peikoff makes that very point in an essay for a 1999 anthology, *Why Businessmen Need Philosophy*. Many businessmen, he says, really are good guys—selfish guys, that is—but try to hide that by saying that they're actually working on behalf of their employees, their customers, and "their stockholders, especially the widows and orphans among them."[5]

Stockholders are, of course, the owners of the company, but Peikoff feels that a CEO should be out for himself, and not work for the benefit of the company as a whole or its shareholders. It was the most honest expression one can find of the mindset that pervaded Wall Street during the greed era that preceded the 2008 fiasco.

It was natural that the Objectivist promotion of laissez-faire capitalism, a belief system predicated on selfishness, would appeal to people in that line of work. So it has become something of a stereotype: the youthful, Ferrari-driving, Ayn Rand-reading hedge fund manager. His compatriots "tend to be instinctively in sync with Objectivism," said Colvin. But that doesn't mean that they are card-carrying Objectivists.

If they were, they might not care for an article by Rand, published in *Cosmopolitan* in April 1963, in which she distinguished between "Money-Makers" and "Money-Appropriators."[6] Rand's views were rooted in the long-gone days of heavy industry, so she admired "Money-Makers" who exemplify "the discoverer who translates his discovery into material goods." The Money-Appropriator, on the other hand, "is essentially noncreative—and his basic goal is to acquire an unearned share of wealth created by others. He seeks to get rich, not by conquering nature, but by manipulating men" and by "social maneuvering."

The Money-Appropriator "does not produce, he redistributes; he merely switches the wealth already in existence from the pockets of its owners to his own." Rand was aiming her ridicule directly at Wall Street. In the article, she quoted her longtime associate Alan Greenspan addressing "what percentage of men in our business world he would regard as authentic Money-Makers—as men of fully sovereign, independent judgment." Greenspan's response, "a little sadly: 'On Wall Street—about five per cent; in industry—about fifteen.'"[7]

Another swipe at today's hedgies in the article: "Most Money-Makers are indifferent to luxury, and their manner of living is startlingly modest in relation to their wealth," she told the readers of *Cosmo*.[8] That certainly doesn't jibe with the conspicuous consumption of many hedge fund managers. But when it comes to the opposite side of the ledger—giving away money—hedgies imbue the values of Ayn Rand.

Financier and former hedge fund manager Warren Buffett, one of the wealthiest people on the planet, drew the wrath of Objectivists in 2010 for his widely publicized decision to give away most of his wealth, and for persuading other super-rich to give away 50 percent of their fortunes.[9] Yaron Brook joined with ARI analyst Don Watkins in attacking Buffett's "giving pledge" as a "guilt pledge" in a Forbes.com column. Citing the less-than-enthusiastic view of philanthropy by "the Greeks' modern heir, Ayn Rand," Brook and Watkins rebuked Buffett and Microsoft's Bill Gates, who joined Buffett in organizing the pledge drive. They reminded the two billionaires that keeping their money was just as moral as giving it away. (Perhaps more so, they implied.) "Every dollar in your bank account came from some individual who voluntarily gave it to you—who gave it to you in exchange for a product he judged to be more valuable than his dollar," they argued. "You have no moral obligation to 'give back,' because you didn't take anything in the first place."[10]*

No worries. Philanthropy of the Buffett, Gates, and Soros variety is rare among hedge fund managers. One museum director I know tells me that the byword among donors from finance today is: "What's in it for me?"—what's in the goody bag, what kind of social recognition they can garner, and what kind of contacts they can make? That sounds petty and mean-spirited until you factor in Rand, who provided ample intellectual ammunition to justify such attitudes.

Traders and bankers are pragmatists, not ideologues. They hesitate to become actively involved in Objectivism. They'd rather profit from statism than agitate against it. "Almost every hedge fund manager doesn't like Obamacare, but in every bill there are winners and losers," said Colvin. The hedgies try to short the losers and buy the winners, rather than fighting what is viewed by the right as a vanguard of socialism. "So it has

* The late Steve Jobs, one of the wealthiest people on the planet, undoubtedly would have agreed. Apple's founder did not sign on to the "giving pledge," and was noted for his lack of interest in philanthropy. Apple cofounder Steve Wozniak, describing Jobs's early "guides in life," said that "*Atlas Shrugged* might have been one of them that he mentioned back then."[11]

been frustrating from that point of view," he confessed, speaking as an Objectivist organizer. Still, he said, the amount of hedgie participation in the Rand movement has been building steadily.

Colvin was a departure from the preppie, yuppie, Yalie, nothing-but-work stereotype of hedge fund managers. He was also an atypical Objectivist, which made him one of the more interesting people I interviewed for this book.

He was the son of a senior noncommissioned officer in the Air Force who moved around a bit when he was young. He attended the University of Missouri, one of those state-supported colleges that would be a dim memory in an Objectivist world. He worked during the day and went to school at night, so it took him seven years to get through college. After graduation he worked studiously through various firms, beginning as a stockbroker at a regional brokerage, and a decade later he was president of Tremont Capital Management, one of the largest operators of "funds of funds"—hedge funds that invest in other hedge funds.

In none of this was he influenced by Rand. Colvin followed the typical post-pubescent route to Objectivism, reading *The Fountainhead* and *Atlas Shrugged* in college. And until recently that was about it. Just a distant reading experience, as it had been for me before I started my research. But over the past few years his interest in Rand has increased sharply. It is one of the activities that he is pursuing in his retirement.

Early retirement doesn't seem to jibe with Rand's work-centric vision of tall, thin men and women living, dying, and screwing in a constant state of creative productivity. Colvin didn't see it that way. "I had an executive coach, and he asked me, 'Would the Barry Colvin of twenty years ago be surprised where Barry Colvin is today?' I said 'No, but neither would he have been surprised if I had been a truck driver.' I honestly believe that."

I didn't quite get his point, but his next comment was good, solid horse sense. "It's a stressful business," he said. "For the last thirteen, fourteen anniversaries my wife and I had, I was only home for two of them because I traveled so much. I looked at our accounts, and I saw that I had enough to retire on. We don't need huge things, but our quality of life, we're very happy with it so we can retire, so why not do that?" Well, that at least would have pleased Rand, with her dislike of conspicuous consumption.

So even though he had the fancy title of vice chairman of Balyasny, he didn't put in a lot of time on the job. He worked out of his home, which was in the less-than-chic suburb of White Plains, much of the time. He told me the kind of stuff that he was doing in his retirement, things like triathlons and rock climbing. Reading Rand wasn't one of them. He didn't seem especially knowledgeable about Objectivism, and wasn't even familiar with the two Rand biographies that had recently been published.

Having been steeped in the intellectual, somber, somewhat imperious, righteous, judgmental, and elitist culture of Objectivism, this exception to the rule was refreshing. I had met my first cool Objectivist. I don't mean to knock the other Objectivists I'd met in the preceding months, but this particular fellow had a sense of proportion to his life that cried out to the depths of my soul.

The disadvantage of a less-than-thorough absorption in Rand lore is that he was something of a babe in the woods when it came to the Machiavellian politics of the Objectivist movement—no crime to be sure, except that he had already swan dived into orthodox Objectivism by becoming the head of the ARI's New York chapter. He had never heard of the Junto. He seemed only vaguely aware of the existence of the Atlas Society, and his view of it was less than favorable. That wasn't surprising, since his source on such things was Yaron Brook.

"From what I understand," said Colvin, "there are a number of groups that subscribe to Objectivism. It seems to me that the difference is that—that's the foundation—but they also have opinions on things that Ayn Rand never wrote about." Foreign policy, for instance. "According to

Yaron, she never actually opined on it. Never directly." Actually she most certainly did. Sniping at the shortcomings of foreign policy was central to the Rand canon. That could be seen by glancing through books like *Capitalism: The Unknown Ideal,* which published the text of her 1967 lecture opposing the Vietnam War.[12] She voiced support for Israel on several occasions, including a 1973 Ford Hall Forum appearance and an interview on the Phil Donahue show in 1979. On *Donahue* she said that "U.S. foreign policy has been disgraceful for years, for decades, I would say roughly since the New Deal, and in part even before that."[13]

Colvin went on to recite the party line that non-ARI Objectivists "use Objectivism as a foundation to build other views that have not been expressly written about by Rand herself. So Yaron says that these are legitimate groups, it's just that the Ayn Rand Institute only focuses on those things that are expressly part of Objectivism."

To be fair, Colvin was new to organized Objectivism—and besides, he was not on the payroll as a visiting scholar. His participation in Objectivism commenced when Dmitry Balyasny, the Russian-born founder of the company and "a big Ayn Rand fan," invited him to dinner in Chicago sometime in 2009. "Yaron was going to speak so I came, and I liked it very much." He discovered that the ARI didn't have a branch in New York. "I thought, wouldn't it be interesting to try to take what ARI is doing on a kind of fifty-thousand feet up level, and try to help execute it on the local level." So he decided to organize the New York chapter, which commenced in the spring of 2010.

"We had a couple of dinners, and one of my first things was that we've got to have a debate series," he said. "I'm not all that interested in putting on a luncheon with people I agree with. So I came up with the idea of a debate with thoughtful people whose ideas are different than mine." Colvin outlined for me the initial plans for the debates, which would explore broad, sweeping themes—"first principles." They had lined up a first-class moderator, Brian Lehrer of the highbrow radio station WNYC. Yaron

Brook and John Allison would be holding the fort for the Objectivists at two of the debates. The other side would be from Demos, a New York think tank that was the cosponsor along with the ARI and WNYC. Demos was a mainstream progressive group, and its early organizers included an obscure Illinois state senator named Barack Obama.

The first debate was set for February 15, 2011, and would discuss "Government: How much do we need?" The second was to be an exploration of "The social safety net: Are we our brother's keeper?" and the third was to tackle "Capitalism: Virtue or Vice?"

Colvin agreed with me that popular opinion tended to fall within the two extremes set forth in each of the debate topics, but he wanted, not unreasonably, lively debates. "Most of the debate you hear is between people who feel it's a terrible thing and people who have this middle ground. And that's usually conservatives, who say, 'Look, there's some good things about capitalism but we need more regulation, we need this, we need that.' So the reality is that it's not a debate between this end and that, it's a debate between this end"—the capitalism-haters, that is—"and the middle ground."

"So where are you going to end up?" he asked. "You're going to end up no better than here," he said, using his hands to demonstrate an imaginary point in space, "much more toward 'vice.' So we think that where the debate would be most successfully held is between both ends of the continuum." That same general logic was applied to the other subjects being debated, with Objectivists taking the position that there should be no social safety net and so on. "At both ends is where you get to the morality of it," Colvin explained. "It's not just questions of policy and compromise on policy. It's trying to get at the moral fiber behind your beliefs and positions on either side."

If the objective was to debate the morality of radical capitalism, that was the way to do it. I was increasingly seeing how morality needed to be on the front burner. It wasn't. However, I wasn't clear this was such a good strategy from the Objectivist perspective. Sure, Objectivists saw radical capitalism as the true repository of morality. They had fifty years experience pushing that line. But to anyone other than fellow radical capitalists, it made them seem like nuts. Similarly, I couldn't see Demos staking out the opposing position that capitalism is a cesspool of all the evil in the world. Only socialists and Communists view capitalism as an unalloyed evil, and Demos was populated by such moderate types as Miles Rapoport, the group's president and a former Connecticut secretary of state, and Demos cofounder David Callahan. Colvin had been in touch with both of these gentlemen to discuss the debates.

The Objectivist debater could be counted upon to provide all the usual excuses to an argument that capitalism's flaws had been on full display during the financial crisis. The pat answer is the "mixed economy ain't really capitalism" argument, perhaps combined with "government policies caused the crash." But squirting Chanel No. 5 onto Ayn Rand's brand of capitalism—the pure, unsullied, poor-people-be-doomed laissez-faire variety—would require delving deep into the shoals of Virtuous Selfishness, which a savvy anti-Rand debater would be sure to exploit for all it's worth.

The black-and-white framing of the debate topics reflected the extremism of the Objectivist position. At one point there was talk about making the social safety net debate a discussion of "how much is enough." But Objectivists believe there should be no social safety net. "How much we should be our brother's keeper is talking about degrees," said Colvin. "You lose the debate when you say that. If both agree there should be a social safety net, then take the question of unemployment checks. Why should it be $1,056 a month? Why shouldn't it be $1,500 a month? Or $2,000? Unemployment shouldn't stop at a year. What if you don't have a job? If we both agree that people should be getting unemployment insurance, why shouldn't it go on indefinitely? Once you agree that there should be something, then you lose a debate entirely, because then the debate is

'How much should people get?' All too often we think the debate starts there, and you're bound to lose that debate."

All that presupposes, of course, that we don't have some ethical or moral obligation to provide a safety net for the unemployed. That's a question of values, which brings us back to Judeo-Christian morality, the brick wall against which Objectivist doctrines have a way of colliding. The theme of the second debate handily summarized, in one cliché, two Objectivist hobby horses: altruism and intra-familial codependence. "There are centuries and centuries feeding into all of us that there is a religious aspect. So there is a huge guilt part that tells us that we should be our brothers' keepers," Colvin pointed out. I agreed with him on the guilt part, as would any son of a Jewish mother.

So, I suggested, why not go whole hog and make this a confrontation between Objectivism and Judeo-Christian morality? Why not stage the second debate with, say, a Catholic priest?

"Well, of course, the way we come out on this—as an Objectivist, you're an atheist," he said. "So before we ever get to a Catholic priest, in terms of the morality behind that, I think an Objectivist would probably discard it on the grounds that their moral basis is rooted in a mysticism, which we completely discount in the first place, so there's really no morality behind something that's based on mysticism."

It was interesting to see two thousand years of Christian doctrine swept so casually into the dustbin, but still I was impressed with Colvin's honesty and forthright attitude. This man was no bullshitter, which I assume must have contributed to his success as a hedge fund guy and his ability to retire at such an early age. (He called it "semiretirement," but I didn't see much "semi" about it. I've seen actual, post-sixty-five retired people working much harder at Wal-Mart and as telephone solicitors.)

Colvin said that he hoped the debates would change the thinking of the people watching them, strengthening or weakening their beliefs. "Either one of them is a good thing. Take for example capitalism. You get somebody who's very thoughtful from Demos and you get John Allison, who's incredibly thoughtful, articulate about capitalism. Let's say they have this debate. Now I know how I feel today, but what if after that debate, whoever their debater is from Demos comes up with wonderful, valid points? I'd take that home and think about it."

At this point in our conversation I reassessed my view of Colvin as not being a bullshitter. People can be persuaded to change their view of peripheral issues in their lives, such as their feelings toward laundry detergents or politicians, but usually aren't swayed by mere chatter to alter their core beliefs. But then he redeemed himself: "If I think about it long and hard and wind up rejecting it for whatever reason, then I've strengthened my own beliefs because I've challenged them." Even if he didn't mean it, this was a far cry from Ayn Rand throwing a fit and trying to push her way out of a hotel auditorium in 1967.

I found myself nodding, not out of feigned agreement or fatigue, but because I believed the guy. Then again, this rational and pleasant retired executive didn't believe in unemployment benefits, a position that, should it come to pass, would send America back to the days of the Dustbowl and Okies starving on the outskirts of indifferent cities. I strongly doubt that the retired hedge fund manager sitting in front of me would have advocated that position if he had, in fact, become a truck driver instead of going into finance. It's not that he'd have been a different person. It's just that it is not in a truck driver's rational self-interest to get rid of unemployment insurance. Just as it wasn't in the rational self-interest of Ayn Rand to turn down Medicare when she was old and sick. But you can bet that it is in the rational self-interests of quite a few hedge fund managers, bankers, and other non-socially-conscious rich people to oppose programs like unemployment insurance, food stamps, and Medicare. What do they care if we go back to the days of Hoovervilles? They'll never have to live in one. That's what selfishness is all about.

"It's a moral thing," he said. "It's a moral discussion."

I couldn't agree more. Ultimately the national debate over entitlements and the social safety net boils down to whether Ayn Rand and her embrace of capitalism, her equating the markets with freedom and government with a "gun," is right or wrong. But the tentacles of her belief system extend well beyond business, finance, and the morality of dismantling the government and slashing programs for the poor. Rand has a way of creeping into controversies that have nothing to do with money or capitalism.

That is where it can really get hairy.

CHAPTER EIGHT

The Agitator

Reading Yaron Brook's interview with the *Jerusalem Post,* in which the Israeli-born Objectivist leader sided with Arabs when private property was at stake,[1] one might conclude that a collision of religion, prejudice, and private property would always lead Objectivists to come down on the side of property.

Not necessarily.

In 2010 a significant property rights issue became a national cause célèbre—the right of New York Muslims to build a mosque and community center a couple of blocks from Ground Zero. The battle lines were unambiguous: private property versus the government, which came under strong and unsuccessful pressure to put a stop to it. New York's mayor Michael Bloomberg said: "The simple fact is this building is private property, and the owners have a right to use the building as a house of worship."[2] Rand took an absolutist stance on private property. "The right to life is the source of all rights—and the right to property is their only implementation. Without property rights, no other rights are possible," she said in *The Virtue of Selfishness.*[3]

Yet Objectivists, the supposed champions of property rights, came out against the Ground Zero mosque, and advocated that government use not just the metaphorical but the *actual* "gun" to put a stop to it. Leonard Peikoff set forth the official Objectivist position in June 2010, in a rambling podcast: "Any way possible permission should be refused, and if they go ahead and build it, the government should bomb it out of existence." After evacuating it, of course, but with "no compensation to any of the property owners."[4]

This was a good example of reason being pitted against what Rand derided as "tribalism"—prejudice against Muslims—with tribalism winning out. It was one thing to oppose the mosque on grounds of sensitivity to the feelings of 9/11 survivors, just as many people opposed establishment of a monastery at Auschwitz in the 1980s. But to refer to it as a kind of enemy outpost, without evidence, seemed to leap into the chasm of prejudice. Rand denounced prejudice of all kinds in a 1963 article on racism, reprinted in the *Virtue* anthology. She called racism "the lowest, most crudely primitive form of collectivism."[5]

Rand was never reluctant to take unpopular positions, so she might have supported the project were she alive in 2010. But I tend to think not, because late in her life she achieved a kind of epiphany on something she suppressed all her life—her Jewish identity. This embrace of her heritage was, I think, reflected in the pro-Israel position that she took publicly in the 1970s—and privately much earlier, Barbara Branden told me, perhaps as early as the late 1950s.

Rand's flight from her ethnic background was one of the most conspicuous aspects of her early life. She came from a family that was secular by Russian-Jewish standards, only celebrating the holiday of Passover—the Jewish festival that, perhaps, comes closest to Objectivist ideology by commemorating the Children of Israel's exercise in rational self-interest (and a Galt-like strike action) by fleeing Egypt.[6] One gets the impression that she was anxious to de-Judaize herself, and to not associate with what might be described as Jewish concerns. She didn't fool the immigration officers when she arrived in the United States—the ship's manifest listed her as "Hebrew"[7]—but she immediately Anglicized her name, which was recognizably Jewish, and did not reveal her birth name (Alyssa Rosenbaum) except to a select few.[8]

Her strenuous effort to distance herself from her heritage was evident in a number of ways, from her atheism to her adoration of Henry Ford to her opposition to U.S. involvement in the war against the Nazis. Her published journals and letters show Rand uttering not a word on the subject of Israel during the pre-independence period or the first years of its existence. Yet something changed in the early 1970s, perhaps because of the Soviet Union's hostility toward the Jewish state. She might have privately supported Israel before then, as Barbara Branden recalled, but only in the 1970s did she become an outspoken admirer of Israel and a fierce critic of its Arab enemies. Being Rand, she expressed her position in a way that was calculated to make everyone but Objectivists feel uncomfortable.

Israelis take pains to emphasize the Jewish people's nativity to the region, their roots as confirmed by archeology and the Bible (and, more recently, DNA analysis). Efforts by anti-Zionists to delegitimize Israel always portray Israel as a foreign body lodged in the gullet of the Middle East. Yet that alleged otherness was what Rand *liked* about Israel. She didn't give a hoot about the Biblical roots of the nation or the painstakingly accumulated archeological evidence of Jewish habitation through the ages. She never traveled to Israel to participate in mystical rituals like praying at the Wailing Wall. No, what appealed to her about Israel was not that it was the fulfillment of three-thousand-year-old promises made in religious texts whose validity she did not recognize, or that Israel was a refuge for persecuted Jews or Holocaust survivors, but that it was an outpost of Western civilization.

In response to a question at the Ford Hall Forum in Boston in 1973, Rand described Arabs as among "the least developed cultures" and said that they "are practically nomads." She called their culture "primitive" and said that they "resent Israel because it's the sole beachhead of modern science and civilization on their continent." When "civilized men [are] fighting savages," she said, "you support the civilized men."[9]

This "pro-Israel" (if you can call it that) attitude was channeled by her followers, differentiating them from the sometimes anti-Israel libertarians. When David Kelley was frog-marched from the ranks of Rand-dom in 1989, the association of some libertarians with the "baby-killing followers of Yassir Arafat" was cited as a reason for his supposed moral lapse.[10] Unlike libertarians such as Ron Paul—who enraged John McCain with his isolationist views during the 2008 primaries—Brook has been a strong opponent of Islamic militancy.[11] Peikoff is even more outspoken on the subject. "End States Who Sponsor Terrorism" is the title of an essay that he wrote not long after September 11. "The choice today is mass death in the United States or mass death in the terrorist nations," he opined.[12]

Yet there is a disconnect between these positions and Rand's anti-interventionist stance toward Nazi Germany and her hero worship of Henry Ford. Perhaps to avoid bringing attention to her own Jewish background, Rand never said a word about anti-Semitic discrimination in American life, which was especially pervasive in the hiring practices of her "persecuted minority," big business. Wall Street, which she adored, was the worst offender. From her arrival in America through the 1960s, commercial and investment banks, except for a tiny number of Jewish firms such as Kuhn, Loeb & Co. and J. & W. Seligman & Co., were almost totally *Judenrein*. In 1933, *Fortune* reported that in the largest commercial banks "there are practically no Jewish employees." That remained the case in 1948, when a study of anti-Semitism in employment found that Jews were systematically excluded from banking, the stock exchanges, and insurance.[13] As late as 1967, the American Jewish Committee found that there was "an apparent pattern of discrimination against Jews" in executive positions in commercial banks.[14] A 1966 AJC study found no Jews in senior positions in forty-five of fifty commercial banks in New York. There were similar complaints through the 1970s.

There is no evidence that Rand, Branden, Peikoff, or any leading Objectivist, all of whom happened to be Jewish—as was Alan Greenspan, who couldn't get a job on Wall Street when he graduated from college in 1948—ever said a word about the persistent anti-Semitism in big business and finance, even though Rand pigeonholed racism as "collectivism."

By 2010, the Objectivist indifference to Jewish issues was over. The Middle East was now the central Jewish concern, and the Ground Zero mosque was being portrayed as radical Islam stabbing New York City in the throat. So when push came to shove, it was no contest. Clear-cut property rights issue be damned—Objectivists were against the mosque.

In the fight over the mosque, the prime mover was an Objectivist, but it wasn't Brook or Peikoff. It was a blogger who represented the intersection of Objectivism with far-right Islam-baiting politics. Her name was Pamela Geller. She was a single mom in her early fifties who lived on the East Side of Manhattan, and became an Internet and media sensation because of her strident anti-Muslim opinions. Her blog was called *Atlas Shrugs*.[15]

The title practically cried out "I'm an Objectivist!" but nobody paid much attention. In all the voluminous media coverage that Pamela received, surprisingly little attention was paid to her strongly Randian ideology. A lengthy and unsympathetic profile in *The New York Times* mentioned Rand only in passing, to explain the title of the blog.[16] It didn't say that Rand was Pamela's primary ideological influence. Left unmentioned was that Pamela had cited Rand at every conceivable opportunity for years, and on subjects having little or nothing to do with Islam.

Commenting on Paul Krugman's Nobel Prize in 2008, for instance, Pamela said: "Who'd a thunk that reality would make Rand's *Atlas Shrugged* look soft? Even Rand couldn't have made this believable. Ellsworth Toohey is dancing in hell. The triumph of the collectivist, aiming at a society that shall be 'an average drawn upon zeroes.'"[17] This was not a casual reader of Rand but a devoted acolyte.

I contacted Pamela Geller by e-mail, and initially the response was the kind that I had grown accustomed to receiving from the ARI, which was no response at all. Had I made some kind of mistake? Should I have called her "Doctor" Geller? (I was careful to refer to Yaron Brook, a PhD in finance, as "Doctor" Brook in my e-mails and phone calls, as is the approved Objectivist practice.) After some weeks, I e-mailed again and this time received some encouraging responses, invariably signed "yours in liberty," a salutation commonly utilized by libertarian and Tea Party types.

"I am proud to have introduced her to hundreds of thousands of new readers," Pamela said of Rand, and forwarded an e-mail from a fan in Germany: "I admire you and the tea party movement, and am very grateful for your recommendation to read 'Atlas shrugged.'" the admirer's e-mail said. "Despite not having read it fully yet (page 748), it's (that is, I am) changing my life already. During my philosophy studies there was no mention of Objectivism but once in a pejorative comment, and no hint at how liberating it is." My request for more examples was rebuffed. "Not rifling through my stuff—I don't keep these," she said. That was a little curt, though not "brassy and vulgar," as the unadmiring *Times* profile quoted some former colleagues as describing her.

We batted e-mails back and forth for a few days, and then I received one that asked, "Do you have someone that can vouch for you? As to who you are? If not let's do it by email or phone." I was taken aback by this request. Did she think I was an imposter? I promptly provided the e-mail address of my publisher, but I was left a bit off-balance.

After I was suitably vouched-for, we met at a coffee shop on East 34th Street. Yes, that street again. I walked by Rand's old apartment building on the way over, past the high school named for Norman Thomas. Pamela arrived, dressed in blue, with a necklace spelling out L-O-V-E around her neck, forming a vivid contrast to her unlovable Internet persona. She spoke with a thick Lawngisland accent. Linguists say that regional accents are on the wane. Hers was refreshingly retro, like a Brooklyn accent but more insistent, with a kind of nagging quality. It gave her a gritty, "street" aura even though she was from the manicured lawns and five-bedroom houses of Hewlett Harbor, an affluent town on the south shore of Long Island.

Like a lot of the people I'd met in the Objectivist sphere, Pamela stumbled upon Rand in young adulthood, while she was attending Hofstra University. A friend recommended that she read *Atlas Shrugged*. Pamela "made a mental note of it" and read the book two years later. "It was not so much enlightening," she said, "but it was revelatory. Somebody put to paper my way of thinking."

Rand seemed to have that effect on people. It was as if she articulated what was already in the American consciousness, just as John Galt's fictional engine generated electrical current from ambient static electricity. "I was shaking my head all the time. 'Yeah, that's right. Yeah.' Commonsensical. Her epistemology was American. I mean, her sense of America. It's based on, for the very first time in history, individual rights. And that's my platform. I'm not Republican or Democratic or certainly not a libertarian. If I had a party, that would be my party."

Certainly not a libertarian? No, she said, "they go too far." She went on to recall Rand's oft-expressed dislike of libertarians and added, "I don't think they get it. I don't think they get Rand." She cited the libertarians' advocacy of drug legalization. That surprised me because Rand embraced drug legalization, along with prostitution, as an area in which the government should not interfere.[18] When I mentioned this to Pamela she dodged a bit, pointing to Rand's more ambiguous position on gun control. Generally, though, she seemed quite well-read on the subject of

Rand. "Succor and logic in a completely insane world," is how she summed it all up.

Pamela showed considerable foresight in naming her blog back in 2004, before Rand became so wildly popular. From the beginning, she has quoted Rand "whenever I get to the heart of the matter." She claimed to get two to three e-mails a week from people who thank her for "turning them on to Ayn Rand." Her sassy and edgy opinions brought her to the attention of organized Objectivism, though to no great effect. She told me that she met Yaron Brook and liked him, but she was sour on Peikoff, feeling that he had "destroyed Ayn Rand's legacy."

How so? "It's hard to get into. I think that he has compromised her vision. I think that many very good people have been thrown under the bus that should never have been," she said. That led us to talk about the Rand–Branden split of 1968. She was definitely a Brandenian. She told me that Barbara Branden had read the blog and been in touch with her, though not for the past couple of years.

Pamela was not up on the latest Randian gossip, even as it concerned her core interest. I was surprised that she had not heard of Peikoff's assertion that the mosque should be blasted to smithereens if it were ever built. Even more surprisingly, she didn't agree. "That's kind of wild," she said. She viewed it as exceptionally bad from a PR perspective. That's saying a lot, because it takes a really *extreme* position to outflank Pamela Geller on the right of that particular issue. Pamela is so off the charts that the conservative blog *Little Green Footballs* has repeatedly flayed her for fostering anti-Muslim bigotry.[19]

I was getting the impression that an internal coup, with Brook overthrowing Peikoff, would have been perfectly OK to a lot of Rand acolytes. It will never happen, of course, because Peikoff controls the rights to Rand's works. ("I almost feel sorry for Yaron Brook," Barbara Branden said to me. "He's in a very difficult position. Leonard holds all the copyrights of Ayn's materials and has all her stuff, Yaron Brook cannot go against him. I think he would if he could.") So far, however, the intra-Randian dissent is muted, partly because Rand supporters like Pamela don't air their misgivings in public. She certainly never said in her blog anything like what she was telling me about Peikoff.

Pamela confined her Objectivism to her blog. She has heard from the dissident Atlas Society and been invited to Objectivist gatherings, but she told me that she simply doesn't have the time. She meant that not as a busy single mother, but in a somewhat more melodramatic context. "I really feel that the clock is ticking. I have a certain amount of time. I think that my blog will be deemed hate speech at some point. Clearly they're taking down sites," she said, and she expected that eventually hers will be one of them. That may seem like paranoia, but she could be right. The Internet payment service PayPal cut her off for a couple of days in mid-2010 on grounds of fomenting "hate speech," but swiftly reversed course a couple of days later.[20] The experience clearly shook her up. Pamela feared "the government" would shut down her Web site, and she lamented the increasing Islamic influence at ICANN, the top-level Internet organization.

Pamela's hyperfocus on Islam is a stark contrast with the relaxed, tolerant perspective that one hears from libertarians like Ron Paul. He was the front-runner among archconservatives in the preliminary presidential machinations, winning a Conservative Political Action Conference presidential straw poll in early 2011 with 30 percent of the vote. To no great surprise he declared his 2012 presidential bid in May 2011.

Pamela and other pro-Israel types (and not just Randers) can't stand Paul because of his unsupportive stance on Israel. "He's horrible. I don't like him at all," she said. When he pushed cutting aid to Israel in February 2011, right after his CPAC triumph, he was savagely attacked by Pamela and blogger and commentator David Horowitz. The latter called him a "vicious anti-Semite." Jewish groups seemed less alarmed—it was just Paul being Paul, without the support of the Republican leadership—and he dropped the issue for the time being.[21]

Paul's hostility to Israel harkened back to the days when Israel was a darling of the left and the Commie-hunter John Foster Dulles pursued a pro-Arab foreign policy under Eisenhower, forcing Israel to withdraw from Egypt after the 1956 Suez campaign. Over time the pendulum swung back, with Republicans and conservatives aligning themselves firmly with Israel, the old Eisenhower era snootiness long forgotten. All of the right lined up for Israel—except for libertarians and oddball Republicans like Pat Buchanan.

One of the reasons for Israel's popularity with the left in bygone days was that the country was run by socialists until the rise of Menachem Begin in the 1970s. I talked with Pamela about the leftist character of Jewish immigrants to the United States early in the twentieth century and the socialist kibbutz movement in Israel. She seized upon that to contrast Rand, "an individual capable of critical thought," versus the "groupthink" of the left (in which she included much of the Israeli media, which she described as "Jewicidal"). "Where are they?" she asked of the kibbutz movement, which she described as a "failed idea." Such communal arrangements, she said, are a form of "slavery." Pamela thought that Israel was too left-leaning, too weak-kneed. "They have to stop apologizing for being alive, for being in their own homeland," she said.

None of her views on the Middle East were particularly gasp-worthy. It was her inflammatory rhetoric on the Ground Zero mosque and on Muslims that made her notorious. What distinguished Pamela from blogs like *Little Green Footballs* was less the content of her positions, or even her Objectivist imagery, than her invective—which was reminiscent of Rand's crossing of red lines and willingness to provoke and offend. It worked for Rand and it was working for Pamela. She succeeded handsomely as an agitator, and a group that she cofounded—Stop Islamization of America—had the distinction of being listed as a hate group by the Southern Poverty Law Center. The group was behind municipal bus ads that urged Muslims to leave the "falsity of Islam."[22]

The sentiment was tribal, the rhetoric pure Rand. But if Rand was a role model for Pamela's verbal excesses—assuming she needed any guidance in that area—she wasn't much of an influence on the subject of religion. Pamela believed in God. "I do believe God created the universe. I think she's wrong," she told me.

Apart from that, Pamela was in lockstep with Objectivist philosophy, including the concept of altruism. People who think the Randian view of altruism differs from Judeo-Christian ethics, she said, "don't understand what she means."

My reading of Rand's essays had led me to a different conclusion. Her view of altruism was entirely different from the reverence for charity and generosity that is drummed into every Jewish kid in Hebrew school, and every observant Christian and Muslim in their religious training. Rand did not believe in any system of morality that she didn't personally commit to writing.

In *The Virtue of Selfishness*, Rand begins constructing her moral code by defining her terms. "In popular usage," Rand says, selfishness is embodied by the "murderous brute who tramples over piles of corpses to achieve his own ends, who cares for no living being and pursues nothing but the mindless whims of any immediate moment." In fact, she claims, the "exact meaning and the dictionary definition of the word 'selfishness' is: *concern with one's own interests.*" (Rand's italics.) That's the totality of the "dictionary definition," according to Rand.[23]

When I first read her definition I pulled out my dictionary, and found that I had a choice: I could believe either Noah Webster or Ayn Rand. One had to be wrong. My 1971 edition of *Webster's Collegiate Dictionary* defines selfishness as the state of being "concerned excessively or exclusively with oneself; seeking or concentrating on one's own advantage, pleasure, or well-being *without regard for others.*" She leaves out the "no regard for others" part, which I think most people would agree is an essential component of selfishness.

But most people can be wrong and there are errors in dictionaries, so I went to the library and got hold of the *Oxford English Dictionary.* I found that it defines selfishness as "Concerned chiefly with one's own personal advantage *to the exclusion of regard for others, deficient in consideration for others.*" (My italics.) I could hardly believe what I was seeing here: Rand had deliberately misquoted the dictionary. In "defining" selfishness she left out the swinish characteristic, the failure to respect other people, which is an essential part of the definition of selfishness.

Rand also made up her own definitions for selflessness and altruism. "Altruism holds *death* as the ultimate goal and standard of value," she says in *Virtue*, "and it is logical that renunciation, resignation, self-denial and every other form of suffering, including self-destruction, are the virtues it advocates."[24] She goes on to claim that selfishness has really been unfairly maligned all these years, that it's actually a worthy pursuit—and that selfless people are the ones whose thinking is defective.

"Ayn Rand and the hardcore objectivists who back her are determined to define selfishness and sacrifice in their own way and ignore customary usage of these terms," Albert Ellis wrote. "Where it might well be shown that it is desirable for most humans, most of the time, to be *relatively* self-interested, [putting] their own interests first and those of others a close second, Rand claims that all of us should be *utterly* selfish."[25]

The part of the definition of selfishness that she left out—acting without regard for others—is what distinguishes a banker engaging in sound business practices from a banker loading up on leveraged derivatives to make a short-term buck to boost his bonus. One banker is pursuing his own interests; the other is *selfishly* showing no regard for the impact his actions may have on his shareholders over the long term, or on the rest of the banking system. But that's fine, as Peikoff pointed out in the passage from *Why Businessmen Need Philosophy* that I quoted earlier. A businessman has to look out for himself, not his shareholders, "widows and orphans" notwithstanding.

Pamela Geller wasn't troubled by Rand misquoting the dictionary. "Nothing she espoused is the standard definition," which she felt had been shaped by "statist, collectivist ideas." She certainly had done her reading, which included the more obscure Rand anthologies such as a compilation of the columns that she briefly wrote for the *Los Angeles Times,* and a more recent book consisting of answers that Rand had given to questions from the audience at various lectures. There had been many books like that over the years, even a book of "marginalia"—writings she scribbled on the books of others. These books, published or sanctioned by the Ayn Rand Institute, aim to satisfy the near-insatiable hunger for her work.

Listening to Pamela as she described for me the delights of Ayn Rand, I could see why every fresh spoonful of new Randisms, when doled out from her estate for publication by the ARI, is so eagerly lapped up by the faithful. There was a definite evangelical fervor among Rand believers. Pamela sincerely felt that Rand's word needed to get out among the multitudes. What wasn't clear to me was exactly why she had become so enthralled with Rand. But as she talked about Rand's influence on her private life, I began to understand. "Ayn Rand has given me the resolve and the confidence to stand alone," she said. "She's the mother ship."

That was an interesting choice of words. *Mother* ship. Rand was the antithesis of a Jewish mother. No Jewish guilt for her. "You can't allow yourself to be used by vultures," Pamela said, referring to the Randian family predators, but she might have been referring to her own. Pamela told me that she was the "black sheep of the family," an underachiever when compared to her sister. "I didn't like how they treated me, so I really disengaged." Pamela worked her way through college when her parents refused to pay her tuition. They certainly could have afforded it—her father was a textile manufacturer—but wouldn't pay the tab unless she lived at home.

When she told me her story I could understand Rand's appeal for her. Her parents had tried a classic control gambit and Pamela wouldn't play along. Rand would have been proud. After she finally got around to reading Rand, "I felt validated. Like, 'Of course. See? This is what I've always thought.'"

She initially thought that Rand was too pessimistic about the future of America, but now she felt that Rand was not pessimistic enough. A frantic undercurrent permeated Pamela Geller's blog, which portrayed an America under siege from radical Islam. But it wasn't just the Muslim threat. Pamela was generally disgusted with the direction the country was taking. She was contemptuous of ecologists and global warming concerns, and disdainful of Obama. She was against taxes and in favor of the right-wing budget-slashing agenda advocated in 2011 by Paul Ryan, the Randian chairman of the House Budget Committee. As a matter of fact, Pamela sounded a lot like one of the Tea Party people, with their nonspecific "small government" agenda and generalized disgruntlement about the direction of America.

When I asked Pamela about the Tea Party, she lit up like a Christmas tree. "What's not to like?" she asked me.

CHAPTER NINE

The First Teabagger

The origins of the Tea Party are usually traced back to Rick Santelli's televised rant, which took place on February 19, 2009—by coincidence exactly eighty-three years to the day after Ayn Rand first set foot on American soil. A few antitax, antigovernment rallies preceded the Santelli rant, and he and his immediate predecessors usually get the nod for originating the movement.

I beg to differ. Ayn Rand was the very first Teabagger—the first person on the national political stage to enunciate views that mesh perfectly with the ones being bandied about by the Tea Party.

Rand was channeling the Tea Party decades before there even was a Tea Party. In 1964 she gave a radio interview that could have been broadcast today, in which she perfectly captured the angst of twenty-first century right-leaning populists.

It's doubtful that Rand would have supported the Tea Party movement if she were living today. That wasn't her style. But it's important to distinguish between Rand's ideology and her knee-jerk opposition to any movement whose views might have competed with her own. In a 1971 newsletter article, she expressed disdain for Birchite groups—similar to today's Tea Party, though far smaller—that opposed the United Nations, foreign aid, international treaties, relations with Communist countries, federal aid to education, and the income tax. She disparaged them as "primitive patriotic groups," even while agreeing with most of their ideas.

"Personally," she said, "I have little sympathy with such groups because they do not know how to uphold their ideas intellectually, because they rush unarmed and unprepared into a deadly battle and do more harm than good to the rightist cause."[1] She was right. Such groups faded into the mists of history without having much impact, while Objectivism has flourished. The Tea Party is different. It's latched on to the disdain for government that is common in the Heartland, and seems to have an almost psychic connection to the grand old lady of radical capitalism.

The most dramatic evidence of that can be found in an interview that she gave to a small chain of radio stations in October 1964. I haven't seen this interview mentioned in any of the anthologies generated by the Ayn Rand Institute over the years. Barbara Branden told me that she had never heard of it either, although she had heard Rand privately express similar opinions. Why the interview has not been widely disseminated, given its topicality, is beyond me.

I obtained tapes of that interview and a 1962 interview, both with the McClendon radio stations, owned by iconoclastic broadcaster Gordon McClendon.* In the 1962 broadcast, Rand was interviewed by McClendon himself. I surmised the date because of references to the imminent publication of *Who Is Ayn Rand?*, a worshipful biography by Nathaniel and Barbara Branden, which was published in that year. Rand expressed contempt for the Kennedy administration throughout the broadcast, repeating themes that she raised elsewhere, such as in her newspaper column

* The provenance of the tapes is worth mentioning. They were in the possession of a friend and colleague of mine, the noted investigative reporter Richard Behar. Rich got them from McClendon in the 1980s, and they've resided in a succession of closets ever since. When he heard I was working on this book, Rich was kind enough to take time out from writing his momentous exploration of the Bernie Madoff scandal, expecting nothing in return, to dig them out of his closet, copy them, and send them to me. In other words, this was a *selfless* act, something that would earn contempt from Rand if she were still alive.

and *The Objectivist Newsletter*. The Kennedy administration, she said, was "fascist" by exerting pressure on the steel industry to roll back prices.

There's no question who has emerged as the ideological victor in that contest—it's Rand, hands down. Five decades later, a U.S. president wouldn't even think about injecting himself into the affairs of a major industry (except to step in with billions of dollars to keep it afloat, if it's considered too big to fail).

Nothing startling there. It was the other interview that resonates with today's struggle over the soul of the nation.

The interview, conducted by a Los Angeles attorney and investor named Roy B. Loftin, was broadcast at the height of the 1964 presidential race, which pitted the ultraconservative Republican Barry Goldwater against the glad-handing, warmongering, unreconstructed New Dealer Lyndon Johnson. These were innocent years compared with today. Vietnam hadn't quite reached the boiling point and the nation was relatively prosperous. The country was on the move. Congress actually did stuff in those pre-gridlock days—passing civil rights legislation and coming to grips with health care for the elderly, as the Medicare bill moved toward enactment. Thanks to Johnson's political skills, within a year this vile example of government gunslinging would benefit Mr. and Mrs. Frank O'Connor and millions of other older Americans.

There was a youthfulness and zest in the nation back then. Some World War II veterans were still in their thirties. The times were changing. Rand didn't see any of that. She saw not prosperity but a dark tide of government oppression. Her bleak vision was of a United States that had been "moving in the direction of statism for over sixty years." Remember that this was broadcast in 1964, so she was talking about the state moving in to strangle business since the beginning of the twentieth century. What she saw was a nation very much like the one seen by the Tea Party today—a country in which freedom was fast eroding. Never mind that the very act of her speaking out against the government, unmolested, refuted her denunciation of "fascism." Reality, as usual, was not Rand's strong point.

Loftin began the 1964 interview by asking Rand about labor unions. Her response was ambivalent. She had no problem with them in principle, but didn't want them to get too uppity. In a remark that foreshadowed the 2011 battle over collective bargaining in Wisconsin, she expressed wariness concerning the power of unions. During the era of heavy industry, unions could shut ports, cripple transportation, and freeze production of vital raw materials. Still, Rand did not take an entirely anti-union stance, and stuck to her belief that unions had a right to negotiate for wages and benefits on an equal footing with corporations.

Rand was asked by Loftin if she saw a "danger in heavy union contributions to candidates, congressmen, and senators?" Her response was hedged and contradictory, but generally lined up with the kind of rhetoric that would be heard, five decades later, from Wisconsin governor Scott Walker and his Tea Party supporters as he stared down unions in 2011.

"Danger?" she said. "No, so long as the membership does not have to vote the way the union wants them to vote." But then, backtracking a bit, she said she saw "an element of enormous injustice and impropriety because the unions have no right to determine the political viewpoint or voting preferences of its members, and therefore have no right to contribute money to one candidate over another without the individual consent of the members."

She distinguished between the unions' moral and legal right to use member dues for political contributions: "They have no moral right. It is unfortunate that today they do have the legal right, which is totally improper. Therefore, it is an injustice but it is not particularly a danger as such. The danger will come when and if the union leaders are able to deliver the vote, so to speak. When they are able to really control the vote of their membership, which so far they have not been able to do." It was tepid by

Randian standards, but still cut right to the heart of an issue that remained unresolved fifty years later.

Loftin shifted to the New York senate race. Robert F. Kennedy was running against Kenneth Keating, a liberal Republican (back when there was such a thing), who had represented New York for years. Again, Rand's reply could have been spoken by a Tea Party activist. Framing her remarks less to chastise Kennedy than to take a swipe at Keating, who refused to support her man Barry Goldwater, she said the New York senate race "is one of the most unfortunate ones that I can remember in a long time, if not the most unfortunate." In addition to Kennedy's move to New York being an "obvious grab for power"—which wouldn't have gotten much of an argument in New York at the time—she viewed it as unfair that right-thinking voters in New York couldn't vote against the dastardly Kennedy. Doing so, she pointed out, would benefit a liberal Republican, a species of politician that she viewed with as much contempt as Tea Partiers despise moderate and less-than-fanatically conservative Republicans.

"The Democrats at least are openly what they are," she said. "Liberal Republicans don't disagree with Democrats in any significant way," but "have kidnapped the Republican party into welfare statism."

Rand had no reason to worry. By the time of her death, liberal Republicans were as obsolete as a 1959 Edsel. Thirty years after she passed on, the ascendancy was in her direction, with candidates seeking to outflank each other on the right like ambitious World War I generals. Her movement, the Tea Party movement, was calling the shots in the Republican Party.

Loftin moved to a subject that is a national obsession today. He asked if Rand believed "our national debt of somewhat over three hundred billion dollars represents a serious national problem for us." That was a lot of money in those days. Today, at an inflation-adjusted $2.1 trillion, it would be a significant reduction in the U.S. debt burden.

Rand's answer could have been pulled from a stump speech before a Tea Party rally: "The idea," she said, "that this debt is no problem merely because we owe it to ourselves, so to speak, or because we will never have to pay up on it, that we can keep passing it on from generation to generation, is a fallacy which can be exposed by a simple, primitive look at economics. Any sensible knowledge of economics would tell you that one cannot spend more than one produces, and that sooner or later that kind of spending will have to catch up with us."

Then came the following prophecy:

"The form in which we will pay for it would be a financial crash that will make the one in 1929 seem like a little trouble. The national debt is going to cause an economic crash. What no economist can predict, of course, is the time when this will happen. No one can tell. But that it will happen is obvious."

When I first heard these tinny words drifting out from the distant past, I could not understand why this startling prediction had not been disseminated by the ARI. It's possible, I guess, that given the volume of her various broadcasts and writings over the years, this comment just fell through cracks. Sure, it's nonsense to suggest that the national debt caused the financial crisis or the crash of 2008. But the debt-ceiling gridlock of 2011 caused a downgrade of the nation's credit rating—and a major market correction. Rand's prediction might have seemed absurd in 1964, or even in 2010. In 2011 it was eerily, frustratingly credible—because of an ideological polarization for which Rand had been a catalyst.

If Rand's 1964 radio interview had become general knowledge, it still would not have eased the primary obstacle impeding the Rand–Tea Party dynamic—faith. That was anathema to Objectivists, and was a dealbreaker for Rand throughout her life. She hated religion, especially Christianity. But faith in God was the essence of life to a great many in the Tea Party.

Tea Party literature sometimes read like hymnals, with copious references to the Almighty and Jesus. In his vest-pocket-sized *The Tea Party*

Manifesto, author and conservative commentator Joseph Farah invokes the Deity on almost every one of its tiny pages. "I know the heart and soul of the tea party movement," he says. "It is populated by people who think just like I do on these big issues. It is a movement of prayerful people, people who love God, people who go to church and synagogue."[2] That would leave Objectivists out in the cold, unless you included the Church of Rand on that list.

If the Tea Party ever wholeheartedly embraced Objectivism it would be the greatest boon for Rand since the publication of *Atlas Shrugged*—and a major challenge for anyone who doesn't care for the right's agenda. Yet little attention has been paid to the Rand–Tea Party relationship. The media instead has focused on secondary issues, such as Tea Party links to groups like Americans for Prosperity, which was financed by David and Charles Koch, the right-wing oil moguls. *New York* magazine called the Koch brothers the "Tea Party's wallet."[3] The implication was that the Tea Party was a conglomeration of "astroturf" groups—phony grassroots outfits—financed by corporate interests that benefit from their low-government, low-tax, deregulatory agenda.

I wasn't sure it mattered who bankrolled the Tea Party. Regardless of its source of funding, the Tea Party reflected a growing sentiment in the Heartland. It lacked a cohesive ideology, which made it ripe for Randian exploitation no matter who was paying the bills. Kate Zernike observed in her book *Boiling Mad* that the first organizers were motivated by ideology, talking about personal property rights, liberty, and such, "but as the rallies grew over the next months, many of the people who joined their ranks were acting on something more visceral—anger, fear."[4]

The question was whether Rand's people could exploit this vaguely motivated but powerful political movement.

CHAPTER TEN

The Organizer

Ayn Rand has a long record of winning over the ideologically adrift. It helps a great deal that Objectivism focuses on more than just capitalism and economics, which can be boring and complex. For a great many people encountering Rand's novels, the appeal lies elsewhere—the individualism of characters like Howard Roark, for instance. Pamela Geller, as a teenage rebel from a critical family, sopped up Rand's hard-headed view of family relationships and felt that Rand made her feel "validated." Teenagers are often spiritually vacant, rootless, and ripe for Rand to guide them. Tea Party rallies were performing much the same function for their members, making them feel good about themselves, surrounded by like-minded individuals mouthing the same vague platitudes.

Yaron Brook's job was to convert all those viscerally angry people into recruits for Objectivism. Were it not for their differences over religion, it would not be an overwhelming task. Randers and Tea Partiers were united by a mutual antigovernment agenda and opposition to the Wall Street bailouts. Dick Armey's "Tea Party manifesto" *Give Us Liberty* devotes an entire chapter to a denunciation of the bailouts,[1] and hostility to them—and to Wall Street in general—was evident at Tea Party rallies long before he put his "manifesto" on paper in 2010.

Armey, the former House of Representatives majority leader, represented what might be described as the Republican wing of the movement, because he was the most forthright in advancing corporate and Wall Street agendas. His organization FreedomWorks received $12 million from a Koch family foundation, making it a prime example of the oil magnates' influence on the Tea Party.[2] Armey blamed the financial crisis of 2008 not on anything Wall Street did, but on the villain that had proven so effective in years past—the government. He sought to deflect the Tea Party's anti-Wall Street anger by pointing to government policies that, he argued, were the root cause of the crisis. Among his solutions: repealing "various distortions in corporate accounting hurriedly drafted during previous legislative panics . . . starting with Sarbanes–Oxley," the law that was passed in a half-hearted attempt to stave off the kind of accounting chicanery that was found at Enron and other early 2000s frauds.[3]

Armey's talking points were straight out of the U.S. Chamber of Commerce and Business Roundtable. Reading Armey's missive—Farah's *The Tea Party Manifesto* generally avoided economic issues—one could understand the act of jujitsu being performed here. The failings of capitalism would be transformed into an endorsement not of unregulated capitalism but of the Bush–Reagan vision of weakly regulated crony capitalism. Most members of the public, unless they'd been closely following the financial news, had no way of knowing how clearly the evidence laid the blame for the crisis on the actions of the major banks, American International Group (AIG), and mortgage lenders, combined with far too little and negligent government regulation. Yet Armey hit on precisely the right note by focusing on the weakness of the bailouts, saying, "Bailing out bad actors who took too many risks was exactly the wrong approach."[4] It was a winning argument because it made a valid point. Moral hazard was disregarded in the bailout because of a rational fear that the system was on the verge of collapse. Banks were given capital that they were not required to lend—and they didn't. It was a fundamental weakness of the bank bailout, necessary though it was at the time.

The bitter irony of the bailouts is that they failed to spur lending because the bankers were acting like good Randians, even if they didn't have copies of *The Virtue of Selfishness* on their bedside tables. By not lending the money they received from the government, they were acting in their own rational self-interests. They were being *selfish*. It was not only incorrect but immoral, from the Rand perspective, for them to behave any differently. If the bankers had been viewed at the outset through a Randian lens, as people who could be counted upon to behave like Objectivists, their failure to be good citizens and loan out the capital they received would have been viewed not as possible, or likely, but inevitable. No other outcome would have been conceivable.

On the other hand, Henry Paulson, Tim Geithner, Ben Bernanke, and the other Treasury and Fed officials involved in the bailouts did not behave like Objectivists. They did not look out for the rational self-interests of the U.S. government. They naively assumed that capital injections would result in money flowing to borrowers. Instead, the money stayed at the banks, and the bailouts wound up as a manifestation of self-sacrifice by the government. They also ran counter to the Randian concept that the markets need to hum along without interference from government—a hollow concept indeed, when you consider that interference was needed to keep the bankers' bad choices from destroying the banking system. The financial crisis was actually a fine example of the markets failing abysmally as a self-correcting mechanism.

None of these nuances were glaringly evident. What the public saw—bankers getting a glorious package of treats that no one else enjoyed—was true, but incomplete. The little that was obvious seemed to argue in favor of Rand. Viewed in outline form, it looked as if bankers got a bailout when they should have failed.

Of course, much would depend on how you define *rational self-interest*. An alternate way of viewing the foregoing is that Paulson, Geithner, Bernanke et al actually did act in their rational self-interests, viewed in the narrow sense, the *selfish* sense—which, come to think of it, is the Randian-approved sense of the word. Hank Paulson retired from government service in comfort. Geithner was inexplicably promoted to Treasury Secretary, Bernanke kept his job, and there were no repercussions for anyone involved, banker or bureaucrat. None of the bankers were prosecuted, at least not in the three years following the crisis. Few were even sued by regulators. The government officials who rode herd over the most unpopular government intervention in business in history were vilified but unscathed. If a bureaucrat's primary function is self-preservation, the bailouts were a smashing success.

The Tea Party hated the bailouts, but who didn't? People from all points on the political spectrum despised them. But only the right—including, especially, the followers of Ayn Rand—seemed to gain because of the bailouts. The record-breaking sales figures of *Atlas Shrugged* attested to that.

The bailouts ran counter to everything that Objectivism stood for. They were a heavy-handed interference by the government in the free markets, crony capitalism at its worst, et cetera. Sure, they saved the system, but it wasn't necessary to acknowledge that, so it wasn't. Randians could exploit the bailouts to spread Objectivism to the Tea Party, and exploit it they did.

But Ayn Rand didn't have to be introduced to the Tea Party by Yaron Brook or anybody else outside the movement. She was already there.

I dashed off a note to a leading Tea Party organizer named Mark Meckler. I chose him based on the size and influence of his organization, and not from any hunch that he might be a Randian. This was totally a shot in the dark. Neither he nor any other Tea Party leader had been publicly identified with Ayn Rand, whether endorsing her views or rejecting them. So I was pleasantly surprised that Meckler wanted to talk. The implication was that he had something to talk about. He did.

Meckler, a lawyer in northern California, was cofounder and national coordinator of the Tea Party Patriots, one of five advocacy/organizing groups that embraced the otherwise disorganized Tea Party cause. His group provided support and training for Tea Party activists, and the buzz was that it was a genuine grassroots group, avoiding the partisan agenda of the Dick Armeys hovering around the movement.[5] Meckler got some heat in *Mother Jones* for his previous job as a distributor for Herbalife, a purveyor of nutritional supplements that uses a "multilevel marketing" approach, which some critics viewed as little more than a pyramid scheme.[6] Though he was quoted as saying that the Tea Party should not become an arm of the GOP, Meckler was criticized for his links to Republican consultants and Dick Armey's FreedomWorks.[7]

The picture that emerged from the hostile media coverage was of an opportunist and hustler, not a committed ideologue. Examining his background with my Rand-educated eye, however, I saw some clues that he was more than just the Sammy Glick of the Tea Party. The Herbalife distributorship showed a Randian entrepreneurial quality, a desire to be a Money-Maker, and its ethical characteristics demonstrated the kind of selfishness that Randers adore. I also found a press clip indicating that he ran something called the Cafe Mekka in Nevada City, California, some years back.[8] Every reader of *Atlas Shrugged* knows that one of its secondary characters (a good guy) ran a chow house.

So I was not surprised when Meckler told me that he read "the entire Rand compendium" during his first year of college, when he was eighteen. "With the influence she's had on my life it's a little embarrassing I can't remember how I first came across her books," he told me. Meckler said he first read *Fountainhead* and *Atlas,* and then worked his way through the other novels.

Meckler's early life was a small-town and suburban tableau. He grew up in Northridge in the San Fernando Valley, the son of a salesman and entrepreneur. His parents were conservative Republicans. He grew up in "massive suburbs," which I imagine might have led to his early ambition to become a real estate developer. In pursuit of that goal he went to law school, and he now lived in a town called Grass Valley in the hills above Sacramento. This was John Steinbeck country, more or less, but as an Ayn Rand follower there wasn't much Steinbeck in his consciousness. His populism was not our grandparents' populism. In his populist vision there were no bindle stiffs exploited by cruel farmers, no Okies striving for a better life, fighting scabs, finding refuge at government migrant worker camps. His was a populism of noble entrepreneurs and non-self-sacrificing shopkeepers and farmers.

Meckler was a serious student of Rand. As a kid he worked his way not just through her novels but her nonfiction books as well, including a book exploring Objectivist epistemology. You had to be true-blue and Randian to the core to plow through that murky tome, which has the literary elegance of a cement mixer. ("The Analytic-Synthetic Dichotomy" is the title of one chapter, written by the always-riveting Leonard Peikoff.) I was surprised to learn that he hadn't gotten hold of bound copies of her newsletters. Absorbing those stirring essays in their original form is a sign of a hard-core Rand follower, I pointed out.

"I've never been a hard-core follower of anything," he said. "For me it was that I was fascinated by the ideas and the philosophy. I'm not a big joiner or signer-up for newsletters, or joiner of clubs, or anything like that." That was odd coming from the organizer of a political movement. Perhaps he was like Gandhi, who I certainly could not imagine joining the local Kiwanis.

I asked him to explain what appealed to him about *The Fountainhead*. He responded that "when I read it there were a few fundamental concepts in there that were important to me. When I read it, it was a clear expression of a lot of philosophies that I already held when I was eighteen and was unable to articulate. One was just the power of the individual to accomplish anything."

Another concept that Rand had clarified for him was "the damage that can be done by collectivism," though he wouldn't have put it in those words at the time. "I saw what happened to people when they got dragged down by the group," he said. "There was a tendency in society to take people who'd accomplished stuff and to tear them down." He already had that perception when he was eighteen, so when he read that book "it was like 'yes!' Pump your first in the air and 'Yes, this is what I believe.' It wasn't so much, 'Wow, these are new ideas and they're expanding my mind.' It was, 'Now what I believe has been articulated, in a way more sophisticated than I could ever do.'"

Yet again I was hearing how Rand had crystallized her readers' opinions into the hard rock of ideology. Again, I heard the same "confirmation factor" that Pamela Geller, Iris Bell, and others had described, almost word-for-word, as if they were comparing notes. Rand spoke to something deep inside these very different people—the Long Island career woman, the Chicago-born graphics designer, and the small-town California lawyer.

Meckler worked just as hard at Objectivism as they did, even though he was not quite as demonstrative. I could find nothing in the public record indicating that he ever mentioned Rand publicly. But Meckler was committed, all right. He told me that he read *Fountainhead* and *Atlas* "six to ten times." That kind of compulsive re-re-rereading was found only among the most dedicated followers of Rand, anxious to relive the joy of reading these two basic texts and, perhaps, to pick up insights they might have missed on earlier readings.

In talking with Meckler I detected a discordant note. He expressed his devotion to Rand using words that seemed odd for an Objectivist: "They're books that for me, in addition to spiritual books, in addition to Scripture, they're books that I read when times are tough. When I need inspiration to continue to stand, those are the books that inspire me." Meckler made Rand sound more like Norman Vincent Peale than the hard-edged collectivist-fighter that she was.

Atlas Shrugged originally inspired him, he said, because it appealed to him that "people who do the right thing, working hard and producing the best they possibly could for the sake of it would seek out other people who were doing the same. To me it was inspiring that there are groups of people who do this. I knew how I was, how I worked. I did my best for the sake of doing my best. I wasn't trying to prove anything to anyone else."

Meckler described himself as not the "quintessential kid who would be reading *Atlas Shrugged,*" which he defined as a preppie "in an argyle vest in an Ivy League school or something." He was into punk rock and normal 1980s kid stuff like that. He wasn't politically active, though he'd been following politics since he was twelve, reading the *Los Angeles Times* and talking about current events with his father. From an early age he felt much as he did as an adult, that "the less that government was involved in our lives the better." Reading *Atlas Shrugged* appealed to those yearnings, much as a kid with a passion for social justice might be lit up by books that are soft on altruism (like just about every other book written since the dawn of time).

"It's almost prophetic now," he said of the Objectivist Good Book. "It's impossible to read *Atlas Shrugged* without seeing today's world." His son, who was twelve, felt the same way when he read it, Meckler pointed out. Now, that was a touching picture, a dad handing down a treasured book to his son. Was that his favorite book? "Other than talking spiritually and scripturally, *Atlas Shrugged* is definitely my all-time favorite and influential book," he responded. Apparently Meckler was one of those Christian Objectivists that John Allison mentioned to me. Meckler told me that he "mostly agreed with" Objectivism. "I say 'mostly' and that's important. I'm not one of these adherents to Objectivism or Randian philosophy per se. I just like a lot of the ideas espoused in the book."

Having repeatedly cited "Scripture," it was no great surprise when Meckler told me that atheism was one area of disagreement with Rand. "There's never been a philosophy that I've bought wholesale," he explained.

"I'm not a follower; it's not my style. Certain things appeal to me and certain things don't." That made sense, of course, though it was not the kind of thinking that would have pleased Rand. But it was obvious that few of Rand's adherents today would have pleased the grand old lady of radical capitalism. Even the so-far unavailable Yaron Brook might have annoyed Rand by associating with the hated libertarian movement. I'm sure that she would have hated the way Meckler and other admirers of her work had a tendency to pick and choose from her teachings, as if they were at the breakfast buffet at the local Marriott. If there were to be a new Objectivist Man, it would be Mark Meckler—Scripture-reading non-atheist, organizer and promoter of mass protests, independent thinker, buffet customer.

"She was not exactly your average human being. She was an incredibly flawed character," he said. "I've been married seventeen years. I can't imagine having affairs. I can't imagine justifying her personal life the way she did." And there is the right to abortion, which, I reminded him, Rand favored.[9] "From a philosophical point of view I am not a follower of Objectivism," Meckler responded. Here we had an Objectivist Man who was *not* an Objectivist Man when uncomfortable issues were broached.

Meckler was familiar with *The Virtue of Selfishness,* which he had in front of him as we talked. I was curious to hear his view of altruism, the hatred of which is, after all, the lynchpin of her entire ethical system. While I could accept his view that it's possible to pick and choose from Rand's works as much as one wishes, it seemed to me that a serious reader of her work would have to either ignore, reject, or swallow whole her belief that altruism is a terrible thing.

Meckler waffled a bit on that. "I probably haven't read that book in twenty years," he said of *The Virtue of Selfishness,* its presence in front of him notwithstanding. "I couldn't define for you the way she defines altruism." As for him, "This is the way I was raised, and I'll throw out a couple of catchphrases that I've always lived by, which are things like, 'If you're not happy you can't make other people happy.' So I'd say that probably falls in line with *Virtue of Selfishness*." People who are not successful, he noted, "are generally not going around, doing for others. It's people who have achieved a measure of personal satisfaction in their lives, and that's what I define as success, who are the ones doing for others and lifting others up."

I didn't see how any of this tracked with Rand, especially the "make other people happy" and "doing for others" aspects. They sounded like song lyrics from the hippie-dippy 1960s.* In *Virtue,* Rand expounds a bit on the subject of happiness, which she defines as "that state of consciousness that proceeds from the achievement of one's values."[10] "Making other people happy" and "lifting others up" don't jibe with this definition and seem like off-the-rack, Sunday School altruism. Still, these were nice and sweet sentiments, so I didn't want to play ogre and disabuse him. If people wanted to impose humanity on the Rand value system where none previously existed, who was I to stop them? Still, at this point in our conversation it seemed Meckler was either not as acquainted with Rand's ideology as he initially appeared to be, or was soft-peddling the more unpalatable aspects.

When I noted that Rand was not big on charity or on lifting people up, Meckler showed again his Rand smarts by alluding to the always-convenient "trader principle," pointing out that "she believed in a value exchange for everything." So it's a question of "how you define value. You can exchange in a way that's completely altruistic and it can still be a value exchange." After all, "you won't find people who give to charity who say it makes them feel miserable to do so. It just doesn't happen. People give to charity because it makes them feel good, and they may not want to define it like this but there's a measure of selfishness in that." Giving to charity "improves their self-concept, it improves how they feel." Writing a big check "makes them feel good to do so." By that tweaking of Objectivist dogma, Warren Buffett's "giving pledge," which Yaron Brook attacked as a "guilt pledge," was just

* They were. "Make Someone Happy" is a song from a long-forgotten 1960 musical, *Do Re Mi.*

fine. In fact, any purely altruistic act would be okay if it makes one feel glad within.

"There's self-interest," Meckler said, "in designing your life in a way that satisfies your personal ideal"—such as Mother Teresa, the altruist's altruist, devoting her life to the poor in Calcutta. Using that modified Rand 2.0 criteria, only a handful of miserable, self-sacrificing nutcases, who'd give away their firstborn and favorite fishing rods to their worst enemies, could be viewed as "selfless." Or would even they be considered selfless? Such people seem like wackos to us, but to them the desire to sacrifice is a deep psychological need. I'm sure an argument can be made that there is a "value exchange" buried in there somewhere.

I'd heard other Randians use similar tortured logic to gloss over Rand's fierce attacks on altruism. Such reasoning always struck me as intellectually fraudulent. You can't have it both ways. If you feel that being selfless is wrong, it seems craven to carve out all kinds of exceptions so that virtually *nothing* is selfless. Those rationalizations seem designed to make the less-appealing parts of Rand's beliefs appear less extreme than they really are, so that the other parts of her dogma—such as zero-government capitalism—can be more readily embraced.

As we chatted and Meckler continued to find selfishness in selfless acts, I found myself admiring his sound political sense, which could serve as a bridge between the Christian right and the doctrinaire free-market atheists of the Randian persuasion. The formula was simple: politely disagree with Rand's beliefs that are repulsive to devout Christians, such as her atheism and approval of abortion, and rationalize her disdain for charity, altruism, and other Judeo-Christian ethical principles.

Even with suitable loopholes carved into Rand's philosophy, it wasn't going to be easy. Meckler agreed that Rand's atheism had turned off a lot of people in the Tea Party. "There's a whole group of people who would say, 'I can't read Ayn Rand because she was a strident atheist,'" he said. And if they knew about her personal life, he said, "they might even be more offended." He struck me as an upright Christian gentleman, with his study of Scripture and all, so I asked him about his upbringing and churchgoing habits, and Meckler disabused me of the Tea Party stereotype I'd formed in my mind. "I'm Jewish," he said. I don't know why I was surprised, but I was. Like many people, I'd assumed a Tea Party leader would be white, middle-American, and definitely Christian.

With his serious intellect and political savvy, this man could be a major asset to the Randers. He was one of the most important figures in the Tea Party circuit, helping to run an organization that, by his reckoning, had 20 million members and 3,000 chapters. So I was surprised when Meckler told me that he had never met or corresponded with anyone from the Ayn Rand Institute or Atlas Society. Not even Yaron Brook, despite all his outreach to the Tea Party. "I wouldn't mind meeting him but I have no particular desire," said Meckler. Brook made a serious effort to link up with the Tea Party since its earliest days, and his efforts were intensifying in 2011. He was projecting a high profile among Tea Partiers throughout the year, including a speech at one Tea Party forum in which he denounced the "morally corrupt scheme" called Social Security that was causing "suffering" throughout the nation (however much it might have helped Ayn Rand in her golden years). "Phasing out Social Security is not going to be easy. It's going to take a little bit of time," Brook said. "But we need to stand on principle."[11]

So what did Meckler surmise from the fact that nobody from the Rand groups ever reached out to this immensely influential kindred spirit? Nothing much, or so he contended. "This is not false humility but I'm nothing special," he said. "I'm a guy who started a Tea Party in Sacramento and just kept raising my hand and volunteering to keep doing the work when others couldn't because they had other things in their lives intervening."

Actually it did strike me as false humility. If he was "nothing special" I wouldn't be interviewing him, and he wouldn't be skewered all over the media. He was clearly a brilliant political operative, no matter what one thought of his politics, and I was interested to get his take on the extent of Rand's influence on the Tea Party movement. His response was an illuminating flip-flop.

"I would say that Objectivism itself, as an overall philosophy that people think about, not at all. Even those I know who read Rand's fiction don't talk about Objectivism," he said. "They talk about Rand, they talk about *Atlas Shrugged* primarily, but they don't talk about it as an expression of Objectivist philosophy." In other words, Objectivism *is* what Tea Partiers talk about, because *Atlas* is the Good Book of Objectivism. Rand spoke through her characters, and let's face it: the minutiae of Objectivist theology are dead boring. Even the Midtown Restaurant Objectivists rarely talked about Objectivism in an abstract sense.

But Meckler had observed "a substantial influence, especially *Atlas Shrugged*, on the way people think." He'd have been right at home at the St. Regis fund-raiser, and Yaron Brook and Tara Smith would have been delighted to hear that. Meckler ranked Rand higher as an influence on the Tea Party movement than the free-market thinkers Friedrich Hayek and Ludwig von Mises, whose books sold briskly throughout 2011. In the Tea Party movement, he said, "You won't find anybody more widely read than Rand."

What the Tea Party was experiencing was not an invasion of John Galt-banner-waving, Rand-praising Objectivists, fanning out from the Midtown Restaurant and other Ayn Rand cells, but rather an influx of what used to be known to 1950s Red-baiters as "fellow travelers"—people influenced by her views without embracing all of them. An analogy was the New Left of the 1960s and 1970s: activists who were influenced by the doctrinaire Marxism embraced by a hard core, but without adopting the entire party platform. Waving Vietcong flags at antiwar rallies was the baby boomer generation's counterpart to the Tea Party's John Galt placards. Both were emblems of an extremist ideology, held by people who felt a deep malaise about the direction in which the country was heading.

There's just one flaw in my analogy, which is that in America only academics, would-be Marxists, and other specialized readers plowed through *Das Kapital*. Rand, of course, has been read by millions of Americans, and as Meckler pointed out with some validity, "It's pretty hard to find somebody who read her work who says that they were not influenced by it." Meckler viewed Rand's impact on the Tea Party in a reasonable fashion: "When you're talking about affecting people's worldview and philosophy, inevitably that has a tangible effect." He then went on to put his finger on the source of her appeal: "She's been able to take very complex philosophical ideas and put them into pop fiction. I think those ideas go into our heads and our hearts."

It's subtle, almost subliminal, as Meckler saw it:

"People don't necessarily say, 'I'm voting for that guy because he reminds me of Ayn Rand's philosophy.' But in their hearts and minds, Ayn Rand's philosophy lives as a part of who they are."

CHAPTER ELEVEN

The Vaguely Dissatisfied

I put out word on the grapevine that I wanted to speak to Randers in the Tea Party movement, and the e-mails started coming quickly. These were regular folks, happy to help a guy understand their movement—which I had a hell of a time trying to figure out. I could understand their dissatisfaction with the status quo, but I could not understand why they favored policies that would have gotten us deeper into the muck we were already in.

Thomas Frank's *What's the Matter with Kansas?* provides a sense of why people in the Heartland felt and voted as they did at the midpoint of the Bush presidency in 2004. Back then the central fixation was social issues, with little attention paid to the economy. Now the economy was horrid and social issues were taking a back seat. Yet we saw millions of ordinary people organizing under the Tea Party banner, directly endorsing economic policies that would slit many of them right across their windpipes. I could understand gut-level rejection of the Eastern elite causing people to vote against their interests. I could understand people ignoring economic issues that they did not understand. But I had trouble comprehending blithe acceptance of the most radical form of no-government capitalism that would directly harm them, their children, and their parents.

It's one thing to refer to the national debt as a burden that one shouldn't pass on to one's grandkids. But if the grandkids are affected by cuts in aid to education, or if they and their parents can't get affordable health insurance, isn't that the most immediate priority? Isn't a strong effort by the government to ensure low-cost health care in the *rational self-interests* of most people? Did these Tea Party activists understand what was in their best interests? Did they know what they were endorsing when they held up those ubiquitous "John Galt" placards at Tea Party rallies? Or was it a vacuous symbol, just the way my generation held up placards at antiwar rallies that sometimes sided with the murderous Vietcong?

From a Randian perspective there was a selfish point to the antiwar rallies of the 1960s. The male participants therein did not want to serve in the Army. "Hell no, we won't go" was the popular chant of the era. But these Tea Party followers were shouting, "Hell no, stop regulating big business!" "Hell no, keep tax cuts for billionaires!" I was looking forward to Tea Party people making sense of all this for me.

The first Tea Partier to get in touch with me after Mark Meckler was a fellow named Mark Herr. He was from "far west Tennessee—home of Elvis and barbecue," and he was with the Mid-South Tea Party, which encompassed northern Mississippi, eastern Arkansas, and most of western Tennessee. The Mid-South Web site described itself as "a nonpartisan organization of grassroots citizens from Memphis, Shelby County, Tennessee, and the surrounding Mid-South area." It went on to say that the group "was born out of a concern that the peoples [sic] government is shifting away from adherence with [sic] the United States Constitution toward the implementation of failed Statist and Socialist policies."[1] Right there, with "statist," we had a bold self-identification with libertarian and Objectivist rhetoric.

Herr received some attention when the NAACP voted in July 2010 to condemn racism in the Tea Party. The resolution was mild, calling upon Tea Party leaders to repudiate "those in their ranks who use racist language in their signs and speeches."[2] But Herr would have none of it. He said that the resolution was political "if they're afraid of the Tea Party because we want to limit size, scope, and power of the government."[3] Herr was variously described in press accounts as an "activist" in, "spokesman" for, and "organizer" of this Tea Party group. I suppose he could have fit all those descriptions. The e-mails that he sent me were from a Mid-South Tea Party e-mail address, replete with an official-looking notice at the bottom, such as one might get from a law firm, that "any dissemination, distribution, or copy of this communication is strictly prohibited." So he obviously had a role with Mid-South significant enough to warrant an e-mail account.

Herr seemed to be part of the Tea Party faction that was nervous about being seen as too cozy with the Republican Party. (I never could understand that; who else were they supposed to be cozy with? Obama? It reminded me of 1968, when the left avoided Hubert Humphrey and helped usher in the age of Nixon.) I noticed one article from the spring of 2010 in which Herr was quoted as saying, "We don't want to become 'Teapublicans.'"[4] But I also noticed that he was a member of Dick Armey's Republican-leaning FreedomWorks, as attested by his own FreedomWorks member page on the Internet.[5]

He was a host with the Mid-South Tea Party's Internet radio operation, which explained why he had a Tea Party e-mail account. As we talked, one of the first things he told me was that had never actually read Ayn Rand.

No problem. Herr could be a one-person control group, like the poor saps in drug trials who get the placebo—a prominent but random Tea Partier who hadn't actually gone the Rand route. He had heard John Galt bandied about at Tea Party meetings, and he was aware of Rand's influence on other Tea Partiers, but he didn't happen to be one of them. Herr could be a useful sounding board. "A baseline," he said, agreeing to participate in my Rand-consciousness experiment.

Herr traced for me, in painstaking detail, the evolution of his thinking back to the early 1990s, when he was in the Air Force. That was when he started to be troubled by the political undercurrents that have bothered him to the present day. In the beginning, his first problem was the epidemic of political correctness. "I was young, I didn't know anything about politics or Democrats or Republicans, conservative, liberal, or whatever. I just thought it was a very strange way to stifle freedom of speech," he said. "Why are we stifling our ability to think freely or speak freely? That's kind of where things began for me. I questioned conventional wisdom and political correctness."

Then came the election of Bill Clinton, which was an eye-opener. Herr recalled for me the really annoying and offensive event that influenced his thinking for years to come. He told me that Clinton went to Japan in 1992, while Herr was stationed there, to sign the Kyoto Protocol on greenhouse gas emissions to curb global warming (a phenomenon whose existence is disbelieved by Objectivists, by the way). During his visit, Herr said, there was an unpleasant incident.

"For whatever reason the president sent Air Force Two to our base. We're all standing there, about thirty-three hundred of us, standing there, waiting for the president to get off the plane. President is about to get off. Somebody walks up to the general, whispers something. He turns around, you could tell he's really pissed off. We find out he sent a decoy to the base, and the president landed at Narita Airport," he said. This was a major breach of protocol as far as the military was concerned. You just don't do that to servicepeople. "There was a lot of discontent because that spread throughout the military quite fast," he said. "That kind of added to my 'Man, what's going on here?' I just didn't understand. Know what I mean?" It seemed to me like a minor snub at most, but I guess you had to be there.*

That was bad enough, but the 2000 elections really knocked him for a

* I'm not sure it matters, but just for the record: Clinton was in Japan for the G7 Summit, not for the Kyoto Protocol, and it was in 1993, not 1992.

loop. For weeks after the election it was . . . well, come on! What a lot of huffing and puffing, a lot of noise and confusion. He was baffled by "the hanging chads and the Supreme Court. I'm like, 'What is all this back and forth going on? Why are they struggling so hard against each other?' You know what I mean? I didn't understand, and I'm still in the process of learning. You know what I mean?" At the time he was out of the Air Force and studying at Middle Tennessee State University for a master's degree in finance and information technology—"greed and propaganda," he quipped. I asked him about his political thinking during that time period, and he responded by going back to that confounding 2000 election. "My thinking at the time was I didn't understand why—what was behind the struggle. Why was it so significant? Why was all this—it seemed like there was so much discourse about the desire to take power between the two sides. You know what I mean?" Yes, I did.

"I was just curious," he continued. "It was all about hanging chads and Supreme Court, I'm going to sue you, you're going to sue me, it just was 'What's the deal here? Why is there so much foment?' "

Then came September 11, and the Patriot Act, Iraq, weapons of mass destruction, and so on, and the "discourse began to switch significantly—it seemed like the folks who lost power in 2000 were very much bent on—not so much on national security matters as much as they were on regaining power.

"That began to affect my thinking more significantly," he recalled. "Now you have to apply this to my thinking about political correctness, the fake Air Force One thingie, then there's 2000, and now you've got 9/11, and the way political discourse changed at that point." Then the Democrats assumed power in Congress in 2006, and his thinking continued to evolve further along that track (I'm not sure exactly how but I'll take his word for it). Herr worked as a counselor at a Memphis college and then went "on hiatus," remodeling his home "and stuff like that."

Then came 2008 and "a whole bunch of little things all at once." One of those was the "mortgage bailout under Bush." That was his name for the bailout of the banks and American International Group, the mammoth insurer. All had suffered because of their exposure to various varieties of toxic subprime mortgages and securities based thereon. In the case of AIG, there was reckless speculation in mortgage-backed derivatives. It was complicated but it boiled down to financial services executives drowning in their own fee lust, and needing to be rescued lest they pull everybody down into the muck.

Herr looked at it this way: He had paid his mortgage on time, that's how he'd been taught to behave, "and here we had a situation where the federal government had put in policies—and I don't know all the names of the policies, all the frickin' details—but I do know the federal government was culpable for putting mortgage lenders in the position where they would have been brought up on discrimination charges for not approving certain types of loans." He called this a "real corrupt situation," in which "the same people who created the problem were the ones who were going to solve the problem. That just bothered me."

I was baffled by this version of events, so I asked him if he was referring to the financial crisis of 2008, which this account vaguely resembled the way a basketball vaguely resembles a cantaloupe. Yes, he was. "I was very disconcerted by the fact that the federal government, which was responsible for the regulations which the mortgage lenders had to follow, were the ones who were blaming the mortgage lenders for the problem and now they were the ones who were going to solve the problem. There's something wrong with that logic." There was. Just to be sure I understood him correctly, I asked him if he was blaming the banks or government policies for creating the crisis. I didn't quite follow his point. Yes, there were regulations that banks had to follow. They didn't, and that was the fault of . . . the government?

He responded that "For me it was the government policies that put the banks in the position where they could be corrupt or make bad financial decisions." That was the central perception, straight out of Dick Armey's talking points: The banks and mortgage issuers were not to blame. The government was. I had heard this kind of thinking before. It was 1960s logic, blaming the "system," only now the logic was turned upside down. The rich and powerful were the ones getting the short end of the stick, not the youthful victims of Johnson/Nixon/Laird. Not to worry; today's wealthy victims of the system had a lot of ordinary people like Mark Herr sticking up for them, in return for . . . nothing, except possibly the shaft. Altruism at its best.

I asked him what government policies he had in mind. Here was a Tea Party leader, a communicator, a broadcaster, so I expected some kind of analysis, or at least a description, of the cause of the crisis and the government's role in it. He was a layperson, not a politician, but laypeople were clogging the Internet with all kinds of theories on the banking system's near-collapse.

"It's very complicated," he responded. "This is the problem with the federal government. It's so complicated, how can you make a transparent discussion about it? It's like this intricate web of confusion." He couldn't name any of the policies that gave rise to these bad banking decisions, but he did know that Barney Frank "was involved in a lot of the discussions in the Clinton era regarding the 'responsible lending act' or something like that in the early nineties where mortgage banks were put in the position where they had to make certain types of loans." He was referring to the Community Reinvestment Act (CRA), which was passed in 1977 and prodded lenders to make loans in low-income and minority areas. The CRA was the whipping boy in the far-right narrative of the financial crisis, pushed by the likes of Dick Armey and Ron Paul.[6] It was much hated by Randians, as it appeared to require that bankers make loans to people who ordinarily wouldn't be eligible—a scenario straight out of *Atlas Shrugged.* Critics of the blame-CRA thesis say it has been refuted "up, down, and sideways," as *New York Times* columnist Paul Krugman once put it. The chief flaw in the argument, Krugman noted, is that the vast bulk of subprime lending was by institutions not subject to the CRA.[7]

By the 2008 elections, Herr's feelings of alienation were reaching a crescendo. He saw how "the Democrats were using the political discourse regarding Iraq and terrorism and Abu Ghraib, and they were starting to just chip away at President Bush." He understood "the need to return to power and make change, but to actually interfere with national security—and you got to understand, the military guys—and I'm going back to my experience in 1992, with Clinton and his fake plane trip—I'm associating his group of Democrat people with the same people who were undermining national security efforts, and CNN is airing terrorists sniping . . ." and so on. That Clinton airfield nonappearance really got his goat. It was an act of disrespect, a snub that grated on him, even though I couldn't understand how being part of a necessary security precaution could have riled him so. It seemed to run a lot deeper than disappointment at not seeing Bill Clinton climb off a plane in Japan twenty years ago.

The Rick Santelli rant crystallized his feelings. "He was saying what I was thinking," he told me. I pointed out to him that Santelli was a Rander. He didn't know that. "I really need to read Ayn Rand," he said, and I agreed. Yes, this man desperately needed Rand. If he's going to feel the way he does, why not have a halfway logical basis for his feelings? I'd been spoiled by hanging out with Randers, who related everything, even ridiculous stuff, to their ideology. Turning my control group to a guinea pig, I suggested that he read some of her works, or at least peruse the ARI Web site. We could chat again afterward, and I could see how much he'd been swayed. Herr readily agreed.

Herr moved on to "auditing the Fed" and other Ron Paul–Dick Armey talking points, and I could feel my eyeballs glazing over. This was pulled right out of the Republican narrative. I felt as if I had fed a Heritage Foundation press release into text-to-audio software. The Tea Party movement was a grassroots movement, but it sometimes seemed to reflect concerns that emerged from corner offices in far-off metropolises. His ideas had no consistent ideological basis. Herr was angry for a bunch of disjointed and rather petty reasons, all of which led him to notions that had the same musty, Barry Goldwaterish smell to them.

The misgivings of my Midtown Restaurant Objectivists seemed to be justified by my talk with Herr. He only seemed to know what he was against, not what he was for. He had no opinion on deregulation, for instance, indicating that whatever he picked up from the right-wing media was incomplete and not very well thought out. This was my control group, and what I was gleaning from our conversation was confusion and lack of information, so as to make it impossible for him to discuss the financial crisis in an informed way (even informed with bad information).

This man needed intellectual ammunition. With some Randian notions under his belt, perhaps he'd stop obsessing about the "fake Air Force One" and focus on stuff that mattered, like the need to be selfish and the moral superiority of no-government capitalism. Listening to him kick around various half ideas, unfocused and not always making much sense, was painful. Not unpleasant, though. He was on the radio and he knew how to talk. He reminded me a bit of the cranky radio talkers of bygone late nights, men like Long John Nebel and Barry Gray, easy to listen to as one drifted off to sleep.

I suspected that there were a lot of Mark Herrs out there: vaguely dissatisfied people who were newly empowered by the Tea Party movement. Back in 2009, as the despised Obama took office, Herr was so inspired by Rick Santelli's rant that he looked around locally in Memphis for the like-minded. He found fifteen people. They started meeting in March 2009 in a Perkins restaurant, and they decided that "tax day was the perfect day to voice our concerns." There was no Rand ideology involved here, no talk of "looters," but the concern was the same: Government had gotten too big, too domineering. It was "us" versus "them," with "them" being the government and "us" being everyone else, from dirt farmers to CEOs of the banks that were charging some of these people 30 percent interest on their credit cards.

The rally was held as planned on April 15, 2009, and the media showed up—along with five thousand people. "It was just a fabulous experience. We didn't know what we were doing. But it was so organic and fresh and fun. It was great to be able to speak your mind and say exactly what you felt." That was an interesting choice of words—as if it was necessary to assemble with other right-thinking, disgruntled people in order to exercise one's right to freedom of speech.

From the beginning, Herr saw "John Galt" on signs and shirts at Tea Party rallies. Never having read Rand, he had only the slightest idea what that meant. One movement regular in particular, Vicki Towles, "would always have these funny little different things, John Galt things. 'Where is John Galt?' and stuff like that."

She would have to be the next one on my list. Meanwhile, I contemplated my interview with Herr. I went into this conversation hoping to find out why people would openly endorse policies that were contrary to their best interests. My impression was that not even Herr understood why he felt the way he did. He just felt emotionally, on a gut level, that things needed to change, that government was to blame for the financial crisis, and that it needed to be curbed.

It was obvious that a lot of people felt just as he did. Five thousand people don't grow on trees. And if those five thousand people aren't too picky about the facts—well, then they would be ripe for conversion to the Objectivist cause.

Vicki Towles was reluctant to talk to me. She e-mailed to say that that she was "more of an *Atlas Shrugged* fan than [an] Ayn Rand [fan]. I've not studied her enough to determine whether or not I'm an a Objectivist, but I do love and am drawn to her theme in *Atlas Shrugged*. I have such excitement and optimism when I think of the power of the individual. John Galt et al had that burning desire to dream and create, which is the choice of every human. Each of us has an innate desire to do good and blaze our own path, but too often that desire is smothered.

"That frustrates me," her e-mail continued, "because no matter the day, man has the ability to begin anew. I'm the eternal optimist and recognize the potential in everyone I meet. We all have unique gifts and talents endowed us by our Creator, that no man can stifle, unless we allow him."

This note made me all the more interested in talking to Vicki. That reference to the "Creator," with a capital "c," was the clincher. To hard-core Rand aficionados, "creators" are people, not deities. Lowercase-c "creator" is a *Fountainhead* term of endearment, the way you or I would use "honeybunch," and is deployed throughout the novel mainly in reference to its hero. I was interested to know how Vicki reconciled faith in the capital-c Creator with her Rand advocacy.

She overcame her hesitation and we connected. Vicki, who lived in Memphis, was an operations analyst at Federal Express. That had a certain symbolic significance. FedEx was sometimes cited by Randers as a shining example of private enterprise making fools of an unpopular government bureaucracy.

Vicki told me that she never actually carried a "Who is John Galt" placard. "I had a little sticker on a satchel bag," she said. "It had the 'Who is John Galt?' sticker that I bought from the John Galt Store." She got her sticker when buying some "Who is John Galt?" T-shirts from JohnGaltGifts.com. There were many Web sites that catered to *Atlas Shrugged* readers desiring to pay tribute to their reading experience. The Web site Vicki named redirected to ProudProducers.com, and was the first hit when I googled "John Galt Store." (I made a mental note that I would altruistically suggest to Yaron Brook, if I ever met him, that he offer "official Ayn Rand souvenirs" on the ARI Web site.)

ProudProducers.com had a line of *Atlas Shrugged*-theme clothing,

T-shirts, ball-point pens, hats, license plate frames, coins, mouse pads, decals, stickers, and dog tags, among other things, all inquiring as to the identity of John Galt, ruminating on Galt's Gulch, and urging passersby to read Ayn Rand. Also available were souvenirs of Rearden Metal, 20th Century Motors, d'Anconia Copper, and other *Atlas Shrugged* totems, characters, concepts, and fictitious companies. As was to be expected, the site had several variations on the "Who is John Galt?" theme, in different typefaces and colors. Also available was a smaller assortment of *Anthem*- and *Fountainhead*-related products. My favorite was the sticker saying, "Ask not what your country can do for you but what you can do for YOURSELF."

Atlas was the only Rand book Vicki had read, though she was about to read *We the Living*, Rand's first novel, which was set in postrevolutionary Russia and was published in 1936. It is considerably shorter than Rand's final two novels and is somewhat more digestible for beginners. Vicki had tried to read *Fountainhead*, but was too busy with Tea Party work to give it proper attention. "I haven't studied Ayn Rand very much, but what little I know about her philosophy I like," she said. "The fact that we are responsible for ourselves, and by being the best we can be, we are going to make it better for everybody else." That vague but all-American be-the-best-that-you-can-be sentiment seemed to resonate with Tea Party people, though it still wasn't clear to me how it was possible to read through *Atlas Shrugged*, with its extremist vision of America, and come away with a trite aphorism. I guess it was just wooly headed lefties like Whittaker Chambers who fixated on the more fascistic aspects of the book.

Vicki told me that she read *Atlas Shrugged* at about the time of the 2008 elections. She saw references to "Going Galt" and other Rand-related slogans in blogs, "so it piqued my interest and I started doing research on it, and I'm like 'What is this?' " Vicki, who was from Mississippi originally, was a liberal in college, but her politics shifted rightward after she graduated in the early nineties. She became hooked on Rush Limbaugh, "so I really started questioning things." Limbaugh, she said, "opened the door to me to know my facts, and if I was ever in a situation where something was happening, and there was a conversation going on and people asking my opinion, I'd feel very confident saying 'OK, here's what I've researched. It's not necessarily what I've heard, but here are the facts as I've seen them and read them and here's where I got them. So I recommend you to find out for yourself. You may not agree with them, but here is where I got the facts.' "

She used to like Bill Clinton, but that faded when she saw him contradicting himself, "like a chameleon," in his stump speeches. Listening to Limbaugh aided her political education, helping her see the light on Clinton. "I started scratching my head, going 'Now that just doesn't make sense.' I don't understand why he's saying it but I wasn't a student of politics enough to get it. So then I started listening to Rush. It wasn't that there was one specific issue. It's just whatever he was talking about he would read an article from a newspaper, he would give his source, and it was all of these different things, it was just *truth*." That "source" bit really impressed her. "He's saying where he's getting his stuff. He's not just throwing these beautiful words into the air and not backing them up."

Vicki was not a regular viewer of the *Glenn Beck* show on Fox News but she traveled to Washington, D.C., to attend his Restoring Honor rally on August 28, 2010—the one that had troubled my Midtown Restaurant Objectivists. She was one of the right-leaning God-believers that Paul Bell viewed as the great hope of the nation. She was not a member of any organized church but called herself a Christian. "I'm one of those Jesus fans," she said, demonstrating again that one can simultaneously be a follower of the man from Galilee and the lady from Murray Hill.

The Beck rally was her sixth trip to D.C. since the Tea Party movement began. "I've never been to Disneyland," she said, "but there's something so magical and beautiful about Washington—not just the scenery, but the history and all of the thinking and the thought that has taken place in that area. It's just the center of the free world."

I wondered if she'd feel that way about the thinking and thought that has taken place in my neighborhood, Greenwich Village. It is the site of the last home of Thomas Paine, the great pamphleteer and philosopher of the American Revolution. His final dwelling is now the site of a tenement at 59 Grove Street. Marie's Crisis, the piano bar on the ground floor, takes its name from Paine's "Crisis" articles, which he wrote during the Revolutionary War.*

Our conversation drifted over to George Washington. He had a much bigger fan base than Paine—who was so radical he couldn't get buried in a churchyard—and hence Washington's final home was commemorated by more than just a plaque. I urged her to visit Mount Vernon on her next trip, as I was surprised she'd never been there. It's a pleasant half-hour drive from the capital. I'd have thought that the Tea Partiers, with their oft-expressed reverence for the Founders, would invariably make a pilgrimage to the home and grave of our first president.

We reminisced about Washington, D.C., a bit. I tantalized her with the time in the early 1980s when any citizen could actually wander around the Capitol building, unescorted, just as the White House was open to visitors in Lincoln's day. She oohed and aahed at that, and one doesn't have to be a Tea Partier to feel a primal, drummed-in-at-an-early age thrill when exposed to Washington in its raw grandeur. This was much the same spirit that her followers found embedded in the works of Ayn Rand, a hold on the American imagination that appealed to people like Vicki Towles, Christian faith notwithstanding.

Could the Objectivist faith ever become a big umbrella, encompassing the religiously devout as well as nonbelievers? People like Vicki

* The first article, published in December 1776, begins, "These are the times that try men's souls. The summer soldier and the sunshine patriot will, in this crisis, shrink from the *service of their country;* but he that stands by it now, deserves the love and thanks of man and woman." On a plaque outside the building are these lines from Paine: "The world is my country, all mankind are my brethren, *and to do good is my religion.*" As you can see from what I've italicized. Thomas Paine was a die-hard altruist and believer in service to the state.

Towles, Pamela Geller, and Mark Meckler seemed to be pushing it in that direction.

The purpose of the Beck rally, she said, was to "recognize our Creator"—again defiling the holiest of Randian terminology. "It was about 'Listen, we have to get back to that. We need to remember what's truly important here and have faith.'" Vicki was definitely not—and did not purport to be—in sync with Objectivist precepts on the all-important issue of altruism. She felt, like the good Christian she was, that "people who are down, having bad luck, we should offer a helping hand, pick 'em up, get 'em on their way." Objectivist dogma did not rule out a helping hand, but Rand felt that charity recipients should be worthy of being helped.[8] The Talmudic concept of giving charity without knowing the recipients was alien to Randian thought.

We talked about the Rand idealization of selfishness. Vicki approved of selfishness in the sense that it helps people "be the best that they can be." She said, "A level of selfishness is good in the sense of you're improving—you're taking time for yourself to become better, and when you become better you're going to bring everybody else around you up. The human being, in my opinion, is one who loves to share the good stuff. We like to see people succeed."

I mentioned to her the concerns expressed by the Midtown Restaurant Objectivists about the religious character of the Restoring Honor rally, and asked her about the atheism of *Atlas Shrugged,* and how she reacted to it. "I'm a live-and-let-live" person, she said. "For me, God is the center of my life. Every day I get up and I'm very thankful and grateful. So I'm very fulfilled. That's for me. But anyone who isn't, I'm fine with that. As long as we're respectful and we're working for the same goal, which is, for me, individual liberty." But the emphasis on mutual respect begged the question of how one can reconcile Christian beliefs, especially profoundly religious ones, with the Ayn Rand vision of selfishness and rejection of altruism. Mark Meckler managed that contradiction by pretending it didn't exist. The impression I got from Vicki was that she simply hadn't quite thought through the implications of Rand's ideology.

You don't have to read *Atlas* very thoroughly to realize the extent to which it is a repudiation of Christianity. But its antireligious character is spelled out in obtuse philosophical jargon, so casual readers like Vicki might not be bothered by it. Instead people tend to be drawn to the John Galt character, and how he forthrightly dropped out when his good work was about to be looted by the socialist managers of his factory. "What really gets me is that he found a different approach to deal with the looters. He let them win on their game board, but this board was much larger . . . he just didn't play their game. And he wins in the end. Good wins, it always wins," Vicki said. When I asked her if there were any parts of the book that she didn't agree with, she responded, "Not offhand."

To her, "Who is John Galt?" is an expression of "liberty." Tea Party supporters talk a lot about liberty, but their use of the term is different from the way Thomas Jefferson and John Adams deployed it in their day. The Founding Fathers were talking about liberty in the simple sense of self-governance and freedom from oppression by a foreign power. The new definition—the Tea Party definition—seeks to expropriate the term in a sense that apes Rand, to oppose use of state resources to "promote the general welfare," an objective of government explicitly included in the preamble to the Constitution that directly repudiates Rand's principles.

As a matter of fact, onetime Greenwich Village resident Thomas Paine had ideas for the "general welfare" that would be considered pinko even today. He argued in his pamphlet *Agrarian Justice* for taxation of landowners to pay for a guaranteed income for all through "a national fund, out of which there shall be paid to every person, when arrived at the age of twenty-one years, the sum of fifteen pounds sterling, as a compensation in part, for the loss of his or her natural inheritance, by the introduction of the system of landed property." In *Rights of Man* he set forth in detail a plan for "comfortable provision for one hundred and forty thousand aged persons." He favored the progressive income tax and even cash gifts for weddings and "live births." All to benefit the *general welfare* of the public.

The Tea Partiers weren't pretending to react to the same, honest-to-goodness oppression and deprivation of liberty, actual liberty, that motivated the Founders. To our latter-day patriots, "liberty" was a slogan, to be used as signature lines in e-mails and otherwise thrown around willy-nilly, cheapened in a way that would have made the Founders flinch in their powdered wigs. The Tea Partiers did not appreciate that these quaintly attired gents were radicals—and not radicals for capitalism. They were hypocrites—some were slave owners—but they were off-the-charts far-left agitators for their day.

In Vicki's case, the applicable infringement of liberty seemed to involve not British bayonets but "all of this spending and the stimulus bill and omnibus bill, and it was like nothing we could do, and Rick Santelli came on CNBC and said something about a Tea Party, and boy, all over the Internet it just took off. Next thing I knew I'm looking for one in Memphis, and taking responsibility to head it up, and we started meetings, and it just took off from there." I was struck by the phrase "nothing we could do." Sure there was, and it was done, and effectively, precisely because the totalitarian United States in *Atlas Shrugged* bears no resemblance to the corporate-dominated, weakly regulated, right-leaning America of today.

Vicki was not the only Christian *Atlas* fan at the Restoring Honor rally. She told me that she saw many Ayn Rand and John Galt stickers and placards. To her, the book resonates because "we're spending money we don't have . . . we should leave this country in a better position than we found it, and he [Obama] is not doing that. He's recklessly spending. He's totally ignored the will of the people. He doesn't respect—when hundreds of thousands of people show up in Washington to say, 'We don't want this.' Instead of going, 'You know what? America, I work for you, I'm going to listen to you, we're going to slow this train down,' he rams it through." She called this a "blatant disregard for those of us who stood up" at the rally, which it probably was. But was it really that big a deal that President Obama didn't change his policies because of a Glenn Beck rally? That's as much of a slap in the face, I suppose, as the "fake Air Force One" that riled Mark Herr.

Vicki told me that she wanted to start an organization—an "individual-type mentor kind of thing" aimed at "empowering people who have been oppressed for so long by the state to become their better selves and realize their dreams." Empowering people is fine, I guess, as is people improving and realizing their dreams. But the bit about people "oppressed by the state" sounded like something that might have come from the Black Panther Party in 1969. The inspiration for this group, which would be more philosophical than political in character, was not too hard to figure out. "It might have a little bit of the teachings of *Atlas Shrugged* in it," she said.

Postscript: I stayed in touch with Mark Herr, and the last I heard from him was that he hadn't gotten around to reading Ayn Rand. I'm keeping my fingers crossed.

CHAPTER TWELVE

The Persuaded

Something remarkable happened early in the formation of the Tea Party: an atheistic philosophy achieved a foothold in a right-wing American political movement. If the Tea Party represented a unique and significant coalition of economic and social issue conservatives, as Scott Rasmussen and Douglas Schoen argue in their book *Mad as Hell*,[1] then by 2011 Objectivists were firmly in place as a silent partner in that coalition.

Objectivism was such a quiet undercurrent that Mark Meckler's devotion to Rand was generally ignored in the copious press coverage that he received. Rand's impact on the Tea Party, except for passing references to John Galt banners, did not get much attention in the media, or in the books that appeared on the movement. In *Boiling Mad*, Kate Zernike only briefly mentions Rand. The grand old lady of the radical right makes a cameo appearance early on, when Zernike identifies a pioneering pre-Santelli Tea Partier, Keli Carender, as having *Atlas Shrugged* on her "to read" list.[2]

It was becoming clear to me that the Rand involvement was low-key because of her atheism. The hard core of the religious right, such as born-again Watergate figure Charles Colson—who produced a video in mid-2011 denouncing Rand—would never accept Objectivism.[3] But Rand's atheism was not an insurmountable problem. It could be finessed, or perhaps just ignored. If the Tea Party were ever to wholeheartedly embrace the Ayn Rand philosophy, what it needed was a core of ideological true believers, a cadre of Rand followers who subscribed to all of Objectivism and could relate to the values of the Heartland.

The Tea Party needed atheists.

I set out in pursuit of my godless quarry. I was in search of the ideal combination, the sociological outlier that the times demanded: grassroots Tea Partiers who were also committed Objectivists, atheism included. Did such a person exist in this great land of ours?

My first candidate was one of the most prominent early Tea Partiers. Sally Oljar, a graphic designer from Seattle in her fifties, was getting a lot of press as a national coordinator of the Tea Party Patriots, along with Mark Meckler and a few others, and had the distinction of being one of the very earliest organizers of the Tea Party. *Boiling Mad* describes how she connected Tea Party pioneer Keli Carender to the national movement.[4] Later she was quoted in *The New York Times* expressing concern that Republicans in Congress might be straying from their promises.[5] Yet in none of the coverage was it pointed out how much of an influence Ayn Rand had on her. She was about as much of an Objectivist as one could find in the Tea Party movement.

Sally described herself as being "very much a child of my time," in the sense of being a "Woodstock kind of kid. I just thought that love made the world go round, and that if everybody shared everything, everything would just be great. I had that kind of naive 'all you need is love' kind of attitude." She recalled the time when she was about seventeen, when her stepfather, who was challenging her on "one harebrained idea or another," suggested that she read Ayn Rand. Sally was flirting with Marxism, feeling, "What a swell system this is. Everybody shares with one another, and everybody's equal and there are no better animals. Every animal was the same. He [her stepfather] was saying, 'No no no, you need to learn something.'"

She decided to give Rand a try, so one day at a bookstore she picked up a copy of *The Fountainhead.* "It struck me very deeply," she said. "Her view of human beings and her role in the world, and how reality really works, struck a real chord in me even at that very young age and inspired me to go on." Reading *Fountainhead*, *Atlas,* and "everything of hers I could get my hands on" not only changed entirely her view of Marxism and capitalism, but led her to major in philosophy in college. "It was like a light bulb went off," she said. "I knew immediately what she was trying to say about human beings and their creative capacities, how money is actually made, what the purpose and value of life is, and why morality is important."

To Sally, Objectivism was in lockstep with the radical capitalism that united all Tea Partiers. She pointed out that "the core principles of the Tea Party are certainly in line with Ayn Rand's views on free markets and fiscal responsibility. Many of us felt in 2009 that Atlas really was shrugging, with the bailout and the stimulus and the collapse of the mortgage industry, that we were seeing the principles that we'd read about in this novel actually acting themselves out in the real world." She went on to describe the events of 2008 much as the non-Rander Mark Herr had done, a narrative that also could be seen on Rand Web sites and increasingly articulated by mainstream Republicans—that regulatory policy was to blame for the banks tipping over, not the banks themselves.

The tip-off was her use of the expression "mortgage industry," just as Herr had. It was as if, through semantics, the connection between the banking crisis and actual *banks* could somehow be disconnected. Sally said that the financial crisis was "the logical outcome of many decades of bad policymaking." She tossed some Objectivist rhetoric at me, saying that the crisis was "built along the collectivist, statist, welfare-state vision, which she [Rand] describes in *Atlas Shrugged* so vividly." You could "take those principles and apply them right along the line probably from about 1960 to 2008," at which time "the jig was up."

As I had with Herr, I asked Sally which policies she was referring to. Sally was also a Tea Party leader, and unlike him she had a good, solid grounding in Objectivism. Surely I could get from her a description of the crisis that went beyond polemics, generalities, and sloganeering.

Sally responded: "In regard to the bailouts I would say the banking system and the regulatory—Fannie Mae, Freddie Mac, the housing bubble, how that was manipulated, the crony capitalism that went along with that, the specifics of policies, public policies, particularly housing policy over the years, lent itself to the kind of moral hazard being created, and that, you know, eventually it collapsed." So, just to be clear, I asked if she was saying that the bankers weren't responsible. "The bankers took advantage of it," she said. "It" referring to whatever it was that she was describing. "I often think that big government and big business are in collusion with one another, and it's the taxpayers left holding the bag." That was a sentiment in which, I'm sure, many non-Objectivists and non-Tea Partiers would concur. "They privatized profit and socialized risk," she continued, in another nod-worthy comment. But I couldn't get Sally to expound more, from an Objectivist standpoint, on the financial crisis.

Sally was a Tea Party leader as well as a devoted follower of Ayn Rand for more than three decades, one who pursued college studies in philosophy because of Rand. Yet she couldn't go beyond superficialities and platitudes in explaining what happened to the banking system, utilizing rhetoric similar to what I had heard from my non-Objectivist Tea Party control group, Mark Herr. There was certainly plenty of free-market spin on the financial crisis, some from Yaron Brook, but she didn't seem familiar with any of it.

Sally reminisced about her origins in the Tea Party movement, describing the protest that Keli Carender organized—the "anti-Porkilus" protest against the stimulus bill on February 16, 2009, three days before the Rick Santelli rant. She attended the protest and met Keli. Sally said that she introduced Keli, a true pioneer of the Tea Party movement, to Rand. "She was aware of her, she knew her work," Sally said. "You couldn't go to those early Tea Party rallies and not know. The signs and quotes from Rand were everywhere, because everyone who's familiar with her work recognized what was happening here." Sally felt that way even before Obama was elected. "He really does want to fundamentally transform the United States." The combination of Obama's election and the bailouts indicated to her that "for the first time in my life, my liberty and my freedom are seriously endangered and I need to stand up now and put a stop to it."

Here we had another victim of liberty infringement. I asked her what precisely was endangering her liberty and freedom. She responded that she's "turning into a debt slave. We're being asked to pay for bad public policy." She and her husband "had lost a tremendous amount in the mortgage meltdown." They lost substantial equity in their home. They built another house on speculation that they no longer could sell and they couldn't pay off the loan. They were fortunate to have renters, "but it never crossed our minds to ask the government, ask my next door neighbor to bail me out of my financial mess."

So by "debt slave" and "endangered liberty and freedom" she was referring to her personal indebtedness. It was straight out of 1960s/1970s "blame the system" consciousness. I remember flunking a math class in high school and the hippie kid in front of me commiserating, "It's the system." The idea was to not accept personal responsibility, but to shift blame to unseen forces, in this case—as in the old days—the government, "the system." Ayn Rand provides a workable ideology for such rationalizing because to her all government is inherently the use of the "gun," a coercive force that is *evil.*

Sally described to me how she, Keli, and their friends called like-minded people after the Santelli rant to organize a Tea Party on February 27, 2009, "and the Tea Party movement was born." Ayn Rand was thus, through Sally Oljar, very much present at the creation of the movement.

The Randian concept of free markets was accepted as a core value by the early organizers. Sally defined the markets pillar of the Tea Party platform as "the primacy and the importance of the free markets, in understanding that economic freedom and property rights are two of the things that have made the United States the greatest nation that it is today—that without that we cannot survive." The other two main pillars, fiscal responsibility and "constitutionally limited government," meshed precisely with the Objectivist worldview.

Another decision that was made early in the movement was to not get involved in the social issues that are important to many on the right. Social issues, she said, are not discussed in weekly conference calls which are held with local Tea Party coordinators from across the country. Abortion, gay marriage, and the like are "best left to the states," she said. Rand, with her atheism and her support of abortion rights, had a dim view of social issue agendas, and this is reflected in the Tea Party. "Our financial life is so much more acute and affects every American," Sally pointed out. Thanks to Rand, the radical capitalist line of thinking, so beneficial to the St. Regis attendees and other wealthy folks but of questionable relevancy to anyone else, now resided in an entire philosophy that could be studied and promoted by millions of Tea Partiers.

Thus the state of affairs spelled out in *What's the Matter with Kansas?* had come full circle. In his book, Thomas Frank describes how a Heartland population energized by social issues voted in politicians dedicated to advancing corporate interests. Thanks to the Tea Party and its Objectivist-leaning organizers and congressional supporters, corporate agendas were now out of the closet. Randian politicians like Paul Ryan cheerfully advocated slashing government spending and advanced a soak-the-poor agenda. Thanks to Rand, radical capitalist doctrine was adopted by the right's new populists. It was just as Mark Meckler had told me: "In their hearts and minds, Ayn Rand's philosophy lives as a part of who they are." And as for the public interest: What of it? Rand did not recognize the concept of "the public," only individuals, and that included corporations, big ones especially. If there is no "public," there can be no "public interest" but only selfish private interests, which means that the strongest—the wealthiest, that is—will always prevail.

The Tea Partiers may have been less articulate and focused than the Ayn Rand Institute, Competitive Enterprise Institute, or U.S. Chamber of Commerce, but these grassroots Randians and their fellow travelers had at least as much political clout. Sally might not have been able to spell out for me the reasons for the 2008 crash with any precision, but she didn't have to. The Tea Party dealt with generalities, with feelings and emotions, very much as the left did when Sally and I were in high school. The slogans were different, but the mindset was the same. Instead of "Hell no, we won't go" it was "Rand was right," and instead of "Ho Ho Ho Chi Minh, the NLF is gonna win" it was "Who is John Galt?" Nobody paid much attention to the real Ho Chi Minh back in those days, or pondered the morality of refusing to submit to the draft, thus shifting the manpower burden to the poor and black. There was a similar mindlessness to the Tea Party in its flirtation with the godless, radical views of Ayn Rand, divorced as they were from conventional concepts of right, wrong, faith, and charity.

This was a movement in which, as in the 1970s, radicals called the shots. The Tea Party was a coalition of people of various political persuasions—from conservatives to libertarians to people tilting in the Randian direction—coalescing over laissez-faire capitalism and limited government, with Rand providing the underlying moral rationale. "We are not allowing other issues to divide us," Sally pointed out.

"The Tea Party is helping her work," Sally said. "It's helping to spread her ideas. Whether or not you end up calling yourself an Objectivist, I think her ideas have a lot of influence." Rand's views on economics, she said, "have absolutely influenced the Tea Party movement," as have "her views on entrepreneurship in general" and "her emphasis on the individual as the prime mover of all that is good in society."

The Tea Party was not as erratic and informal as it was sometimes portrayed. At the weekly Tea Party Patriot conference calls, the number of participants was as high as eight hundred or nine hundred. "We discuss pending legislation and what our response to it should be, how we should express that response—should we do a rally, should we do a letter-writing campaign," Sally said. It was certainly serendipitous, to put it mildly, that two of the national coordinators of the Tea Party Patriots, perhaps the largest of the Tea Party groups, happened to be steeped in the ideology of Ayn Rand. Not ARI plants, not some kind of external force, but intrinsic to the movement.

The Tea Party–Rand synergy was here to stay. It certainly wasn't going to evaporate after the 2012 elections. The Tea Party was taking a long view. "We have what we think of as our forty-year plan," Sally said. "It's taken forty years for the modern left to make its long march through the institutions. It started in the 1960s with the baby boom generation of which I fall smack dab in the middle of, took about forty years for them to reach their apotheosis in Barack Obama. He to me is just a figurehead. It's his ideas that frighten me."

In every respect so far, Sally Oljar met my ideal—the 100 percent Objectivist Tea Partier. But my hope for that faded when we discussed the all-important "a-word." She explained that while she was "solidly on board" with Rand's views on capitalism, reason, individuality, and such, she parted company with her on religion. Sally "used to share her very strong atheism, but as I get older I'm backing off from that a little bit." She said that she was "exploring that own part of my personal journey. I haven't signed on with a formal religion; I'm not a born-again anything and I don't go to church. That's been an interesting journey for me, and part of it is because of the way I got involved in the Tea Party."

There was, she said, "something that seemed very Providential about it for me, that at this time in my life this specific set of events would happen. I guess what I'm talking about is synchronicity than anything else." When it comes to atheism, "I'm just not sure. I'm not as sure as she was, let's put it that way."

Sally was an agnostic. I filed that under "close but no cigar."

I was getting desperate by the time I spoke with Peter Calandruccio. I'd been lucking out with every prominent Tea Partier who crossed my path. I was a latter-day Diogenes, searching for an honest-to-gosh atheistic, Objectivist Tea Partier, so far without success.

Peter was kind enough to invite me to join Vicki Towles in one of the periodic meetings of Objectivists that convene in Memphis. I was unable to attend so we talked by phone. I knew that this was going to be a difficult conversation when I saw the signature at the bottom of his e-mail. Peter was editor and publisher of *Memphis Q—THE Bar-B-Q Directory*. He also had a Web site devoted to the "smoke, sauce, and the love of BBQ." I adore barbecue but was on a strict diet. I gritted my teeth and tried to ignore the delectable smell of barbecue wafting over the phone lines.

Like the other prominent Tea Partiers I'd encountered, Peter had gotten his share of local publicity. In his case, he appeared with Vicki in *The Commercial Appeal* in April 2010, when the two were among a group of Tea Party protesters who confronted Congressman Steve Cohen, a Democrat, at a Memphis coffee shop.[6] Cohen, who was being challenged in the Democratic primary, had bashed the Tea Party a few days earlier. He said that the Tea Party people "are kind of—without robes and hoods—they have really shown a very hard-core angry side of America that is against any type of diversity. And we saw opposition to African Americans, hostility toward gays, hostility to anybody who wasn't just, you know, a clone of George Wallace's fan club. And I'm afraid they've taken over the Republican Party."[7]

Vicki Towles confronted him on his comments as he addressed a small group of people at the coffee shop, and succeeded in putting Cohen on the defensive. "I know that you're not a racist. I suspect that you're not a racist," Cohen was quoted as saying. Peter asked for an apology, which Cohen didn't give, though he did say that he could have handled himself better (which is questionable, since he defeated his primary opponent in a landslide, and went on to win reelection). Cohen received an e-mail threat after his "robes and hoods" remark, but the set-to at the coffee shop seemed civil enough. Peter made a mild and reasonable comment to the local paper that "to characterize a whole group with those terms doesn't speak well of the office." In the future, he said, "it'd be best to refrain from such inflammatory comments."

Peter hadn't forgotten the incident when we talked, though he might have forgotten his "inflammatory comments" plea for civility. "He's pretty vocal, and I consider him the personification of evil," he said of his representative in Congress.

Why is that? "First of all," Peter replied, "I would assume that any educated person has at least a cursory understanding of history, and in that historical understanding you would see that regimes that tend to siphon off the assets, the capital of the people that they serve as governments end up causing great harm and despair and destruction and ultimately death. That seems to be what the history of mankind has been, whether it's been under an imperial situation, a totalitarian situation, a monarchy, a socialist, a Communist. That's the great contrast with the American system of law by which government's authority, power has been limited. . . ."

And on he went in that vein for a little while. He gave me a good, Objectivist analysis of the role of government, all in answer to a question as to why he considered his congressman to be evil. He didn't quite address that specific point, except to the extent that he considered Cohen to be representative of an evil system—evil for exceeding the inherent power of government, which he believed should be limited to "protecting and defending the rights of the individual to care for him or herself."

I brought up the subject of atheism, despair welling up within me. Peter put my mind to rest, bless his heart. He didn't put the creamer of religion or altruism in his Objectivist coffee. He took it black. He was a committed atheist. He tossed off the term casually. It was not a big deal with him, as it wouldn't be to a true-believer Objectivist.

All of the concepts and phraseology he enunciated, and especially the liberal use of "evil," could have come straight from the lips of Rand herself. At the time, upheaval was spreading across the Middle East, for which he gave me an Objectivist analysis. "The global sentiment," he said, "is that people want more for themselves. There's the ignorance of assuming that there's some candy box to go get it out of, and I think that's where Ayn Rand's philosophy and a deeper understanding of the nature of man, the condition of existence as it is, is beneficial." I could well have been among my Midtown Restaurant Objectivists. This fellow knew his Rand. No fumbling around for words by this guy.

Peter, who was in his late fifties, came upon Rand in the usual way—almost. "*Atlas Shrugged* sat on my mother's bookshelf in her sewing room when I was a kid doing homework," he said. "I never pulled it off the shelf, didn't know what the title meant, and I didn't know if Atlas was the object of somebody shrugging him or Atlas was the subject shrugging something else. It always perplexed me." But not enough, because he didn't read it until 2004, when he found a copy at a used bookstore in a dingy strip mall in Phoenix. He and his wife were on a year-and-a-half-long camper trip, during which they traveled for thousands of miles in the western United States, Canada, and Mexico. He previously held a teaching job in Savannah, Georgia, and they "decided to take a proactive stance in our lives, which is Randian though I hadn't read Rand yet."

He picked up the book to pass the time while he was doing the laundry and, well, needless to say, it changed his life. The "thread of her philosophy," he said, "was one I was already starting to formulate in my own assessment of life." There it was again, Randian concepts floating in the ether, so that readers were pre-sold before they ever picked up her books and followed the exciting adventures of Dagny, John, Hank, and the rest of the gang. This was a man who didn't like to get pinned down, having held a variety of occupations over the past decades—college teacher, architect, and developer as well as BBQ connoisseur and entrepreneur. So there he was, now middle aged, and he thought, "God, this is the same kind of stuff I've been concluding," same understanding of the "primacy of the individual." *The Fountainhead* held a great deal of appeal for him, as it does for all architects. "Everybody wants to be a Howard Roark; nobody wants to be a Peter Keating," he said.

He had found his philosophical calling greatly appealing, as do all architects. From there he plunged into Rand, digesting the "metaphysical stuff" like a moist and tender baby back rib. "Existing preceding consciousness. Are you aware of that?" he asked me. This whole existing-before-consciousness stuff was crucial to his accepting the validity of Rand's beliefs. This man had studied philosophy, so he was familiar with that issue in classical philosophy. Rand, he said, "stripped things to their essentials: What do we know and how do we know it." And she concluded, Peter said, quoting Rand, that "existence is—existence exists." She indeed had said that many times. It may sound tautological to an outsider, and it was ridiculed by Albert Ellis, but for some reason this catchphrase really stuck to the ribs of die-hard Objectivists.

"Not subject to the individual's mind," Peter pointed out. Beginning with that as the essential building block came a "philosophy that says you can't have your cake and eat it, too," which is how he characterized the philosophy of those who "believe you can feed at the public trough."

We chatted about the protests in Egypt, which had managed to oust Hosni Mubarak. Some of the protesters were fed up with the wide income disparities in Egypt, and I asked him how he felt Rand would have reacted to that. "It would be ironic to say that she would say what Jesus Christ said, which was 'The poor are always amongst you.' Remember that popular Christian quote?" he asked. "And I'm not a Christian."

"I think there's a popularized notion that there's a pie to be divided up," he said, "so when people talk about income disparity, it's like, I would say to them 'What the hell do you expect? Do you expect everybody to be wealthy?' [Rand] put the microscope on what is, existence as it is. And the fact of the matter is, some people will be poor." I had heard that expression quite a lot in India, where grinding poverty breeds a kind of routine callousness among the citizenry—to such an extent that female beggars in rags holding up their starving babies are ignored at traffic lights.

Peter pointed out to me that in a relatively free-market economy like Hong Kong, hardworking youngsters have been known to advance from waiters to clerks to "maybe owning a hotel." It's all about opportunity and individual initiative. On the opposing side of the argument, as he framed it, is the view that "your highest good is to give your life up for another person, regardless of how much they are or are not doing for themselves." That, he said, "is the evil which I referenced Steve Cohen, for example."

The conversation had abruptly circled back to that bad man, who really stuck in Peter's craw. Cohen "knows the history of mankind, and to my mind, I don't see how anybody with enough intelligence can come away with believing that to sell the populace on the notion that they can get something for free, by being black or female or gay or heterosexual or whatever. That person is doing an injustice to fundamental logic, to history, and they're certainly doing an injustice to their constituents by promoting that political ideology."

Later I searched high and low for statements by Cohen that could be interpreted as endorsing extreme self-sacrifice and racial preferences, and couldn't find any. But it didn't really matter, because anti-empiricism was essential to the Rand mind-set, without which Objectivism could not possibly survive.

Peter found that Rand's writings broadened his understanding of conditions he experienced when he lived for a while in a rundown, largely black neighborhood of Savannah, Georgia. At the time, he was buying properties to renovate and develop. "I didn't have a problem with it," he said of living among racial minorities. "Didn't mind that, but frankly what I found, unfortunately, and you have to analyze this, is that most of the black people had this attitude of victimization. There was very little male presence in the home if any. There was neglect of children, there were abused women, a lot of alcoholism, drug use"—but "plenty of money through the welfare system for cigarettes, alcohol, lottery tickets, and criminality." He pondered how this came to be. He concluded that "they have been victimized by people like Steve Cohen, who say, 'Oh, you've been done a great wrong, and you're too stupid to wipe your ass. Therefore, we'll take care of you.'"

When the Tea Party came along, he felt right at home. "As the Tea Party began to foment, become this *thing*, I saw not only an expression of my frustrations with pop, sixties-era stuff ruling politics," but also "something to latch on to as a vehicle for expression." He had just moved back home to Memphis and was looking around for something that might interest him—Ayn Rand groups, atheist groups, and there it was, the Tea Party. He saw creativity within the movement, which surprised him. "Conservative people are creative also? That invigorated me," he said.

It was February 2009, and the Tea Party was the hottest thing on the right since Ronald Reagan and his jelly beans. Peter started going to Tea Party meetings, and "contrary to the propaganda, it's not a bunch of homophobic, racist people; it's just a bunch of people who are saying, 'I'm tired of trying to be politically correct, and appeasing everybody and giving everybody the benefit of the doubt, and being so altruistically self-flagellating. Enough is enough.'" He was an atheist in an organization that has a "Christian right aspect to it," but he stood his ground. When he talked with people on religion, "I say, 'You know, the purpose of the Tea

Party is to return us to the Constitutionality in which we can all decide our own religion, our own preferences sexually, all those social issues. We don't need a theocratic government to take over what the social left has tried to present us.'"

Most religious people are so theocratic, he said, that it's "hard for people who have grown up with a God belief to give that up. The guilt and all that overburdening makes them go into a defense position." So that if you're an atheist, "everything you have to say must be wrong." Peter agreed with Rand that "logic and reason supersede superstition and mysticism." The latter, he said, continues "a legacy of killing and maiming each other, wherein our God is better than your God. She is so, excuse the expression, so fucking right-on I can't help but just go, 'Hey, I have to speak the truth.' I cannot compromise and say, 'Yes, I'm a Christian' in order to win somebody over to her way of thinking, because they are mutually exclusive."

While Peter didn't meet many other atheists at the Tea Party, at least he was able to get to know fellow Rand admirers like Vicki Towles. At the first rally that he attended, back in February 2009, the Rand influence was already strongly in evidence. "Pretty early on," he said, "there were enough people where a percentage of them held signs like 'Who is John Galt?' and 'Atlas Shrugs.' I remember the first time I saw Vicki she had a T-shirt on that said 'I (Heart) John Galt.'" Peter himself wasn't wearing any Galt or Rand accoutrements. Instead, being a "shameless capitalist," he was selling T-shirts that said, "Welcome to the USSR, a Socialized Obama Nation." At one point he was confronted by "an altruistic Tea Partier who said, 'You're selling those here? Get out of my face.' As if I'm supposed to give them away. I said, 'Dude, I'm a capitalist.'"

Despite that experience, Peter believed that Tea Partiers understood free enterprise. Across the board, he said, "It may not get down into Austrian economics or anything like that with them, but I think they have the fundamental understanding that capitalism is the source of all assets." I mentioned to him the views of Objectivists that the Tea Partiers were lacking in gravitas and a proper philosophical grounding. He viewed that as elitist, and also disheartening.

I sensed a bit of a culture clash at work here. "That's something that all of us have who feel we are right," he said. "If your objective is, as with some of these people, to be right, and smarmy, in and of yourself, and if your individualism is satisfied in that, have at it." But to him, he said, carefully choosing his words, "it is important if there is new information to add to, not the collective, but the cumulative knowledge of man. That I ought to do that with finesse and some understanding, as opposed to just be—a jerk." He told me that he liked the Ayn Rand Institute, and attended an ARI seminar one summer in Telluride, "but I do find some of the personalities to be elitist." This seemed to rub a raw nerve for Peter. Sometimes, he said, it would be best if such people simply don't attend Tea Party conferences. But "if you want to talk with people, part of existence as it is, is an understanding that the cumulative knowledge of man has not come about by just declaring something and ruling everybody else a fool."

Peter's disdain didn't extend to the most visible Objectivist personality, the stubbornly unavailable (to me) Yaron Brook. "I like him a lot," he said. "He does a good job of unabashedly expressing, for want of a better word, the extreme aspects of Objectivism to people," and without being snooty or condescending. He had a less glorious view of another Objectivist spokesman, whom he suggested would be well advised to "go home and read *Atlas Shrugged* over and over," but mercifully forgot his name.

Listening to Peter's iconoclastic view of the Tea Party and his sophisticated take on Objectivism, I felt more than ever that the left was foolish to dismiss this groundswell of right-wing populism as a group of simple-minded, corporate-funded rednecks. Peter was no simpleton by any means, no redneck, no knee-jerk Republican operative or knee-jerk anything. I could see why Randers like Mark Meckler were moving into leadership positions at the Tea Party. Sure they had their differences, especially over religion, but I didn't think that was quite the obstacle it seemed to be at first blush.

The overarching factor, the reason Objectivists were so prominent in the Tea Party, was that the Randers had been exposed to some degree of ideological preparation—not necessarily very much, but enough—and had a sense of direction that non-Randers in the movement didn't have. Non-Randers are unlikely to have an entire philosophy to buttress their views, and to disseminate to their comrades.

Rand distilled vague anger and unhappiness into a sense of purpose. Yes, it was extremist and drew inspiration from her early days in Russia, but it reflected values of individualism and free enterprise that were native to the Heartland. I couldn't help but think about the appeal to the German people of Nazism—another radical ideology whose roots could be found in the soul of a people. The Nazis had corporate sponsors, too, but they are just footnotes to history. Today, nobody but a die-hard Marxist would say that the Nazi Party was a tool of Thyssen and Krupp.

I had yet to see much evidence that opponents of Rand—either conservatives or liberals—were willing to take Objectivism seriously, much less engage in the hard work required to effectively counter its teachings. There had been no true ideological confrontation, no head-to-head clash of ideas. The White House was seeking compromise, sacrificing principle. Democrats and progressives were not arguing convincingly (or arguing at all, in most cases) that their concept of government was *morally* right. Going into the 2012 elections, Rand was winning the moral argument by default. Yet it was becoming apparent that Americans weren't happy with the right's agenda when it affected their personal interests. The May 2011 special election in New York's Twenty-sixth Congressional District, which saw a Democrat win by exploiting unease over Ryan's Medicare plan, was evidence of that.[8]

I wasn't sure that fear was enough to prevail in the war of ideas. As Thomas Frank pointed out in 2004, voters had a way of ignoring their self-interests when suitably manipulated. Obama would have to make it an ideological contest if he was to win against radical capitalism, because the founding principles of the Republic—as enunciated by every prominent American from Thomas Paine through Franklin D. Roosevelt—were on his side. But there was no sign that he was prepared to do that.

Thankfully, one of the rare confrontations between Objectivists and progressives was about to take place. The first of three debates between Ayn Rand followers and members of Demos, a progressive think tank, was fast approaching. Perhaps this peanut-scale skirmish would be a harbinger of things to come.

CHAPTER THIRTEEN

The Great Debate

As was demonstrated by the St. Regis fund-raiser, which was held in a room named for a monarch Rand despised, Objectivists weren't sensitive to unintentional irony. That pattern continued at the first Objectivist–Demos debate, which was delayed a few weeks from mid-February to March 10, 2011.

It was hard to imagine a less hospitable venue for Objectivists on the North American continent. The debate was cosponsored by a festering monster of leftism, the National Public Radio-affiliated radio station WNYC. It was held at the liberal-infested New York University. NYU is adjacent to Washington Square Park, a longtime hangout for left-wing radicals and guitar-strumming beatniks harboring noxious altruistic notions, singing songs glorifying parasites. Overlooking the park is One Fifth Avenue, home of the famous lefty playwright Clifford Odets during his most Commie-leaning years. And then we have the venue, NYU's Skirball Center, named for *Rabbi* Jack H. Skirball, founder of the Los Angeles School of Hebrew Union College, noted philanthropist and producer of 1940s films.[1] There, in one location, was mysticism, collectivism, statism, altruism, Communism, Hollywoodism, Judaism, and every other ism hostile to Objectivism and vice versa.

There had been some subtle changes in the debate topics that Barry Colvin outlined for me at the Yale Club. The first debate, originally conceived as "Government: How much do we need?" was now fine-tuned to "Government: What is its proper role?" A more drastic change was made in the second debate, which originally was to be "The social safety net: Are we our brother's keeper?" Now it was "Freedom: For Whom and From What?" Demos, it seemed, had taken a stronger role in the formulation of the debates, because now the issues were framed in a manner that liberals would find easier to grapple with. The third debate, originally "Capitalism: Virtue or Vice?" was now "Capitalism: Is It Moral?" The title of the third debate was a semantic change but, I thought, one that was skewed toward the traditional liberal view of capitalism as a caged animal, necessary but requiring control, lest it jeopardize the rights of the general public. "Virtue or Vice" was a more black-and-white, either-or question. The way the issue was presented now, a solid "maybe" or "it depends" could be offered as the answer.

While Demos may have had the home-arena advantage, that didn't do Joe Louis much good in his first bout with Max Schmeling. And it was plain that the Objectivists had the edge at the weigh-in. Literature tables were set up for the Ayn Rand Institute and Demos, and a far greater number of people gathered around the ARI table, which featured free pamphlets expounding upon Rand's views. Hardly anyone stopped by the Demos table, which featured a dense pamphlet with the sexy title *Good Rules: 10 Stories of Successful Regulation*. The ARI offerings, such as Peikoff's *Religion vs. America* and Rand's *Man's Rights* and *The Nature of Government*, seemed more abstract, less grounded in reality, but more likely to appeal to an ivory tower audience. The Rand pamphlets were more slickly produced, bound and printed on expensive glossy paper, while the Demos pamphlet was on standard eight-and-a-half-by-eleven plain paper, with a red border and stapled. Were I a young stripling, anxious to find navigable ideas as I gazed across the shattered landscape of a recession-weary postgraduate America, I might have leaned in the Rand direction rather than following the conventional-sounding nostrums advanced by Demos.

One member of the audience was a young filmmaker named Jimi Patterson, who was waiting patiently outside the building in the chilly air before the doors opened. He had already graduated and was there with his girlfriend, who attended Yale and seemed a bit less dedicated to the ultimate victory of Objectivism than Jimi. He had just met Yaron Brook a few minutes before, an experience he likened to meeting John Lennon. "No, Mick Jagger," he corrected himself. Jimi expected the upcoming debate to be a hands-down victory for Brook, who was scheduled to face off in the first debate against Miles Rapoport, president of Demos.

Having seen Brook in action at the St. Regis fund-raiser, I had no reason to doubt that he was the Muhammad Ali of this contest, while Rapoport was the solid, serious Joe Frazier. Inhospitable as the arena may have been from an Objectivist standpoint, Brook was a cool customer used to the visitors' dugout, a riveting speaker and experienced debater. Rapoport was a lesser-known quantity. He was not the same TV presence as Brook, who appeared constantly on Fox News, and he declined an opportunity to allow me to handicap the fight by granting an interview prior to the debate. Instead he handed me off to David Callahan, who was a cofounder of Demos and head of its international division. Callahan was also the author of a well-received book on society's ethical shortcomings, *The Cheating Culture*, which by no means counts "failure to worship capitalism" as among said shortcomings.

When I talked with Callahan a few weeks before the debate, he told me that there was "hesitancy in the organization as to whether we should be debating them, versus, say, the Cato Institute or Heritage Foundation or somebody more mainstream." But ultimately it was decided to go with debating Objectivists, whom he described as "taking libertarianism to its logical extreme." The reason, he said, was that "it's useful to show where this logic goes." For the ARI, there would be the advantage of reaching a new audience, "preaching to the unconverted, and having a respectable platform for their extreme ideas."

That was the chief downside of the debate from the Demos perspective. Another potential danger for the Demosians was that a flaccid liberal debater would get blown away by the sharp and pungent radical arguments of Objectivists.

The passions of the 1967 Branden–Ellis slugfest were not evident at Skirball Center. Perhaps the spirit of the good rabbi kept the audience from getting too rowdy. A show of hands before the debate indicated that, by my reckoning, about six-tenths of the people in the audience identified themselves as Objectivists.

Rapoport was the first out of the corner. He didn't come out swinging. He was a solid-looking man in his fifties, a bit plodding, taking his time, trying to land light jabs rather than knockout punches. He seemed to be reading from his notes during his opening statement, for which, were I the scorekeeper, I would have deducted points. He kept it clean. No hitting below the belt. In contrast to the Branden–Ellis bout, there was no criticism of Rand or her books or the characters thereof. In fact, it wasn't clear to me at first if he had ever read Rand, not that the debate required such knowledge. "Let's keep this at a really high level," moderator Brian Lehrer urged at the outset, and to a high level it was kept.

Rapoport began by observing that the old liberal consensus no longer held. The ideas of Ronald Reagan had been dominant since 1980. "From my point of view, those ideas, applied in serious governance, have driven the country into a ditch, and almost off a cliff," he said, doubling up on his metaphors. Now, he said, we're entering a new period whose character had not yet been defined. Brook, perhaps unnecessarily, was taking notes while Rapoport landed feeble blows ("strong public sector," "fair rules of the road") against his solar plexus. But then Rapoport slipped in a rabbit punch, showing that perhaps he might have a solid working knowledge of the Objectivist weak spot: "It is possible, by the way, to have this debate at too high of a philosophical level, divorced from the real decisions and the real public debates." That was a thumb in the eye of the Objectivists' tendency toward anti-empiricism. It's necessary, he said, to be "relevant to the public debates that we're having." One's principles had to be grounded, he said, "in the reality of how they're applied."

Reality—the untied shoelace that always seemed to trip up Objectivists—would be a potent weapon, if Rapoport knew how to use it.

He quoted Jean Jacques Rousseau: "Finally, each man, in giving himself to all, gives himself to nobody; and as there is no associate over whom he does not acquire the same right as he yields others over himself, he gains an equivalent for everything he loses, and an increase in force for the preservation of what he has." From that stirring defense of altruism/collectivism/public spiritedness Rapoport went straight to brass tacks: "When a mortgage broker persuades an unsuspecting home buyer to take a mortgage he knows will fail, and is paid on the basis of the spread between what that mortgage holder could get in a mortgage and what he was able to persuade them to buy, we need a government agency that's prepared to stop that."

A blow to the jaw had landed. Brook looked uncomfortable and plainly peeved, as Rapoport talked of for the need for government to intervene against polluters, operators of unsafe mines, and other corporate villains. Then he went on to list the positive impact government can have—in fostering the growth of public universities (like the University of Texas, he might have added, where Objectivism is on the curriculum). He went on like that, listing programs that had once been taken for granted, but which were now lying prone before the bulldozer of small-government fanatics.

These were visceral arguments. Objectivists and many conservatives would have gagged as Rapoport went on to say that the backward trend of the last thirty years had threatened the middle class, turning it into an endangered species. "We risk becoming a country with a small sliver of highly successful people," he said, "the 'plutonomy,' as Goldman Sachs [sic] describes it, and a substantial majority of people with low education, inadequate health care, insecure incomes," and so on. The shift of income to a tiny number of superwealthy, the "plutonomy," was first described by an analyst at Citigroup, not Goldman, but Rapoport could be forgiven for this minor error.

Brook, like the old club fighter that he was, showed from round one that he was the better orator. He spoke without notes, using expansive gestures. It sometimes seemed as if he wanted to step away from the podium in a frenzy of expressiveness, like a TV evangelist. He argued his case on personal terms, making judicious use of rhetorical questions. He was an immigrant from Israel. He came to the United States. Why? "What is it that makes this country special? What is it that makes this country *different*?" he asked in college-lecturer fashion, giving emphasis to the last word, already differentiating himself from the steady but colorless, sometimes stumbling Rapoport. His opponent rarely used the word "I," instead taking an institutional, communal approach, saying several times "we at Demos." Brook was making this a personal appeal, never saying "we at the Ayn Rand Institute."

You have to go back to the founding of this country, Brook said. Actually, Rapoport had done just that. Rousseau, whom he could have identified a bit more clearly, was one of the philosophers who influenced the American Revolution. My mental scorekeeper docked Rapoport a point for failing to make that clear. Brook went on, in his Boston-ish accent, to wrap Rand in the flag and call the American Revolution "a fundamental, historical, moral-political revolution. An ideological revolution." Which it was; just read Rousseau's "Social Contract," which Rapoport had quoted. But Brook didn't bring that up. Instead he pointed out that "the Founding Fathers identified a principle" which answered the question: "Who does your life belong to?" The "answer, historically, forever, had always been 'Your life belongs to the tribe, it belongs to the king, it belongs to the state, it belongs to the pope, it belongs to some group outside of the individual,' " using repetition, once again, to drive home his point. But, he said, enlightenment figures, including the Founding Fathers, concluded that "that's not true. Your life belongs to you." Which even rhymes. The audience was rapt, as well it should have been.

Brook then took an immense leap—over Rousseau, that is—saying that the Founders of this nation "rejected the notion of collectivism. They rejected the notion that you as an individual owe your primary duty to some entity external of you."

Actually one might argue that Rand was out of step with the Founders, and that they embraced collectivism in a number of ways, not just in Paine's "Crisis" essays but in their own lives and in the Declaration of Independence and the Constitution, beginning with "We the people." Rand explicitly rejected such collectivist nomenclature, saying that the public "is merely a number of individuals."[2] Brook's argument seemed to be with James Madison, not Rapoport.

Brook went on blithely like that, saying that the purpose of the Founders was "not merely to maximize social utility—that's not in the Declaration." Yet the Declaration of Independence is the quintessential collectivist document. It is a "we" document recounting the *collective* grievances of the general public of the colonies, contending, for instance, that the king of England had "refused his Assent to Laws, the most wholesome and necessary for the public good" (a concept whose existence was denied by the public-phobic Rand). Prominent reference to the capital-c Creator makes the Declaration of Independence an unlikely object of atheistic Objectivist praise. Washington himself was anything but a selfish, Randian figure; he was renowned for the selflessness of his character. And then we have the radical lefty Thomas Paine, who would have turned Brook into a bloody mess had Rapoport stuck that razor in his boxing glove.

Brook flailed away at the silent, prone figure of Rapoport, landing rights and lefts as he rewrote the early history of the Republic. The founding principle of this country is "not to sacrifice for your neighbor, but to live your life. And that is the revolution," Brook told the hushed and impressed Skirball audience. But was it? The signers of the Declaration of Independence were privileged men; they weren't living off their salaries from the Continental Congress. They acted out of great personal risk, which could have been avoided by the simple act of staying home and "living their lives." They risked their lives for their neighbors. They *sacrificed*. All one has to do is to visit Mount Vernon, as I had urged Vicki Towles, and see how Washington's self-sacrifice by not retiring, his failure to selfishly exploit his fame and office, resulted in the need to sell off most of his family's holdings in that part of Virginia. That's why the home of our first president is in the hands of a nonprofit association, not Washington's descendants, and has been for over 150 years.

Brook continued to hammer away, superimposing Objectivism retroactively on those old parchment documents at the National Archives, pressing the thorned crown of Rand notions on long-decomposed Founders, and repeating the old Randian maxim that "government is force." Then he moved on to the list of government functions—"goodies," he called them—that Rapoport suggested were worthy of this naked use of force, including government dictating "what kind of mortgage contract to okay for us to engage in."

What followed was a Randian view of consumer protection, which Brook defined as a choice between freedom (no protection for consumers except the benevolence of business) and the ogre-like forces of government (malevolently interfering with the wholly satisfactory consumer-business relationship). Protecting mortgage customers from rapacious lenders would mean that "we're not free to go in and negotiate for whatever we think."

"We might be mistaken," said Brook, "we might be right, we might be wrong, but assuming fraud is out of this, because I assume we both agree that fraud is a violation of rights, fraud is a form of force. We are not, according to the argument made, we are not free to negotiate whatever makes sense in terms of a mortgage contract. Government is going to tell us what mortgage to have."

Brook went on to explain the consequences of the loss of this cherished freedom to negotiate with banks:

"And what does it mean when government is going to tell us what mortgage to have? It means government is going to *force* us, and it means if we don't do exactly what government's going to say, you know, we're going to be dragged off to somewhere. The gun comes out. Government is force." To the Objectivists in the audience, it was plain what was going on here. Rapoport wasn't suggesting that these were unequal power relationships, and that history has taught us that the government needs to intervene to prohibit grossly unfair terms in consumer contracts. He wasn't saying any of that. He was depriving people of their freedom to sit down and negotiate terrific terms with banks.

I pondered several ways I could exercise my "freedom" to "negotiate" with my bank. I could do a bit of horse-trading on credit card terms, for instance. Instead of signing a card application with unsatisfactory terms, I could dash off a note saying, "I want that interest rate to be 14 percent, not 40. Please come back to me with your best offer. Yours, etc." Just behaving like a trader, with a possible win-win situation here. If 40 million consumers did that, it might work. But in a one-on-one "bargaining" situation, the consumer had as much bargaining power as an ant trying to negotiate with my shoe. Forty million ants would make the difference in that situation, too.

The debate on consumer protection continued along those general lines, with Rapoport and Brook talking past each other. But with so little common ground, how else could it have gone? The only way Brook could possibly "win" was by convincingly portraying government as an all-purpose ogre, turning consumer protection into a use of government force. However, the debate did serve the Demos purpose, which was to bring out the disconnection to reality that characterizes much Objectivist rhetoric. Rapoport, replying later, did not exercise much in the way of oratorical skills, but was simple and unaffected, as if he were addressing the Kiwanis in New Haven and not several hundred smirking Objectivists. He mildly referred to Brook's analysis of the Founders as being a "narrow view," and said that the Constitution, in its pledge to "promote the general welfare," was much broader than a simple effort to prevent citizens from being harmed by force. There are many other things that do harm to people and therefore are the responsibility of government, including poverty, sickness, and unequal access to education. The Constitution mandates that government "do something about that, and not sit back and say 'that is how the free market has distributed happiness. So we're going to allow that to happen.' "

Brook hit the canvas, but he was not out for the count. No one was going to score a knockout, not with an almost evenly divided crowd, but the style and substance of the two had become evident. Rapoport reiterated the moral argument that government needed to be proactive, to help people, a position that was supported by the reality of life in America. Brook took the more abstract position that glorified free markets not as a license for large corporations to do what they wanted, but as a manifestation of "freedom."

It seemed that the debate would end that way, in a stalemate, when Brook gave a roundhouse belt to his own solar plexus. He contended that democracy was not a first principal of the nation. He was questioned about that by the moderator, who suggested that he might have "gone off the rails," but Brook made no effort to set his mind at rest on that point. "I think the broad dissatisfaction that we have today is to a large extent a consequence of democracy and the notion that the majority can force the minority—in this case, the only real minority, which is the individual—to do what he does not want to do." Brook was not going to budge on that point, since Ayn Rand had expressed grave misgivings about majority rule in an interview with Mike Wallace decades before.[3] He was in no position to alter Objectivist dogma any more than a priest could edit the Catechism.

Rapoport responded like an old trooper, not evidently gleeful at his opponent's Rand-mandated plunge into ideological quicksand. He said that the "decisions that people make affect other people" almost all the time. What Brook was suggesting, he said, "did not correspond to reality in an interdependent world." Rapoport said that the problem was not democracy but the distortion of democracy by money and people prevented from voting.

This was fourth-grade civics. But what else was there to say? I guess Rapoport could have thrown the Founders right back at Brook, pointing out that they were the tax-and-spend Democrats of their era. From 1792 to 1811, per capita taxes were ten times higher than were imposed by the British from 1765 to 1775.[4] If I were his cut man, that's what I'd have told him when he retreated to his corner at the end of the round.

Brook trotted out again the shopworn "trader principle" Randism about people relating to each other by the "voluntary mechanism of trade. It's win-win." Rapoport replied that trade "connotes two equal partners. But in our society, in commerce, in the marketplace, we don't have equal partners." And it's government's role, he said, to see to it that those roles are somewhat equalized. He was low-key and stating the obvious, but it was necessary because Rand's dogma is predicated on ignoring the obvious. Or saying, as Brook did, that one achieves income equality by giving poor people "the opportunity to rise up and make a fortune." That brought to mind Anatole France and "The law, in its majestic equality, forbids the rich as well as the poor to sleep under bridges, to beg in the streets, and to steal bread."

As the debate droned on, I saw laid out before me the pattern Rand and her successors had perpetuated over the years in books, essays, columns, and Internet tracts. The old Rand practice of ignoring the obvious and misrepresenting reality was happening right before our eyes, here in the performing arts center named for that movie producer-rabbi. Nothing had changed since 1967, when Ellis debated Branden, except that the cast of characters was different, the tone was more polite—and Randism, while just as extreme, was far more deeply engrained in society. The lesson of the evening was that Objectivism can only be effectively debated by reminding the listeners that, as Rand put it, "existence exists." Reality exists, and reality does not work in her favor most of the time. Rapoport was more than holding his own because he recognized that.

Brook continued in his predecessors' footsteps by repeating the official Objectivist version of the history of the Industrial Revolution, that it was an era in which the great unwashed came from the farms to the cities and found ample jobs in factories owned by noble capitalists. Rapoport, reminding the audience that the history of the Industrial Revolution exists, called that "an interesting history but leaves out a huge portion of it," receiving enthusiastic applause and cheers from the non-Objectivist minority in the auditorium. Sure, it created great wealth, but "it also created great misery if you read any of the histories of England in the 1830s and 1840s." A miserable, downtrodden urban proletariat was created; their fate alleviated only when "the dynamism of capitalism was harnessed." He quoted an early twentieth-century commentator who called child labor laws a Communist plot. Rapoport said that "I suppose one could take Yaron's argument and say, since everyone's in control of their life, if a seven-year-old child wants to go to work in a factory, and work sixteen hours and be paid pennies, that's his or her right to do."

Yep, he had read his Rand. I could see that Rapoport was setting up Brook for a sucker punch. Rand explicitly dealt with the issue of child labor in the *Capitalism* anthology, in an essay by Robert Hessen, "The Effects of the Industrial Revolution on Women and Children" (originally published in 1962 in *The Objectivist Newsletter*). According to Hessen's alternate version of history, capitalism actually improved the working conditions of children compared to the preindustrial age, as they performed "easy work" like tending to looms in factories. "One is both morally unjust and ignorant of history if one blames capitalism for the condition of children during the Industrial Revolution," Hessen wrote. Once his essay appeared in the newsletter, then under Rand's direct control, it passed immediately into black-letter Objectivist law.

"There's this mythology that capitalism created child labor," said Brook, channeling what Hessen had written forty-nine years earlier. Of course, he allowed, "I'm not saying it was pleasant." No, children tending to looms in cotton mills and cutting sugar cane, rather than going to school, is not a pleasant prospect. But hey, that's capitalism. Brook received a scattering of applause from the faithful, but Rapoport won that round. The extremism of Brook's position had been exposed. Lehrer, the moderator, asked Brook if he would repeal child labor laws and "let it exist around the edges." Brook cheerfully responded in the affirmative.

"I would not repeal child labor laws, just for the record," Rapoport deadpanned.

Brook fared much better responding to an ill-informed anti-Objectivist, who tried to portray Brook as a defender of slavery, which he said would be consistent with his position on child labor. Brook easily parried that one, repeating Rand's oft-proclaimed disdain for the use of force against individuals, as well as her view that there was no such thing as state's rights. Then Brook returned to the red lines, crossing them jauntily by saying that "If I had to start with getting rid of government from our lives, I would probably start with public education." That left him open for a head butt from Rapoport. There was some fire in his belly now: "If you eliminate public education, if you allow everyone to fend for themselves in the private market, those people who can afford education, their kids will have a good education. Those people who cannot afford it, will not. And that's not a society in which we want to live. It's not America. It's un-American in my opinion."

It was starting to become exasperating to watch this. Here we were in the twenty-first century. Did we really have to debate not how to improve the public education system, but whether we should have a public education system at all? It was a debate that had been resolved in the mid-nineteenth century, just as the debate over child labor was pretty well over by the 1920s, when there was general agreement that child labor was an evil of the Industrial Revolution that needed to be curbed. Why were we debating these issues again, these first principles? Was it necessary?

The tragedy is that it was.

"When we first picked up this debate," Rapoport said, "some people said 'Why are you debating with the Ayn Rand Institute? They're all the way over on the far right, not really representative of the conservative movement today.' " But he didn't agree. All the things Brook was saying "have in fact been picked up in the mainstream of the Republican Party today." All were "straight from the fundamental set of principles that Yaron has articulated."

Brook was in total agreement. "We have helped reshape the debate, and pushed some in the Republican Party and some in the conservatives, to positions that they traditionally would not have taken" he said. *Atlas Shrugged* "inspires them to have a little bit more confidence, to push their agenda a little more to a radical direction than they would otherwise.

"And," he said, "I think that's saving our country."

CHAPTER FOURTEEN

The Murray Hill Candidate

Yaron Brook had considerable reason for optimism.

The Ayn Rand Institute finally agreed to send me the raw numbers from that Zogby poll, the one that contended nearly a third of Americans had read *Atlas Shrugged*. The ARI held out for so long that I expected to see undisguised pollster bias—slanted questions to yield a preordained result. I was wrong. The questions were framed in a neutral fashion. The results were startlingly clear: America was in love with Ayn Rand.

It made perfect sense. After seven decades of popularity, Rand continued to haunt the best-seller rankings, and still clung tenaciously to the American consciousness. All the Zogby poll did was confirm what we already knew.

Of 2,100 adults surveyed between October 8 and 10, 2010, 29 percent said that they had read *Atlas Shrugged*, 69 percent said they hadn't, and 1 percent said "not sure." If this poll was within spitting distance of the truth, then three out of ten Americans were exposed to Rand's radical capitalism by reading her immense magnum opus. The poll confirmed the stereotype of *Atlas* as being a young person's obsession: 22 percent said they read *Atlas* when they were twelve to seventeen years of age; 51 percent when they were eighteen to twenty-nine; just 20 percent when they were thirty to forty-nine; 5 percent when they were fifty to sixty-four; 1 percent when they were over sixty-five; and another 1 percent weren't sure.

Another stunner was the impact of Rand on her readers' political views. Asked if they "agree or disagree that reading *Atlas Shrugged* changed the way you think about political or ethical issues," 11 percent percent marked "strongly agree," 38 percent "somewhat agree," 22 percent said "strongly disagree," and the same percentage said "somewhat disagree." That's 49 percent of *Atlas* readers who were swayed by Rand, 44 percent who were not. An impressive showing, considering her atheism and extreme views. Evidently a sizable number of Americans are suckers for a good, long yarn with plenty of sex, scads of speeches, and a heavy dose of radical capitalism.

Clearly the ARI's school programs and John Allison's college efforts were having an effect. They were controversial—some colleges had turned down the Allison foundation's money.[1] No matter. The poll numbers attested to his impact: 21 percent said *Atlas* was "assigned or recommended in school," versus 38 percent who said it was recommended by a friend or colleague. The study also found that 21 percent of Americans had read *The Fountainhead,* which was also a hefty number; 7 percent had read *Anthem*; 4 percent *We the Living*; and, surprisingly—astoundingly—3 percent of the American people have read the definitionally deficient *Virtue of Selfishness,* and an equal percentage claimed they had consumed the extremist *Capitalism* anthology.

You could cut those numbers in half and they would still show Rand having a strong influence on the American psyche.

There was one American who exemplified what you could call the Rand Effect, a reader whose views were permanently altered by Ayn Rand. That would be the former chairman of the Federal Reserve, Alan Greenspan. Rand's relationship with Greenspan had intrigued me since I first saw the Oval Office photograph. Were they as closely linked as the picture implied?

Alas, Greenspan, whom I'd interviewed in early 2008 when the subject was an up-and-coming Timothy Geithner, was too busy to give me his account of the impact Rand had on his life and lengthy career. He signaled through a spokesperson that he was "currently heavily committed and is not available for an interview." But not to worry: The public record is more than ample. Perusing his writings and talking to people who knew Greenspan and the Collective, two pictures emerge: One is the story told by Greenspan in the autobiography that he wrote after he left the Fed, *The Age of Turbulence*. The other is what actually happened.

Most accounts of Greenspan's Rand years emphasize Rand's intellectual influence on the future Oracle. But it was considerably deeper than that. For much of its existence the Collective was for all intents and purposes a cult. It had an unquestioned leader, it demanded absolute loyalty, it intruded into the personal lives of its members, it had its own rote expressions and catchphrases, it expelled transgressors for deviation from accepted norms, and expellees were "fair game" for vicious personal attacks. In the manner of all cults, it attracted into its midst an isolated, homely man—who, Barbara Branden told me, had few friends outside the Collective. "None of us did, really," said Barbara. "If they were close friends they became part of the movement, but we didn't have close friends outside of the movement."

Just as Ed Nash consulted the Rand circle before splitting with Iris Bell, Greenspan did the same when he considered leaving his job at the Conference Board to strike out on his own as an economic consultant. Nathaniel Branden recounts in his Rand memoir that he spent hours talking with Greenspan when he was weighing the move. That was a big step in those Organization Man days. Branden encouraged him to take the plunge, which turned him from just another industrial economist into a sought-after, prosperous, economic forecaster. "Take the leap," he recalled urging Greenspan.[2] Yet there is not a word on those marathon conversations in Greenspan's book, which was lavishly detailed—except when it came to Rand and her circle. Instead, Greenspan contends in *The Age of Turbulence* that "changing jobs was a remarkably easy decision" because of freelance income that he was getting at the time.[3] If it was an "easy decision," why did it require hours of discussion? The only mention of Branden is a fleeting reference to him as "Rand's young collaborator and, years later, her lover." Barbara Branden's existence is acknowledged just once, and she is not even named. He makes no reference to his conversation with Barbara in which she converted him to the undesirability of government-chartered banks.

Yet his ties to Rand were so strong in the 1950s that not even the breakup of his marriage to Joan Mitchell, an old friend of Barbara's, induced him to leave the Collective. He stayed with it even when his attractive ex-wife began dating and then married Allan Blumenthal, a cousin of Nathaniel's. A photograph from Joan and Allan's 1957 wedding shows the ex-husband happily in attendance, along with other members of the Collective.

His close association with Rand continued through the 1960s. Greenspan, though ambitious and working for conservative corporations, was unfazed by the pariah status of his leader. He wrote articles for the Objectivist newsletter, and in 1958 volunteered as a lecturer at the Nathaniel Branden Institute, speaking on "The Economics of a Free Society," doing his bit to attract outsiders to the Objectivist cause. These were not entirely altruistic exercises, by the way. Barbara Branden told me that Greenspan and the other lecturers were paid a lump sum plus a percentage of ticket sales. According to Barbara, Peikoff once said that he earned more from the NBI lectures than he would have from teaching college. So there was a monetary element, possibly a substantial one, that helped bind Greenspan to Rand.

Greenspan remained a member of the Collective until it disintegrated in the wake of the Branden excommunication. By then his writings held an honored place alongside Rand's in the Objectivist canon. It would be Greenspan who would be called upon to explain to the world how Objectivists view the role of government in business. According to Nathaniel Branden, Greenspan ranked right after the Brandens in Rand's esteem, putting him on a par with the current spiritual leader of Objectivism, Leonard Peikoff. Sometimes Greenspan was on top, sometimes Peikoff, depending on Rand's whims.[4]

In his memoirs, published in 2007 and updated a year later, Greenspan is silent on his exalted place in the Objectivist hierarchy. He gives short shrift to his Objectivist comrades, doesn't mention his lectures at the Nathaniel Branden Institute, and generally doesn't have much to say about the woman who was his guiding light for three decades. In his only allusion to the essays he wrote for Rand, he says that he "wrote spirited commentary for her newsletter with the fervor of a young acolyte drawn to a whole new set of ideas." He goes on to say that "like any young convert, I tended to frame the concepts in their starkest, simplest terms. Most everyone sees the simple outline of an idea before complexity and qualification set in. If we didn't, there would be nothing to qualify, nothing to learn. It was only as contradictions inherent in my new notions began to emerge that my fervor receded."[5] Does he still believe what he wrote? He chooses not to say.

There isn't much else of substance about his years with Rand in his 200,000-word autobiography. We get only a superficial sense from Greenspan of the kind of person that Rand was, no discussion of her virtues and flaws, no perspective on the controversies in which Rand was embroiled—sometimes dragging in Greenspan—in his thirty years as one of her lieutenants. That would seem bizarre when you consider the detail he lavishes on everyone else in his life and the length of time that Greenspan spent in Rand's orbit, experiencing her at close range. But it was really not strange at all if the objective was to downplay this seminal chapter of his life, mask the extremist positions that he advanced as a Rand insider from the 1950s through the 1980s—and, above all, downplay her influence on his behavior as Fed chairman.

The ambiguous "my fervor receded" remark seems to imply that his devotion to Rand receded over the years. Did it?

A clue to Greenspan's loyalty to Rand at the height of her notoriety can be found in a letter to the editor he wrote to *The New York Times Book Review* in 1957, responding to one of the many critical thrashings of *Atlas Shrugged*. Of the three letters that made it into print—the others were from Barbara Branden and another Collective member—Greenspan's was the most impassioned, the most liberal in its use of Randian catchphrases. "*Atlas Shrugged* is a celebration of life and happiness," he wrote. "Justice is unrelenting. Creative individuals and undeviating purpose and rationality achieve joy and fulfillment. Parasites who persistently avoid either purpose or reason perish as they should."[6]

He was arguably a youthful acolyte when he wrote those words, just thirty-one years old. But what about the rest of his writings and actions? Were they a kind of youthful lark in the distant past of a now chastened old man? Or are they part of an unbroken record of Rand advocacy? The 1966 Rand anthology *Capitalism: The Unknown Ideal* contained three of his essays, and reading them makes it clear that Greenspan's ideology had not shifted at all in the nearly ten years since he had denounced "parasites" in his 1957 letter.

If *Atlas Shrugged* is the Bible of the Objectivist movement, the *Capitalism* anthology is its Catechism. It is the same ideological battering ram as the Rand fiction, but lacks the literary pretentions of her novels. It goes into detail, applying Rand's teachings to the practical problems facing America, such as, "What kind of government shall we have?" The answer can be summed up as, "Practically nothing, and certainly nothing that might discomfit businessmen." There were essays on other subjects, but its primary purpose was to grapple with the always-bedeviling problem of a government that just won't keep its cotton-picking hands off business.

Greenspan received coauthor credit with Rand, her deputy Branden, and Robert Hessen. It was a sign of Greenspan's importance to Rand that compared to his three essays for the anthology, Branden wrote two and Hessen just one.

Greenspan's essays for this volume present a radical vision of America. The gold standard would return. Antitrust laws would go, and so would every form of regulation. The book—still in print, still selling handsomely—is as strident in tone and content, and as filled with Objectivist jargon, as the letter he wrote to *The New York Times Book Review.*

Greenspan's essay "The Assault on Integrity" equates coherent government regulation with a breakdown in society's morals. It presents Greenspan as a kind of Ralph Nader in reverse, arguing against the need for government to protect consumers from dishonest and unscrupulous business practices. The Securities and Exchange Commission and Food and Drug Administration are superfluous in Greenspan's view. Consumer protection is a "cardinal ingredient of welfare statism." All regulations that protect the public from unscrupulous businessmen, even building codes, are unnecessary, he argues. Greenspan maintains that potential damage to reputation is sufficient to keep a contractor in an unregulated environment from building shoddy structures.

He goes on to talk about the "greed" (his scare quotes) of the businessman being the unexcelled protector of the consumer. A drug company's reputation, as reflected in the salability of its brand name, is "often its major asset." And that is even truer for a securities firm. "Securities worth hundreds of millions of dollars are traded every day over the telephone," said Greenspan. "The slightest doubt as to the trustworthiness of a broker's word or commitment would put him out of business overnight."

What's interesting about these passages is that they're not conditioned on how the market would behave in an unregulated economy. No, Greenspan was stating his view of reality as he perceived it when this essay was originally written for *The Objectivist Newsletter* in 1963 (when he was a youthful acolyte of thirty-seven). That's what makes his comments so remarkable: The essay ignores the market's proven tendency to turn a blind eye toward long-term, routine fraudulent conduct. Indeed, fraud is such a regular feature of the financial markets that it is only rarely prosecuted as a crime, and usually is dealt with only by civil actions—private arbitrations and class actions, and SEC lawsuits that are almost always settled without the target admitting or denying guilt. Objectivists say that they are opposed to fraud, but their opposition to regulation would strip away the only mechanism that can tackle systemic, widespread fraud.

The best recent example of this was the Bernard Madoff ponzi scheme, which lasted for at least two decades. Regulation failed, not because regulation is inherently wrong but because the regulators involved were inept. The markets themselves were utterly unable to comprehend the existence of this massive fraud, functioning for years at the heart of the securities markets. Over the years, market participants—including executives at major banks—grew suspicious. But they did not communicate their concerns to other market participants or the public, let alone regulators or law enforcement, so the Madoff scheme continued until the very end. The only thing that would have caught Madoff was a vigorous regulator monitoring the securities industry on a routine basis, and competently investigating complaints—such as the ones from a whistleblower, Harry Markopolos, who insisted that Madoff was a fraud.

On a less grand scale, a host of dishonest practices—from pay-for-play to procure municipal bond business to lying to investors to trading ahead of customers on the floors of the stock exchanges—all have been standard on Wall Street for decades without the market interfering with them. Some of them were prevalent when Greenspan wrote "Assault on Integrity." These were ordinary methods of doing business.[7] Recent history has brought new examples of individuals and firms that profited from pushing hard at the ethical envelope and getting away with it. The credit binge, financial crisis and resulting scandals provided hundreds, perhaps thousands of examples of capitalism failing to self-police.

Underlying Greenspan's argument, ironically, is the implication that businessmen are fundamentally dishonest, and that regulation only brings out the worst in them. "Minimum standards tend to become maximum standards as well," he said. By Greenspan's logic, it is the regulators, not the businessmen, who are to blame for any ethical transgressions that occur, because "regulation—which is based on force and fear—undermines the moral base of business dealings." This view is echoed in the far right's contention—which I heard often from Tea Party people—that government policies and regulations, not banks, were responsible for the 2008 financial crisis. To Greenspan, a future bank regulator, people in the job he was soon to hold are a corrupting influence. Even building codes, he maintains, are counterproductive: "It becomes cheaper to bribe the building inspector than to meet his standards of construction. A fly-by-night securities operator can quickly meet the SEC requirements, gain the inference of respectability, and proceed to fleece the public." That last part is correct—and the Madoff scandal proved that. But it's a stretch to say that removing all regulation and all regulators, instead of making them more effective, is the best way to deal with securities fraud.

A simple way of dealing with weak regulators and regulations is to hire better regulators and write stronger regulations. But Greenspan has a better idea: Get rid of them altogether. "In an unregulated economy," Greenspan wrote, "the [securities] operator would have had to spend a number of years in reputable dealings before he could earn a position of trust sufficient to induce a number of investors to place funds with him." The problem with this statement is that we don't live in an unregulated economy, no unregulated economy has ever existed, and there is virtually zero probability that one will ever come to pass. But such arguments can be—and are—used to weaken regulation in today's regulated economy.

There were certainly enough business scandals during Greenspan's lifetime to demonstrate that self-interest often motivated businessmen to break the law and violate the rights of others, and frequently to bring themselves down. It isn't all that clear if Greenspan cared. His opposition to regulation was ideological—religious, as Albert Ellis would have put it. It was based not only on the morality of free-market capitalism but on the *immorality* of restraining capitalism. His view, codified in *Capitalism* as official Objectivist doctrine, was that government interference in business was not just bad public policy but *evil,* a form of physical force.

Greenspan waxes rhapsodic on the subject in his essay, making regulators seem not like the meek, often corporate-influenced government bureaucrats they often are, but more like brutal NKVD operatives: "The euphemism of government press releases to the contrary notwithstanding, the basis of regulation is armed force. At the bottom of the endless pile of paper work which characterizes all regulation lies a gun." That had been Rand's hobbyhorse, too, and Brook and other Randians have continued that theme to this day.

The "gun" metaphor has always confounded me. I had seen many regulators in action and occasionally detected a whiff of talcum, but never gunpowder. Time and again, companies large and small have violated government regulations and nothing has happened to them. It happened in Greenspan's time, when he was a bright young economist sitting on Rand's sofa, and it certainly has happened in ours.

Greenspan continued to behave like a loyal apparatchik in 1968, during the Break with the Brandens. In a statement published in the official Objectivist newsletter, signed by Greenspan, Branden's cousin Allan Blumenthal, Peikoff, and another Collective member, the Rand loyalists said the following: "We, the undersigned, former Associate Lecturers at Nathaniel Branden Institute, wish the following to be on record: Because Nathaniel Branden and Barbara Branden, in a series of actions, have betrayed fundamental principles of Objectivism, we condemn and repudiate these two persons irrevocably, and have terminated all association with them and with Nathaniel Branden Institute."[8] Greenspan makes no mention in his memoirs of this Stalinist-style denunciation, which he signed when he was a youthful acolyte of forty-two.

Greenspan dabbled in government service during the Nixon administration, serving as an advisor during the 1968 campaign and on a government panel that recommended abolition of the draft—a longtime Rand priority. To her, a military draft was never to be imposed, not even in time of world war. Writing in the *Capitalism* anthology, she contended that the draft "negates man's fundamental right—the right to life—and establishes the fundamental principle of statism: that a man's life belongs to the state, and the state may claim it by compelling him to sacrifice it in battle."[9] Greenspan was brought into the draft panel by Martin Anderson, a White House aide and fellow Rand acolyte.

Greenspan declined a White House position in 1968. We don't know if this was Rand's influence at work, but we do know her role in his appointment as chairman of the Council of Economic Advisors by President Richard Nixon. Were it not for her, he might not have taken the job.

At the time Greenspan was appointed in July 1974,* *New York Times* reporter Soma Golden quoted both Greenspan and Rand in a remarkable, long-overlooked page-one story that put his agenda—and Rand's involvement in his appointment—in black and white. For more than twenty years, the article pointed out, Greenspan had been a "friend and follower" of Rand. It was one of the few interviews that Rand granted to the detested Eastern liberal media at the time, and one of even fewer that was relatively sympathetic. "Like others of this persuasion," the *Times* reported, Greenspan "believes in the morality and ultimate desirability of complete laissez-faire capitalism." Greenspan told the *Times* that when he met Rand he was

* He was sworn in, and photographed with Rand, shortly after Nixon resigned and was succeeded by Gerald Ford.

a "free enterpriser in the Adam Smith sense—impressed with the theoretical structure and efficiency of the market." What Rand did, "through long discussions and lots of arguments into the night, was to make me think why capitalism is not only efficient and practical but also moral."

Rand was candid about how why Greenspan took the job—it was her influence. "I helped Alan to analyze what was involved, but of course the decision was his own," she said. If it truly was his own decision, why even say that?

Greenspan did not want to take the job. He was making a fortune as an economic consultant, and he points out in *The Age of Turbulence* that he didn't agree with many of Nixon's policies.[10] But Rand wanted him there, in government, even though his employment in such a high government capacity conflicted with her entire philosophy. She wanted access to power, through her youthful acolyte, and she got it.

In *Turbulence,* Greenspan talks about his old mentor Arthur Burns, the former Fed chairman, persuading him to take the job. But there's not one word on Rand's role, her assistance in helping him "analyze what was involved"—even though it was discussed on page one of *The New York Times.*

"I think it's an heroic undertaking on his part," the *Times* quoted Rand as saying—peculiar language to describe a person accepting a high-level government position, "Alan is my disciple, philosophically. He is an advocate of laissez-faire capitalism. But neither he nor I expect it to happen overnight."

"I don't believe he would stay if he if he is asked to compromise his principles," Rand said. "Inconsistency is a moral crime."[11]

As I pored through Greenspan's writings and utterances, I concluded that his "my fervor receded" comment in *The Age of Turbulence* was not misleading, not mealy-mouthed, but simply not true. I saw no change in his fealty to Rand, no change in his determination to implement her objectives, from the early 1950s, when he attended her salon at 36 East 36th Street, continuing through his years at the Fed, and slogging through the calendar to the present day. I was reminded of Richard Condon's 1959 novel, *The Manchurian Candidate*, which was about prisoners of war brainwashed in North Korea, with one programmed to become an assassin. It was an image that I could not get out of my head. I couldn't help thinking that Greenspan was the Murray Hill Candidate, wired at an early age to become a killer—to go forth and assassinate government regulation of business.

I know, it's not a terribly kind image. But it's the best metaphor I could find for Greenspan's single-minded pursuit of Rand's agenda before, during, and after his years at the Fed. Objectivists have long since disowned him, deriding him as a traitor, and Yaron Brook has castigated him for supposedly betraying Rand,[12] but I think that Greenspan's record of achievement, his long years of service to Ayn Rand, speaks for itself.

CHAPTER FIFTEEN

The Bill for Collection

Alan Greenspan remained close to Rand until her death in 1982. In that year, her loyal subaltern Leonard Peikoff authored a book—written with Rand's painstaking interference—which had the title *The Ominous Parallels.* In it, Peikoff identified supposed similarities between the prelude to Nazism in Germany and the intellectual history of the United States in the late twentieth century. Rand wrote an introduction to this strident book, and it received a glowing blurb from the man who, along with Peikoff, was closest to her:

> Dr. Peikoff has produced an extraordinarily perceptive thesis. His insights into the parallel philosophical tracks of pre-Nazi Germany and contemporary America are frightening. Everyone concerned with the collectivist trend in today's world should read this book.
>
> —*Alan Greenspan*

As a leader of the Objectivist movement, Greenspan could do no less. Once again, he risked his reputation by speaking up for Objectivism, in this instance a book that compared the United States to the Weimar Republic. Greenspan was an esteemed economist, still a youthful acolyte at the age of fifty-six.

The previous year he became an advisor to Ronald Reagan, and he advanced Objectivism in government as one of the strongest backers of the Kemp–Roth tax cuts of 1981. These slashed the top marginal tax rate and forever changed the progressive character of the income tax system—a system whose very existence Rand opposed. He could not end income taxes, just as he could not put an end to the minimum wage that she also opposed, but he could make the system more favorable to the creators and entrepreneurs who were more valuable to society than people lower down on the ladder of success. Two years later, as head of a commission weighing changes to the Social Security system, he engineered an increase in the most regressive tax on the poor and middle class—the Social Security payroll tax—combined with a cut in benefits. This was no contradiction. Social Security was a system of altruism at its worst. Its beneficiaries were looters. Raising their taxes and cutting their benefits was no loss to society.

In 1987, Alan Greenspan was Reagan's choice as the next chairman of the Federal Reserve Board of Governors. Greenspan had often talked with Branden about the destructive potential of the Fed and the necessity of having a completely free banking system.[1] So his activities at the Fed were either a betrayal of Objectivist principles or a reprise of his role at the Council of Economic Advisors—to advance Randian principles from within.

In his essays in *Capitalism: The Unknown Ideal,* Greenspan laid out three main goals. Two were fast becoming reality as he took the helm at the Fed. The gold standard was dead—the notion of reviving it was too extreme even for Reagan—but enforcement of antitrust laws had been steadily weakened in the preceding six years, and he would personally see to it that financial regulation would be chipped away in the years to come.

Regressive tax policies supported by Greenspan, and Wall Street and corporate compensation practices, widened the gap between rich and poor to an extent that would have made the robber barons blanche. Between 1979 and 2004, middle-income people saw their after-tax income increase by one-fifth, while the income of the top 1 percent, adjusted for inflation, climbed 176 percent.[2] In 1980, CEOs earned 42 times the wage of the average production worker. In 1990 that number had climbed to 107. By 2010, CEO pay was 343 times the wages earned by average Americans.[3]

Greenspan advocated repeal of Glass–Steagall, the Depression-era law that separated commercial from investment banks, from almost the moment he was named Fed chairman. Under his leadership, the Fed chipped away at the law until its repeal in 1999. Repeal allowed commercial banks to underwrite complex mortgage-backed securities, a crucial step on the road to the 2008 financial crisis.

In 2000, when a Fed governor named Edward M. Gramlich brought to Greenspan's attention the growing problem of predatory lending—mortgage companies pushing subprime loans with tricky provisions on poor people who could ill-afford them—Greenspan was opposed to sending examiners into the mortgage affiliates of national banks.[4] Protecting the public from exploitation by powerful banks was directly contrary to the precepts he set forth in "Assault on Integrity." It never happened.

What was predatory lending anyway? From an Objectivist perspective it was about as consequential as a baker selling a loaf of bread. Mortgage companies were offering subprime loans with grotesquely complex, inequitable terms, sold to poor people who often did not understand them. Under Objectivist doctrine, as promulgated by Alan Greenspan, it was in their rational self-interest to do so. So was investment banks packaging those mortgages as securities of daunting complexity, with credit ratings that tended to be of the highest caliber even when not warranted. It was in the rational self-interest of the credit rating agencies to place the highest possible ratings on mortgage-backed securities, because doing so encouraged a flow of revenues.

There would be no regulation of any of this—not subprime lending, not credit rating agencies, not the derivatives that spilled forth from the mortgages. Greenspan, true to his long-dead leader, stood solidly behind derivatives, and frustrated efforts to regulate them. To do so, he told the Senate Banking Committee in 2003, "would be a mistake."[5] A year later, he said at a banking convention: "Not only have individual financial institutions become less vulnerable to shocks from underlying risk factors, but also the financial system as a whole has become more resilient."[6]

When Congress tried to close a derivatives loophole that had abetted the Enron scandal, Greenspan was opposed. And as usual, his opposition carried the day. "Public disclosure of pricing data for customized OTC transactions would not improve the overall price discovery process," he and several Bush administration officials argued in a letter to members of Congress in 2002.[7] Despite the abuses of Enron, Greenspan and the others did not "believe a public policy case exists to justify this government intervention." The derivatives that were byproducts of the housing boom, such as collateralized debt obligations, were now regulated only by the best possible regulator, "the greed of the businessman."

Greenspan's memoir *The Age of Turbulence* was published in 2007, a year before his reputation was shredded by the financial crisis. In the book's brief discussion of Rand, Greenspan tries to put daylight between himself and his mentor by emphasizing his disagreement with Rand on income taxes, which she opposed. But shortly thereafter, as if conflicted, he declares himself one with her on the central focus of Objectivism: "I still found the broader philosophy of unfettered market competition compelling, as I do to this day."

That's it. Not a word withdrawing anything he said in his three *Capitalism* essays, even though the Randian anthology was still in print and selling briskly. *The Age of Turbulence* was a golden opportunity to repudiate the radical capitalist agenda set forth in his essays. He could have done that by saying so in his memoir, just as he could have distanced himself from his essays years before, by asking for them to be omitted from the anthology or issuing a public statement saying that those essays no longer reflected his opinions. He never did. It's reasonable to assume that he didn't do any of that because he still believed every word he wrote in those essays.

Greenspan also could have used his memoir to make amends to the Brandens for signing a statement at the time of the Break in 1968 that he now knew to be false and defamatory. Barbara Branden told me that she met with Greenspan and told him the whole story while researching her book in the 1980s. "He was flabbergasted," she said. "He told me that he had heard rumors [of the affair with Nathaniel], but didn't believe them." He was apologetic, she said. "He was very nice." For Barbara Branden, that was enough. When I talked to her she harbored no hard feelings. But as an indication of his attitude toward his long-dead mentor, it's significant that Greenspan didn't devote a few sentences in his book to setting the record straight, and expressing regret for signing the statement.

As for his ideological evolution—or lack thereof—Barbara Branden has watched Greenspan as he has soared in power, and says that she "knows that for a long time [Rand's philosophy] continued to influence him for many years." As for today, "I don't doubt that it's a significant influence still."

One might see that as jumping to conclusions, and perhaps wishful thinking. After all, what about his famous congressional testimony in 2008, in which he confessed to a "flaw" in his worldview?

It was one of the seminal events in the history of the financial crisis. On October 23, 2008, Greenspan was summoned to appear before Congressman Henry Waxman's Oversight and Government Reform Committee. During his tense appearance before this normally friendly committee of the House of Representatives, Greenspan performed a public self-denunciation that brought to mind the friendly witnesses who appeared before congressional committees in the McCarthy era. They would plead and cajole, denounce and betray, conceal and lie, seeking to purge themselves of ideological errors, abandoning all self-respect as they repudiated their previous, flawed thinking—not because they had changed their beliefs, but to keep their careers alive.

Greenspan fit snugly into that mold. He told Waxman that he had found a "flaw in the model that I perceived is the critical functioning structure that defines how the world works, so to speak." He said that "those of us who have looked to the self-interest of lending institutions to protect shareholders' equity, myself included, are in a state of shocked disbelief."[8]

The "flaw" speech made headlines around the world. It was almost universally interpreted as a repudiation of his free-market ideology, and to this day it is one of the seminal moments of the financial crisis. But as I studied his public comments, I came to realize that it wasn't quite the mea culpa that it was portrayed as being. The word "doubletalk" came to mind. Yes, he admitted a "flaw." He used that word. Asked if he was wrong, he said "partially." But he backtracked almost as soon as those words left his mouth. Remarkably little attention was paid to his dissembling and backsliding on his personal, ideologically driven culpability.

Greenspan began flip-flopping during the Waxman committee hearing. The "flaw" in his worldview, he said later in an oft-overlooked portion of his appearance before Waxman, was possibly transitory and not meaningful—"I don't know how significant or permanent it is," he said. He always upheld "the laws of the land passed by the Congress, not my own predilections," he said. "I voted for virtually every regulatory action that the Federal Reserve board moved forward on.... I felt required by my oath of office to adhere to what I am supposed to do, not what I would like to do."

That much was true. Greenspan ruled the Fed by consensus, and avoided being on the losing side of a vote. Instead Greenspan discouraged unpalatable proposals—such as Fed governor Ed Gramlich's attempt in

2000 to rein in predatory lending—from ever coming to a vote. At every opportunity he used his unchallenged leadership at the Fed, and his influence over Congress as economic oracle, to frustrate regulation whenever it reared its head, very much as Ayn Rand would have wanted.

His continued devotion to Rand was confirmed by another remark before the Waxman hearing. Responding to Waxman's prodding on the shortcomings of his ideology (whose identity and characteristics were not probed by the committee), Greenspan gave the congressmen a little lecture on the importance of ideology in modern life. He said that "ideology is a conceptual framework with the way people deal with reality. Everyone has one. You have to. *To exist, you need an ideology.*" (My italics.)

Unlike the "flaw" comment, this was spontaneous, and was not in his prepared testimony. It was also dubious. Millions, perhaps billions of people throughout the world live unremarkable and sometimes even happy lives, under every conceivable system of government, without a strongly held belief system. It's safe to assume that the vast majority of people are too consumed with the daily struggle to survive.

It occurred to me that his remark had a familiar ring to it. I glanced through some books on my desk and there it was, in Ayn Rand's introduction to *The Virtue of Selfishness.* "The first step," she wrote, "is to acknowledge man's right to a moral existence—that is, *his need for a moral code to guide the course and fulfillment of his own life.*" (My italics.) A few pages later she drove the point home: "Does an arbitrary human convention, a mere custom, decree that man must guide his actions by a set of principles—or is there a fact of reality that demands it? Is ethics the province of whims: of personal emotions, social edicts and mystic revelations—or is it the province of reason? Is ethics a subjective luxury—or an objective necessity?"[9]

That was not some isolated remark but a consistent theme that Rand repeated often:

A human being needs a frame of reference, a comprehensive view of existence, no matter how rudimentary.[10]

As a human being, you have no choice about the fact that you need a philosophy.[11]

In a rare burst of spontaneity, Greenspan had let his guard down and was telling us that Ayn Rand remained at the core of his thinking. While attention focused on his famous "flaw" comment—there was even a British documentary in 2010 called *The Flaw*—the "ideology" remark was overlooked. Rand was so little understood that Greenspan's public embrace of his mentor largely escaped notice.

Greenspan wasn't repudiating his ideology; he was reaffirming it. And he continued to do so, again and again. Shortly before his appearance before the Waxman committee, Greenspan the Objectivist materialized, giving a speech at Georgetown University. He reminded his Georgetown audience that "the vast majority of transactions must be voluntary, which, of necessity, presupposes trust in the word of those with whom we do business—in almost all cases, strangers. It is remarkable that large numbers of contracts, especially in financial markets, until recent advances in information technology, were initially oral, confirmed by a written document only at a later time, even after much price movement. . . . We bank on the self-interest of our counterparties with whom we trade to foster and protect their reputation for producing quality goods and services."[12]

Unknown to his audience, unless they were among the 3 percent of Americans who have read the *Capitalism* anthology, Greenspan was returning to the same theme that he explored in his "Assault on Integrity" essay four decades before. Greenspan plowed directly to the point of his speech, which was that Ayn Rand was right. He was right.

"In a market system based on trust, reputation has a significant economic value. I am therefore distressed at how far we have let concerns for reputation slip in recent years. When trust is lost, a nation's ability to transact business is palpably undermined." That was the crux of the financial crisis, he said. "During the past year, lack of trust in the validity of accounting records of banks and other financial institutions in the context of inadequate capital led to a massive hesitancy in lending to them. The result has been a freezing up of credit."

So by his account, the financial agony wasn't caused by the greed and selfishness of the banks, the predatory subprime lenders, or the traders in mortgage-backed securities. It wasn't a breakdown in regulation by people like Alan Greenspan. It was lack of faith in the people Ayn Rand had worshiped as heroes of capitalism.

Two years later, in 2010, the Lehman Brothers bankruptcy trustee demolished Greenspan's entire thesis, revealing that the problem at this pivotal investment bank was not lack of trust in the firm's accounting records but dodgy accounting. Lehman had engaged in accounting gimmickry that pushed much of its derivatives exposure off its balance sheet. Greenspan, undeterred, published a paper advancing his view that the crisis of 2008 could not have been averted—in other words, that he and Ayn Rand had not failed. The fault was elsewhere—inadequate bank capital levels, poorly functioning credit rating agencies. Replete with opaque prose and mathematical formulas, it was classic Greenspan, for buried in its verbiage was the same message he had advanced throughout his career in government: Whatever the question, regulation is not the answer. Greenspan argued that a central facet of President Obama's regulatory overhaul proposal, a regulator keeping watch over systemic risks, was "ill-advised." Greenspan pinned his entire analysis on the shortcomings of economic forecasting, ignoring that a regulator of systemic risk would do considerably more than make economic projections.[13]

Greenspan continued to infuriate his critics throughout 2010 and 2011 by pushing his free-markets-at-any-cost agenda. He was being loyal and ideologically consistent. One has to give him credit for that. Greenspan was no turncoat. He was still the Greenspan of the Collective, still the Rand pal and close supporter, the essay-writer and lecturer, the blurb-writer for Peikoff, the draft-opponent, payroll-tax-raiser, and dedicated assassin of any regulations that might cross his path. Still a youthful acolyte at the age of eighty-five.

In April 2010, he made a spate of media appearances in which he sought to simultaneously assert his ideology and rescue his reputation, reassuring the public that the crisis that he had helped to create showed signs of abating. He was now advancing the line that he was but a cog in a vast and inefficient machine, just another victim of a rare global economic calamity with roots dating back to the fall of the Berlin Wall.

In an appearance on ABC News, he was asked if the market crisis had repudiated laissez-faire capitalism or Ayn Rand's belief that the markets can be trusted to police themselves. It was one of the few times in recent years that Rand's name would be invoked in his presence, and he took it in stride. If Greenspan really believed that there had been a flaw in his thinking, this would have been an opportunity to reassert it. "Not at all," he said without hesitation, as if he had expected the question, forthrightly standing up for radical capitalism. He went on to say that he and other policy makers had "no experience of the types of risks that arose following the default of Lehman Brothers."[14] Greenspan apparently forgot that the Fed, under his leadership, coordinated the bailout of Long Term Capital Management (LTCM), a hedge fund that collapsed in 1998, threatening the solvency of its counterparties, which included all of the major Wall Street banks. It was a dress rehearsal for one of the crucial events of the 2008 financial crisis, when AIG's derivatives exposure threatened to bring down its counterparties—again including all of the major investment banks. Once again, the financial system was endangered by the recklessness of a single player. LTCM was far smaller than AIG, but still needed to be bailed out to avoid systemic collapse.

Three days after the ABC News appearance, on April 7, 2010, he returned to Capitol Hill for the first time since he was grilled by Waxman in 2008. This time he appeared before the Financial Crisis Inquiry Commission.[15] There was to be no mea culpa this time, not even a *faux* one, not even one that he would repudiate in his next breath or at his next public appearance. His stance was not apologetic but defiant. With the public temper cooled and the market rebounding, Greenspan was in a position to go on the offensive. He used this opportunity to explicitly repudiate his October 2008 not-quite mea culpa.

The Fed, he said, had acted to prevent subprime lending abuses. He provided the commission with a handout entitled "Federal Reserve Initiatives to Curb 'Abusive' Practices." Even now, Greenspan could not resist the temptation to use scare quotes questioning whether the practices were in fact abusive. What he described as initiatives were a succession of guidance documents. All were issued in conjunction with other agencies, sometimes as many as five. None were binding. The regulators had set forth their expectations, but, contrary to Greenspan's account, they had not directed the banks to do anything. There were no requirements. The "gun" of regulation was never used.

Commission member Brooksley Born, who headed the Commodity Futures Trading Commission when Greenspan thwarted her plan to regulate derivatives,[16] honed in on the Maestro's ideology: "Your ideology has essentially been that financial markets . . . are self-regulatory and that government regulation is either unnecessary or harmful," she said. "You've also stated that as a result of the financial crisis you have now found a flaw in that ideology. You served as chairman of the Federal Reserve Board for more than eighteen years, retiring in 2000 [sic], and became during that period the most respected sage on the financial markets in the world. I wonder if your belief in deregulation had any impact on the level of regulation over the financial markets in the United States and in the world."

Born continued to neatly outline the case against Alan Greenspan—

the failure to regulate, the failure to prevent banks from combining to the point that they were too big to fail. "Didn't the Federal Reserve System fail to meet its responsibilities, fail to carry out its mandates?"

Greenspan was in no mood for any admission of guilt or regret. He seemed grateful for the opportunity to withdraw the impression that he had ever turned his back on Ayn Rand. He denied that he ever repudiated his ideology in the first place.

"First of all," he said forcefully, his voice gravelly and determined, "the flaw in the system that I acknowledged was inability to fully understand the state and extent of potential risks that were as yet untested." Having falsely characterized his October 2008 testimony, Greenspan continued to rewrite history by disputing the very idea that he had been the Maestro. "The idea that my ideas on regulation were predominant and effective as influencing the Congress is something you may have perceived. It didn't look that way from my point of view."

Born's time expired and there was no follow up. No commission member read to Greenspan from the transcript of his testimony in 2008. None contradicted his amazing statement concerning his influence on Congress. His effort to rewrite history slipped by, all but unnoticed. Greenspan had fallen back on a time-honored Objectivist technique: denying reality.

Greenspan was right in one respect: He had never repudiated his ideology in the "flaw" speech. His appearance before the Waxman committee gave a different impression, of course. But obfuscating was an art, and Greenspan was a virtuoso. His appearance before Waxman's committee had served its purpose, deflecting public and congressional anger without admitting, or recanting, a blessed thing.

He left the commission's hearing room and resumed his place of honor in public life, continuing to push the agenda of Ayn Rand.

As the recession that his policies helped foster lingered on, he authored an article in March 2011 for the journal *International Finance* in which he contended that government "activism" was slowing recovery.[17]

Why all the high unemployment and lack of business investment? "I infer," he said in summation, "that a minimum of half and possibly as much as three-fourths of the effect can be explained by the shock of vastly greater uncertainties embedded in the competitive, regulatory and financial environments faced by businesses since the collapse of Lehman Brothers, deriving from the surge in government activism." He concluded that "the current government activism is hampering what should be a broad-based robust economic recovery."

Greenspan made the same point in a *Financial Times* op-ed piece, published in March 2011.[18] His mission was to attack Dodd–Frank, the half-formed legislation that was Congress's much-diluted legislative response to the horrors of 2008. Weak as it was, even that was too much for Alan Greenspan. The Greenspan of the 36th Street salon, the Greenspan of the *Capitalism* anthology, opposing all forms of government regulation, was back. Not that he had ever gone anywhere.

First came a brief history of the financial crisis as seen by Alan Greenspan: "Regulators were caught 'flat-footed' by a breakdown we had erroneously thought was more than adequately reserved against." The problem, in other words, was not the banks/AIG recklessness abetted by lax regulation, but failure of banks to hold reserves sufficient to offset their own incompetence. Ever since the financial crisis, that had been his mantra—that the fault was not runaway deregulation or the misconduct of bankers, but the failure of banking authorities to require adequate reserves against the very misconduct he had encouraged. It was like blaming a security fence for the burglars who kept cutting through it.

Then came this jaw-dropper: "Today's competitive markets, whether we seek to recognise it or not, are driven by an international version of Adam Smith's 'invisible hand' that is unredeemably [sic] opaque. *With notably rare exceptions (2008, for example),* the global 'invisible hand' has created relatively stable exchange rates, interest rates, prices, and wage rates [emphasis added]." Finance, he said, was too complex to be regulated.

There was apoplectic reaction to "notably rare exceptions" from commentators like academic-blogger Henry Farrell, who asked his readers to find other examples of "notably rare exceptions," such as "With notably rare exceptions, Russian Roulette is a fun, safe game for all the family to play."[19] Sniffed Paul Krugman in his *New York Times* blog: "Alan Greenspan continues his efforts to cement his reputation as the worst ex-Fed chairman in history."[20]

Greenspan could seek to escape reality, but his words and his actions could not be so neatly erased. The fact was that Rand had failed. Her ideas had collided with the real world, a world in which monomaniacal selfishness is not beneficial but harmful, in which businessmen are driven by the scent of money to act recklessly, and in which capitalism requires government oversight lest capitalist excesses hurt the financial system and society as a whole.

Existence still existed, and everyone but the Randers seemed to notice. Nathaniel Branden had framed the issue well in his memoirs: "Today, it seems painfully obvious that if respect for reality was the ultimate Objectivist virtue, it was not one we practiced consistently, and it was inevitable that one day reality would present a bill for collection."[21]

CHAPTER SIXTEEN

The Prophecy

Leonard Peikoff was Ayn Rand's heir, but only by default. He was too much of a sycophant—even by Randian standards—to be a credible leader of a movement, and too much of a lightweight to fill her shoes. That role fell into the capable hands of the man who took charge of the Ayn Rand Institute at the end of 2000.

By any measure, Yaron Brook has been a remarkable leader. He is a stirring speaker, an articulate spokesman, and a sharp writer. He has the keen edge of fanaticism that was the hallmark of Ayn Rand, without actually coming across as a fanatic, as Peikoff does. He is a forceful spokesman for unapologetic, guilt-free radical capitalism.

My efforts to interview Brook were rebuffed for months. My e-mails went unanswered, my calls left to languish in far-off voicemail boxes. That abruptly changed after a telephone conversation I had one day with John Allison. I mentioned in passing that I hadn't been able to speak with Brook despite repeated attempts, but *had* interviewed his archrival David Kelley. Allison was not happy with that state of affairs. The very next day—almost seven months to the day after my initial interview request—I received an e-mail from the ARI's Kurt Kramer. "Sorry it took so long to get back with you," he said. "Yaron will give you an interview." Lord knows what would have happened if I'd told Allison I'd interviewed the Brandens. Would they have sent a private plane?

I met Brook at the restaurant of the W Hotel on Union Square, where he was staying during one of his frequent trips to New York. Brook set me at ease at once. The friendly, casual Israeli in him emerged. I did not have to call him "Doctor," which was a relief. On the podium he seemed fierce at times, with his wire-rimmed glasses and skull-like visage, and I practically expected him to smack me the first time we met. But up close his edges softened considerably.

Yaron Brook was born in 1961 in a neighborhood in southern Jerusalem, but lived only a few years in that divided and religiously conservative city. He was raised in Haifa, a port city on the Mediterranean with a more liberal atmosphere. His parents were immigrants from South Africa of Lithuanian extraction, and his father was a physician. "Still is," he said. "He was forced to retire because of socialized medicine." The elder Brook was chief of medicine at Rambam, a major medical center in Haifa. "He would have loved to stay on," said Brook. I later confirmed that Brook was right—physicians are forcibly retired from Israel's government-run hospitals to make way for younger doctors, and there are few private hospitals where they can seek employment. There were shades of Rand's early life in this: Brook watching his father, an esteemed physician, ousted from his hospital position by government fiat.

Brook's father traveled overseas a lot, as is common for Israeli professionals, so Brook lived for a time in London and in Boston, where he attended high school. He was not impressed. He found Americans to be "ignorant, stupid, and immature." It was at the end of the Vietnam War and "they didn't know where Vietnam was. Kids couldn't point to Vietnam on a map. I knew where Vietnam was."

For Brook, the Rand initiation came when he was sixteen. This was the late 1970s, and he was "a committed socialist and a committed Zionist at the time." So were most Israelis and so were his parents. But, fortunately for his Objectivist destiny, he had a friend who was slightly older than he was who liked to talk. "He started spouting these pro-capitalist ideas.

I asked him where this was coming from, and he handed me a copy of *Atlas Shrugged*."

In the beginning he "fought the book." Brook was not only a committed socialist but, far worse, "I'd say even a committed altruist." He found *Atlas* incomprehensible, as his only exposure to America was at a high school in Brookline and "drugs, sex, and rock 'n' roll." But by the time he finished the book, he wasn't arguing anymore, at least not with Ayn Rand. He was, however, arguing with everyone around him about the ideas he picked up in *Atlas*. It wasn't just his newfound aversion to socialism that put him at odds with his friends and relations, but also what he began to see as Israel's "Jewish collectivism."

Before reading Rand, he said, "one of the ways I'd have identified myself would have been by my belonging to, if you will, the tribe." Rand taught him that "you're not a member of the tribe. You're predominantly yourself. You're who you are." Since then he has come to understand Zionism in a different way, despite its tribal and collectivist roots, as an "act of self-defense. A people who, whether they want to define themselves as Jews, it doesn't matter, because the world wants to define them that way." But in the absence of anti-Semitism, "What difference does being Jewish or non-Jewish make?" I was impressed by this example of the Objectivist faculty for obliterating thousands of years of religious tradition with one sweeping statement.

Atlas did not exactly reinforce his Israeli identity. "Israel's small," he said, "it's full of your relatives, it's limited opportunities, it's tense, it's very tense. After reading *Atlas Shrugged* it became clear to me, it crystallized the idea that you live once, and your moral responsibility is to make your life the best that it can be."

He became sensitized to the principal problem with the country, which was heavy-handed oppression by government and the attitude of the Israeli people. They were simply too altruistic. They wanted to help others, to sacrifice themselves for the nation. It's a persistent problem in the Jewish state. "Who are the ultimate heroes in Israel?" he asked. "It's the people who've sacrificed for the group. It's the people who give up their lives. Israel is about the sacrifice of the few to the many. That's the whole mythology, not just of Israel but of Jews. It's not about fighting, not about the few fighting, but about the few sacrificing."

I was surprised—pleasantly—to hear Brook say this. I'd become weary of the rationalizations that Randians employed to whitewash the Objectivist view of altruism, especially when it comes to patriotic acts. It takes a lot of gumption to take the bull by the horns and repudiate people who give their lives for their country. Every American schoolchild learns the story of Nathan Hale, the Revolutionary War spy who said, before being hanged by the British, "I only regret that I have but one life to lose for my country." That kind of sentiment cannot be allowed to stand unchallenged.

Usually Objectivists play it safe. In a newspaper op-ed on Memorial Day 2006, the ARI's Alex Epstein said that U.S. soldiers do not "'sacrifice' for a 'higher cause.' When there is a true threat to America, it is a threat to *all* of our lives and loved ones, soldiers included."[1] Brook's denunciation of selflessness was refreshingly straightforward by comparison.

"It's engrained in you," he said of the land of his birth. "You're part of a tribe. And your responsibility is to the tribe. And nobility and morality are associated with sacrificing for that tribe." But what about here in the United States, I said to him. Don't we observe Memorial Day? "So we go out and picnic," he responded. "In Israel you mourn." It must be quite a drag, as he described it. No beer. No baseball games. "Songs on the radio all about sacrifice—the music of *Yom Hazikaron*. All the songs and I know them by heart, because they give you an infusion when you're born of all this patriotic stuff in Israel. You learn all the songs by heart and they're all songs about, you know, sacrifice and loss and greatness.

"It's the motivation," he said. "The motivation is a sense of duty or the motivation is *selfless*. Then I think it's a sacrifice. I don't believe in sacrifice." I could just imagine an Objectivist soldier contemplating his motives as he is given an order to attack an enemy position. "But sarge," he might say, like a diligent student of Method acting, "what is my motivation here? Are you asking me to do this for something I believe in, or are you suggesting that I sacrifice myself for a statist goal?" It would be a new battlefield—a *selfish* battlefield. No more soldiers falling on grenades to save their comrades, not on an Objectivist battlefield. I could see pages ripped out of history textbooks in an Objectivist world, with all those dead Medal of Honor winners replaced by the real heroes—the selfish, the greedy, the non-sacrificers, the Quislings and Pétains.

Rand opened his eyes to the evils of sacrifice, as well as the omnipresence of government in Israel, where Brook now could see the heavy hand of the state "inhibiting freedom at every corner." He read as many of Rand's books as he could, and had his father pick up books on his trips abroad. "I had no sense that there was a movement, that there was anybody else reading these books except me," he said. It wasn't until 1980 that he connected with other Objectivists in Israel through a libertarian party, strongly influenced by Rand, that fielded candidates in the national elections. It didn't win even a single seat in the Knesset. The party lingered for a while but eventually was dissolved. Israel was not ready for Ayn Rand.

Brook was certainly ready, but at eighteen he was subjected to the usual Israeli revocation of freedom and was drafted into the Israel Defense Forces. He became a sergeant in military intelligence carrying out low-level tasks, such as analyzing targets in enemy territory. After discharge he trained in civil engineering at the Technion, the Israeli institute of technology, and then traveled to the United States in 1987 to attend graduate school. He began teaching finance. Wall Street beckoned, and in the late 1990s he and another college finance professor founded BH Equity Research, which serviced hedge funds but eventually morphed into a private equity fund, providing start-up capital for companies.

Brook was involved in the Objectivist movement from almost the moment he stepped off the plane in the United States. He attended a two-week

Objectivist conference while he was enrolled at the University of Texas. That put him in touch with Michael Berliner, a cofounder of the ARI; the other cofounder Leonard Peikoff; and various Randian luminaries. In Austin he became involved with local Objectivists, and joined with a few Texans in founding a local Rand group. He ticked off for me a flurry of seminars and conferences that he organized over the next few years, including an Objectivist Greek Island Cruise ("on a crummy little boat"). That built up his credibility in the Objectivist movement, so in the summer of 1999, when Berliner retired, Brook was offered the job of running the ARI. He didn't start until the following year. He kept his job at BH Equity, though he told me that he doesn't work more than ten hours a week at that firm, along with "sixty for the Institute." That sounds true enough if one were to judge by his media appearances and lectures, which are frequent.

Brook's most notable achievement, at least from the standpoint of right-wing politics, has been his reconciliation with libertarians. The official Objectivist position on libertarians has gone from total shunning to a kind of genial collegiality over the years. So it seems from the outside. As Brook sees it, the Objectivist position hasn't changed at all. "Libertarianism has changed," he said. "I suspect—and I wasn't here, I wasn't aware in the 1980s—Murray Rothbard was still alive, and it was a much more cohesive, at least its intellectuals were much more vocal and cohesive, much more anarchy based, much more anti-American." Libertarians, he said, have splintered and become more diverse, so "it's not a movement anymore." The Objectivist attitude toward the Libertarian Party hasn't changed. "We want nothing to do with them," he said.

Objectivists still abhor a faction in the libertarian movement that has adopted positions that Brook described as "anti-U.S." He said, "You saw that after 9/11, very strongly." He described the latter as being "primarily concentrated in the von Mises Institute, which should be called the 'Murray Rothbard Institute,' because von Mises was not an anarchist, not an anti-American." There is no love lost between Randians and the late Murray

Rothbard, a libertarian economist who was briefly in the Rand circle but departed acrimoniously. He was the author of a 1972 article that eloquently made the case that the Rand movement was a cult.[2]

Brook differentiated the aforementioned rascals from a "more mainstream, limited government, what I would view as a classical liberal wing of the libertarian movement"—classical liberal in the sense of the free-market thinkers of the nineteenth century. "So I do think there is a more respectable, if you will, more mainstream, non-anarchist element" in the libertarian movement. "Our attitude toward them is definitely as potential fellow travelers."

That attitude of good fellowship does not apply to the leading libertarian figure in the United States, serial presidential candidate Ron Paul. The Texas congressman, who ran for president on the Libertarian Party ticket in 1988, has said that he "read all her novels and received her objectivist newsletter essentially the whole time it was published"—which would put him in the ranks of Rand's followers as far back as the early 1960s. Paul acknowledges Rand's influence on his thinking in his book *End the Fed*, but also says he never contemplated becoming an Objectivist. In the Webster–Rand conflict that I mentioned earlier, he chose the dictionary: "She never convinced me of her definition and application of altruism."[3]

Brook didn't mince words about anyone, least of all this guy. "I don't think very highly of Ron Paul," he said. Brook described Paul's foreign policy views as "almost instinctual anti-Americanism." During the 2008 campaign, Paul said that American foreign policy contributed to the September 11 attacks, and once wrote that "the real reasons [for the attacks] are either denied or ignored: oil, neo-conservative empire building, and our support for Israel over the Palestinians."[4]

"I also suspect that deep down he's an anarchist, though I can't prove that," Brook said. He wasn't thrilled about Paul's embrace of religion, either. He felt that Paul didn't really believe in the separation of church and state. "His position on abortion"—Paul was opposed—"is one we wouldn't agree with," he said. So in general, "I just honestly don't find him a very credible personality."

Religion also influenced Brook's profoundly mixed view of Glenn Beck, whose Fox show he graced on a number of occasions: "He's just way too religious for my taste, and he's bringing in religion into his advocacy way, way too much, and it's increasing, and it's getting more and more aggressive, and that worries me a lot with Glenn. I also think that this taints his ability to understand key concepts that are crucial for the fight for freedom, like individual rights and the morality of self-interest. I don't think he gets those, because I think his views are tainted by religion." The chapter on individual rights in one of his latest books, he said, is "awful. He can't get away from the idea of religion. It's filled with God everywhere."

He didn't think very highly of Sarah Palin: "I think Sarah's terrible. I think she's a populist, her political ideas are mostly mindless, she repeats ideas she hears from others. Generally I don't think she's very intelligent. She was right on the bandwagon attacking big business and big oil and big drugs and Wall Street when that was popular and she thought she could get political advancement through that, and she's defending Wall Street when she thinks that works. So I have almost no respect for Sarah Palin." He didn't think much of her prospects in 2012: "I don't think she'll run, and I think if she does she'll be wiped out."

In fact, he didn't care for any of the Republican presidential hopefuls. "I think it's going to be dull," he said. "I think the Republicans are going to shoot themselves in the foot. They're not going to have an interesting candidate. I think it's going to be pretty boring." He wanted to see someone in the race more in the mold of Mitch Daniels, the governor of Indiana who emerged in 2011 as a possible contender from the GOP right wing. Daniels was known for his aversion to social issues diverting from the task of slashing government programs, an attitude that would seem to naturally attract Randians. Brook wanted to see a candidate willing to "put religion and social issues to the side, and really focus on more fundamental economic and political issues." The problem is that "Mitch Daniels has no charisma, and my sense is they're advising him now not to run."*

Mitt Romney? "He's awful. He brought Obamacare to Massachusetts. That's a killer in my view. How can you run for the Republican nomination, which is anti-Obamacare, when you're responsible for it?"

Brook had similar concerns about Rand Paul as with his father, except that he wasn't sure about his views on foreign policy, which he thought might be a little bit better than his father's. He was aghast at Rand Paul's anti-abortion posturing. "I worry about his religiosity and the extent to which he'd let that interfere with governing," he said. "On the other hand, he's the only guy in Congress who has the guts to stand up and say, 'This is a joke what the Republicans are proposing to cut. We should cut half a trillion dollars, and here's how.'" Brook wasn't upset about Paul backing off from his opposition to the 1964 civil rights act. "He's a politician," he said blandly.

Brook felt that the Tea Party movement still hadn't quite gotten its act together. In fact, he didn't really view it as a movement, as the Tea Party was plagued by infighting and didn't have a unifying theme. "People are still testing out different things," he said. "Why they're fighting, I don't know." He did have a positive view of the Tea Party as "a group of Americans who stood up and said, 'Enough is enough. Government has gotten too big.' Imagine if that wouldn't have happened. That would have been very very depressing. It's testament to what Ayn Rand called the 'American sense of life' is still well, still exists, that Americans will only tolerate government up to a certain level of intervention in their lives."

What they lack, he said, returning to the theme he raised at the St. Regis, "is an intellectual foundation for what they believe. They don't have

* Brook's instincts were correct. In May 2011, Daniels decided not to run. Palin made the same decision in October.

one. They're searching for it, but they don't have one. And of course the danger is that they get that intellectual foundation from people like Glenn Beck and the religious right. I would like them to get that intellectual foundation from Ayn Rand."

"It's a battle," he said. "We have very limited resources compared to the religious right. But we're doing what we can to try to infuse the Tea Party movement with as good ideas as possible."

So he's out on the hustings, speaking frequently before Tea Party groups, and gave three talks at the 2011 Tea Party Summit in Phoenix. That included one address to all 1,800 delegates, and two breakout sessions on *Atlas Shrugged* to 200 people at each. "And at all the sessions," he said, "I got a standing ovation."

Brook briefly met with Mark Meckler at a Tea Party convention not long after my interview with Meckler. He was aware of Meckler's religious qualms, and that they were shared by many Tea Partiers. They didn't bother him in the least. "My view is whatever Ayn Rand they absorb into their system, the world is a better place for that. If they absorbed all of it, it would be much better. But if they absorbed some of it, we're that much better than if they absorbed none of it." So even though the ARI's Objectivism may be "closed," as David Kelley would put it, that was immaterial as far as outside alliances were concerned. Tea Party people, libertarians, and other useful fellow travelers were definitely part of the ARI network of allies.

But there were limits to Objectivist ecumenism. Brook put the final nail in the coffin of the possibility of the ARI and Atlas Society joining forces to make war against the evil forces of collectivism and selflessness. "I don't like the Atlas Society," he said. "If they called themselves something different I wouldn't care. But they call themselves Objectivists—'Open Objectivists.' The only reason to do that is to assume that we're 'Closed Objectivists,' and to paint us into a corner that's not real." He said that the group's whole claim to fame is "not being us" and has been "disrespectful to Ayn Rand." He went on like that a bit, warming to the subject. "A lot of people have called them 'Objectivist Lite.' If you read them they're kind of soft and wooshy. They don't take a strong position on things that strong positions should be taken on."

But the Atlas Society had an asset that the ARI did not, which was the movie version of *Atlas Shrugged*, in which Kelley served as a consultant and was produced by Atlas Society board member John Aglialoro. While greeted ecstatically by the far right, it was a box office bomb which opened to one of the most unanimously negative critical receptions since *Plan 9 from Outer Space*. The picture had been in development hell for decades. At one point Albert Ruddy, producer of *The Godfather*, had an interest in it. But that collapsed when Rand insisted on creative control. So it languished for years and what resulted was an independent production with a no-star cast and direct-to-video production values. The film was extensively marketed in Tea Party circles and had a strong opening weekend, but afterward its box office receipts plummeted. It was one of the few Rand-worshiping commercial ventures to fall flat on its face. Nevertheless, a second installment of the film was slated for 2012.

Brook said he thought the movie was "OK. I don't think it's great," which was far more generous than the critical consensus. The real test, he said, was whether the movie would get more people to read the book. Brook said he had just been interviewed by a reporter for the *Los Angeles Times* on the movie. He asked her if, having seen the movie, she was more or less likely to read the book. "She said 'less,'" Brook said. "The movie flattens the story, it dulls it." I had to agree with that. The movie was boring and static, with the only action consisting of people occasionally raising their voices. But it was successful in the sense that sales of the book spiked after the film's premiere—which benefited not the Atlas Society but Rand's heir, David Kelley's bitter enemy Leonard Peikoff. The two groups were briefly united in this odd way by the film, but it was such a flop that it didn't really matter.

Brook turned out to be more relaxed and forthcoming, less defensive about Objectivism, than Kelley. He was coy about the disposition of the rights to Ayn Rand's works after Peikoff's demise, though I got the impression that they are likely to stay within the ARI family. That was his only moment of evasiveness. Otherwise I was impressed with his candor, so I expected, and received, a forthright answer when I asked him about the Objectivist endgame. Was this to be an endless, never-ending quest for the unimaginable—an Objectivist nirvana that will never come to pass?

"I think in fifteen years, Ayn Rand will be everywhere," he said. "She'll be taught, her standards, in many universities. She'll be in a significant proportion of high school English classes. Her ideas will be debated on television, in classrooms, and in the public forums. It will be hard to escape, not so much her, but her ideas.

"Fifty years from now, I think Objectivism will be viewed as the primary challenge to whatever the status quo is.

"A hundred years from now, I think Objectivism will be the dominant secular philosophy in the United States."

Brook likes to think that way, taking the long view. The Ayn Rand endgame is much like the Tea Party forty-year plan, only more ambitious. "It's a hundred to hundred-twenty-year-long struggle that we will win," he said, "if civilization doesn't buckle, which is a real possibility. This country's bankrupt. The West, the whole West is bankrupt." He defined it as a "monetary, moral, cultural, philosophical bankruptcy.

"It's just a question of time."

CHAPTER SEVENTEEN

The Vision

Yaron Brook is a realist. He's not a dreamer. When this man draws up a timetable, you can set your watch to it. His Rand timetable is realistic because the Republican Party has become more the party of Ayn Rand than the party of Teddy Roosevelt or Abraham Lincoln. It's realistic because Rand's philosophy appeals not just to the complacent rich but to the Tea Party masses as well as a significant segment of the right-wing and libertarian-leaning intelligentsia and political establishment.

It's realistic because not everything that Rand advocates is the work of the Devil. Her embrace of rational self-interest, if stripped of its extremism and overstatements, meshes well with the currents in modern psychobabble that advocate people standing up for themselves at work and at home. Her idealization of the individual is over the top, but appeals to the celebration of individualism that is engrained in American popular culture. Her ideal of the noble, suffering creator is appealing not because Rand is a sorcerer, but because what she writes often conveys truths and is not invariably destructive or mean-spirited.

The millions of Americans drawn to *Atlas Shrugged* and *The Fountainhead* see in her works an expression of their own deeply held feelings and beliefs. Her books appeal to the best instincts of Americans, as well as some of the worst. Reading Rand's books again recently, even as I was put off by her dogma, made me feel better about myself. I regret not having read *Fountainhead* more carefully when I was a kid. That book and perhaps *Atlas* might have changed my life for the better, and might have given me greater confidence to identify and pursue my own self-interests over the years. It certainly would have made it possible for me to identify Randian traits in others, and made their behavior more understandable. But I'd have had to read her books selectively, with discernment. If not, I might have turned into one of the selfish, cold, money-grubbing nightmares I've written about over the years. I'll never know.

One might say that Objectivism's individual parts are considerably more useful, and certainly less amoral, than they are when taken in the aggregate, as Objectivism. *The Fountainhead* and *Atlas Shrugged* are beguiling as they conflate self-esteem with self-indulgence, enlightened self-interest with selfishness, discarding the ethical concepts that make life bearable. They make it seem so natural, so easy, so *moral*, to be utterly self-centered and greedy. Our most fundamental religious teachings—*out*. Service to the nation—*out*. Aid to the poor and elderly, whether they are "worthy" or not—*out*. Selflessness—*out*. Altruism—*out*. By any reasonable ethical standard—in other words, any standard other than one enunciated by Rand herself—taken as a whole these are staggeringly immoral books, presenting an ideology that appeals to American values but is simply not American. Yet now they are taught in our schools, force-fed to willing and unwilling kids who might benefit—or be corrupted—by Rand's vision.

For those of us who refuse to accept Randian morality, how do we deal with this mixed picture of Objectivism? Do we continue the practice of her critics since the 1940s and chuck out all of her works? Is that the best way to counter a set of beliefs that is clearly gaining ground, to the point that Brook's prediction of Objectivism conquering America makes logical sense? Is there another way?

In my research it became apparent Ayn Rand had to be engaged. Ignoring her was not working. Every day came new evidence that she was winning. By the start of the presidential campaign in 2011 it was evident that no matter who the Republican Party nominated, the successful candidate would toe the Tea Party line, which in its essence was the Rand line. With Obama vulnerable, Brook's prediction was making greater sense with every passing day. We were moving closer to that inevitable endgame. It was a war for America's soul, one that only the Objectivists seemed to recognize and demonstrate a willingness to fight.

It was a grand drama as one might have seen in the movie palaces of old. For convinced Randians, today's America is an early version of the socialist nightmare world of George Orwell's *1984*. But to people who had no such worldview, the consequences for America of an Ayn Rand victory brought to mind the dystopian hell of *Metropolis*, Fritz Lang's 1927 film, with dull-eyed masses slaving away in the underworld to support the privileged classes.

A battle of that magnitude required a great leader. We had no great leader, so I reached out to the next best thing: a great movie director.

Oliver Stone met me at a noisy café in Greenwich Village. "Your favorite place?" he asked me congenially. It wasn't. His office asked me to arrange a meeting near his last appointment at 14th Street and Fifth Avenue, but I couldn't think of any more discreet place to meet a recognizable person in the vicinity. The Subway takeout on 14th Street was quieter, but it seemed a bit too shabby, a bit too cloak-and-dagger. Arranging this rendezvous already gave a conspiratorial character to our meeting, reminding me a little of the encounter between Jim Garrison and "X" in *JFK*.

I was enthralled by *JFK* when I first saw it in 1991, and my fascination continued in subsequent viewings. I am a firm nonbeliever in Kennedy assassination conspiracy theories, and knew that the film's plotline was woven out of thin air. Yet I was willing to accept, for the three hours of its runtime, that black was white, a faker and a con man was a hero, and even that Newman from *Seinfeld* could be an investigator. I was similarly willing to go against my better judgment, suspend disbelief, and enjoy both *Atlas Shrugged* and *The Fountainhead* when I reread those two massive books. Ayn Rand was a hell of a storyteller, and so was Oliver Stone.

Over the years, reports had surfaced that Stone was tackling a remake of *The Fountainhead*. Rights to the film resided with Warner Bros., which purchased them from Rand not long after its publication in 1943. The 1949 version had a modest commercial success, but was artistically notable only as the first major film to star Patricia Neal (and perhaps secondarily because of her on-screen chemistry with Gary Cooper that extended to an offscreen affair). Cooper received mixed reviews as Howard Roark, and yet it wasn't clear that anyone could have coped with the script that Rand had written, replete with a six-minute courtroom speech that she refused to cut.

King Vidor's direction was lifeless. He seemed to be going through the motions. This was the director of the populist classic *Our Daily Bread* (1934), the story of an agricultural commune in the Great Depression. Vidor put his heart and soul in that film, which stood for the values of altruism, collectivism, and self-sacrifice that Rand opposed. In one scene, an escaped convict gives himself up so that the reward money can go to the commune. That kind of self-sacrifice, so contrary to Rand's values, permeates *Our Daily Bread*. But I guess King Vidor had to make a living like everybody else, so he filmed *The Fountainhead*.

I thought that *The Fountainhead* would be an equally poor fit for Stone. He was avowedly left wing in his views, and I couldn't see him working up much enthusiasm for anything written by Rand. The feeling was mutual from the Rand side. Leonard Peikoff called Stone's 1987 film *Wall Street* one of the "obviously left-wing movies" that were "the product of avowed radicals and business haters."[1] Yet there were reports as recently as 2006 that Stone was hard at work on a *Fountainhead* remake, with Brad Pitt in line for the Roark role.[2] The studio system was no more; Stone had his own production company and could work on any project he desired. Why *The Fountainhead*?

Stone seemed a bit fatigued from his earlier appointments, and ordered black coffee. He asked who my publisher was. "So you're not doing one of those worship jobs?" he asked. He seemed relieved by my answer. And mind you, this was a man who had spent years working on a Rand movie.

His involvement with *The Fountainhead* had begun in the 1990s. Since many of his projects don't pan out, just as this one didn't, he never announces projects at such an early stage. But word leaked out. He was hazy on the dates, but he was certain about this much: The rights were no longer in the hands of Rand's heirs, because "I wouldn't have gone into it if the rights weren't available." And I imagine that Peikoff would have eaten mud rather than let the "business hater" Oliver Stone get his hands on *Fountainhead*.

Stone liked Ayn Rand's screenplay. "The script was good," he said. "The script was interesting." The book was immense, and "Ayn Rand had done a great job of cutting through with clarity to what she wanted to say." But he didn't think it came out very well on film. "King Vidor did an interesting job but it's curiously wooden. Gary Cooper is a wonderful actor but he also could be curiously wooden. So sometimes you don't feel the humanity of the man. I think Patricia Neal brings a certain amount of emotion and spiritual warmth, but there's something wooden about the movie. I think it's stiff; it doesn't seem real."

I had difficulty seeing it any other way. The Howard Roark character is an automaton, cold as a mortician's slab, utterly selfish, almost impossible to like, and devoid of humanity. The sadistic and cold-hearted Dominique Francon is so repulsive that she almost seems like a character from a horror movie. Yet Stone saw something in these characters that I, and probably most people, was unable to discern.

He acknowledged the novel's flaws. "People make speeches," he continued. "That's a criticism of Ayn Rand. It's true about the book, certainly.

It's lucid and cogent but people do make speeches." But that was no obstacle. He had a vision for this film.

When he first read her novels he saw some of Roark's characteristics in himself. "I identified. I was a struggling screenwriter. I wanted to be a great filmmaker. I had a hard time," he recalled. For a while our talk reminded me of the interviews I'd had with die-hard Ayn Randers. "Fascinating book," he said of *The Fountainhead,* "I read it as a young man, reread it. I thought it was a great book." He liked *Atlas Shrugged,* too. He described it as "weird, sci-fi—like a Philip Dick story." But the underlying ideology, the endorsement of laissez-faire capitalism, never yanked his chain. It's interesting to speculate how much closer we would be to Rand's vision of heaven if Stone had warmed a bit more to *Atlas,* and used his creative energies to churn out movies with Objectivist themes. The mind boggles, in fact. Such is fate or, perhaps, the intervention of a merciful Deity, that Oliver Stone never put his gifts at the disposal of Leonard Peikoff.

"I'm not wedded to a political philosophy, compared to what you'd think," he said, sipping his black coffee. "I'm a dramatist, first of all. As a citizen I speak out. I say some things that are progressive I think. But as a dramatist, I look at things without politics, because it wouldn't make for a good screenplay. Whether you're talking about George Bush or Richard Nixon, I didn't set out to attack either one. I let them try to speak for themselves."

People are sometimes surprised, he said, and think that he was too sympathetic to Bush or Nixon in his films about them, and the reason is that "often the side of me that's political, that's a private citizen, is confused with the dramatist." He had a point. *World Trade Center* surprised a lot of people by not taking a conspiratorial view of the September 11 attacks. But that film was a straightforward, largely true account. It was not an adaptation of one of the most controversial and deeply political novels of our age.

Stone had a nuanced view of Rand, one that carefully separated Rand the author from Rand the philosopher, much as one would pick out pieces of herring from between the bones. He admired Rand as a person. "It's her mind that I enjoy," he said. "The size of her mind and her outspokenness and her strength of opinion. She's not a novelist as much as she is an essayist disguised as a novelist." A lot of novels, he said, are so ambivalent that they lose focus. "So much of literature washes away, and Ayn Rand does remain, and those thoughts are tremendously popular because they said something."

The problem from an artistic standpoint was that Rand was just too political. It overwhelmed her books.

"She hates Communism, Russia with a passion. She hates totalitarianism," and rightly so, he said. "She hated it the same way we hate to be told what to do by the state. And in that regard I understand her passion about Russia, but of course, it being a passion she carries it too far.

"She equates things in America as if it were a Stalinist decision in her time," he said. "Everything becomes Stalinist in her book."

It was a perceptive observation, and it articulated a feeling that had been germinating in me since I began rereading her books. It seemed that everything she said about government was aimed not at the reality of America but the Russia that she left in 1926. What appears to others as anti-empiricism was, to her mind, reality—the reality of the totalitarian, half-starved, brutal Russia she knew.

It was the Russia of her childhood, the Russia of privation and oppression—and not the United States of her era or ours—in which government could be described as a "gun"; one that could be spiked without causing harm. Indeed, Eastern Europeans gladly overthrew their Communist governments when they wearied of them strangling their freedom. Her acolytes, not fully comprehending the nature of her dogma, blithely accepted her vision of an American Gulag archipelago. Then they used it to rationalize another kind of oppression: the economic subjugation of the poor by large corporations. Only a narcissistic mogul or an escapee from postrevolutionary Russia could say that big business was a "persecuted minority" in this country, and mean it.

Stone, recognizing Rand's Stalinist preoccupation, focused on *The Fountainhead*'s story line. He saw it as a compelling story once it was divorced from Rand's opinions. "When I came to it I saw it as a strong story, great characters, but above all a way to say something about the new architecture that was brewing in the 1990s. There were whole new schools of architecture. So I wanted to make an architecture movie, essentially with drama, and I thought this was perfect," he said.

Rand aficionados (and many non-aficionados) have long rejected the notion that *The Fountainhead* was a novel about architecture, but rather view it as about individuality and integrity set in the world of architecture. *The New York Times Book Review,* in one of the few major reviews that was not negative, described it as a "long but absorbing story of man's enduring battle against evil."[3] One of the criticisms of the 1949 movie was that it was a film about architecture that featured poor-quality architecture. "Trash," *Times* critic Bosley Crowther said of the movie-Roark's buildings.[4]

But Stone didn't care about any of that (in fact, he rather liked the architecture in the 1949 film), so he set out to make his architecture movie. Being a glutton for research—he practically lived on Wall Street while preparing his *Wall Street* sequel—he spent long amounts of time with Frank Gehry, the Canadian-born architect who was at the height of a distinguished career.

"My idea," he said, "was to modernize the story and deal with it in a new way, get to the strength of her character, Howard Roark; strengthen his vision, the suffering he had to go through to make his impact, his unconventionality, his tremendous amount of spirit, and then he becomes successful and then he's destroyed again. And then he rises again.

"It's an amazing story," he said, "an up and down story. I think it's a great story of a man."

Stone was under no obligation to be faithful to the book, and that allowed him to cope with an obstacle that he encountered in working on the adaptation. "The problem I had with the book was that Howard Roark wants to build for reasons of profit," he said. That's like saying that the problem with *Moby-Dick* is that it's about a whale. Or at least it is if you accept the Randian interpretation of the book and its characters.

In the novel, Rand's "whole argument is that the nonprofit motive—altruism—is bad for society," he said. That was understandable, he felt, if one's view of altruism was forged while living in a Communist country, where altruism is used as an excuse for tyranny. He went behind the Iron Curtain years ago to research a movie about dissidents and "saw some of the worst behavior of those regimes." He interviewed twenty dissidents who had been in prisons and mental hospitals, so he understood where Rand was coming from and her deep-rooted hatred of anything that smacked of Communism. "When you leave that country," he said, "you carry that anger with you." Stone saw that same anger in Rand's works, just as he saw it in those dissidents and Cuban exiles.

"I can understand the passion, but it does require one to transcend, to go beyond, to transform oneself, to be above the bitterness and the anger," he said.

Stone told me that some of his early films dealt with that same theme: *Born on the Fourth of July, Platoon,* and *Heaven and Earth.* "The hero or heroine suffers greatly and has to rise above that suffering and not be devoured by the bitterness. But with Ayn Rand I never felt that she was able to overcome bitterness," he said. He's found that to be true among others on the right. There's always some "early hurt, betrayal, whether it was the Communist movement of the thirties, that allows them to practice hatred and bitterness the rest of their lives." In the case of Rand, he said, "It can be argued that despite her brilliance there's a lack of warmth and humanity in her posture, the way she's perceived, and in her writing."

Yet Rand did put forward a view of individuality as a heroic ideal that appealed to him. "She glommed on to that and she uses it well," he said.

"You can like that part of her without going into the other stuff." Stone planned to detach the Roark character from the dialogue Rand stuffed in his mouth. He didn't view that as Roark talking, but the grand old lady of radical capitalism hijacking his voice box.

"See, Roark may talk all that shit but that's her talk. It's what he does—he builds, and he suffers for his building. That's an artist, whatever it is. Doesn't matter whether it's Picasso, Wagner, or Beethoven. He is that. That's why I like him," he said. "If he stands there and talks about the virtue of selfishness, that's not a character to me."

Stone spent considerable time on the project, writing a draft of his own and hiring two writers to work on the screenplay. Meanwhile, he noticed "a lot of shit on the Internet that I was going to fuck it up because I was a liberal, because I was a left-wing conspiracy nut, blah blah blah." But why, I asked him, would he care about what people say about him on the Internet? "There is such a thing as the perception of a movie. It can kill a movie before it comes out," he responded. "Perception is an important part of this game." He likened it to the negative reaction that greeted his plans to make a film about Martin Luther King, though the King film never quite got to the same stage.

The bad buzz wasn't enough to abort the *Fountainhead* project, which otherwise was moving along fairly well. He was getting "hard information from Frank Gehry on how to build differently," which he was going to deploy in the movie. "His materials, how he was doing it, and how he could build at cost. How you can make things cheaper," he said, a bit wistfully. All kinds of new alloys were coming on the market at the time. "This was all new. You could build buildings that were no longer straight. They could bend. And they could be done at a price," he said. "However, as I was getting this story together it was ironic. Events overtook me."

A plethora of new architects was coming on the scene that were doing dramatically different things. "The theory of a Howard Roark standing out in society no longer was valid," he said. Not with Rem Koolhaas and other architects vying with Gehry, similarly challenging the status quo in architecture. "They were all Howard Roarks, you see," he said. So that was that. The project was shelved, but not before attracting the attention of Brad Pitt, who was interested in playing Roark. "He's an architecture buff," Stone pointed out.

As he described it, the Oliver Stone adaptation of *The Fountainhead* would have extracted the essence of the Roark character without the Randian baggage, and brought the story into the real world of contemporary architecture. It would have been a far cry from the listless *Atlas Shrugged* adaptation that briefly slogged through theaters in the spring of 2011, weighed down by Objectivist ideology and bereft of production values or compelling characterizations.

What made it a true misfortune was the next thing that Stone told me: He was going to give Roark a transfusion of humanity.

"My bigger story, my bigger issue, and this would have been the one I would have crossed the Rubicon for, was that because people were building for profit in the eighties and the nineties, there was a significant amount of development, selfishness, and we saw the greed era described in *Wall Street*. I went the other way," he said. "I was having Howard Roark building for social purposes. I was having him building for communities. I wanted him to do parks, I wanted him to build schools, playgrounds. The concept and the theme I was developing was that he was building for the social good."

The Rand people would have had kittens, I pointed out to him. Sure, he said. "They'd have hated it, but if she had been alive and vibrant and free in her thinking, she would have realized that the state could still play a significant role in bettering the community. I think that if Rand had lived, she would have seen the excesses of Milton Friedman, and the excesses of Greenspan, and what they did to our economy. I don't think she would have liked what she saw, and I think, because she was a passionate woman, she may well have gone back, and said we need to have a coordinated policy by the government, city government, state and federal government, to build buildings in a beautiful way."

I felt that he was dead wrong on that point, but it didn't really matter, as movies are about suspension of disbelief. Listening to Stone I felt as if the movie was playing right in front of me.

"The WPA [the 1930s public works program]," he said "built some of the most astonishing, best built buildings of the thirties, and that was because of you know who—federal programs. So the idea of the movie was to keep the individualism of this guy, the Frank Gehry quality, turn it on its head and make him do good things. Instead of the ugly fucking housing developments that we have that are hideous and diminish life, what if Howard Roark built a huge housing project that could house six thousand people in a way that allowed them freedom and air and beauty?"

That was the idea—"To flip *Fountainhead* the other way."

Stone was going to get all the top architects of the world to contribute to his grand remake of *The Fountainhead.* And as he told me about it, I recognized why it fascinated him then, and obviously continued to enthrall him years later. He was going to be Howard Roark; the movie character was going to reflect his vision of public service. "I was going to build a city for the public good," he said. "That was the idea for the movie." His Howard Roark would have been *un*selfish. "He has to build, that's the character. He sees the selfishness of all these architects making fortunes, and there's a lot of them. But because he knows how to build an apartment well, he can do it at a cost saving of fifty dollars a foot"—and that's his preoccupation, because he is a builder, not a capitalist. (And that part of it would have been consistent with the novel because, as I mentioned earlier, Roark did not like money.)

Rand would have hated all of this, I pointed out.

"I don't care if she'd have ate her hat," Stone replied. The Rand people would have had no right to alter the script. They'd have protested, but what of it? Roark would not have allowed interference, and neither would Stone. He would have imposed his vision on *The Fountainhead*, replacing selfishness with selflessness, radical capitalism with humanity, and underlined the need for government at a time when government is under attack. It's an alluring vision, one that becomes more and more remote as Rand's ideas spread across the nation.

"We need the state," Stone said. "We need the community. We desperately need it."

EPILOGUE

> The whole damned history of the world is a story of the struggle between the selfish and the unselfish! . . . All the bad around us is bred by selfishness. Sometimes selfishness even gets to be a cause, an organized force, even a government. Then it's called Fascism.
>
> —Garson Kanin, *Born Yesterday*

There is no real doubt what an Objectivist America would mean. We may not be around to see it, but it's likely we'll be here for its earliest manifestations. They may have already arrived.

The shape of a future Objectivist world has been a matter of public record for the past half century, since Ayn Rand, the Brandens, Alan Greenspan, and other Objectivist theoreticians began to set down their views in Objectivist newsletters. When he casually defended repeal of child labor laws in the debate with Miles Rapoport, Brook was merely repeating long-established Objectivist doctrine, summarized by Leonard Peikoff as "Government is inherently negative."[1] It is a worldview that has been static through the decades, its tenets reiterated endlessly by Rand and her apostles:

No government except the police, courts of law, and the armed services.

No regulation of anything by any government.

No Medicare or Medicaid.

No Social Security.

No public schools.

No public hospitals.

No public anything, in fact. Just individuals, each looking out for himself, not asking for help or giving help to anyone.

An Objectivist America would be a dark age of unhindered free enterprise, far more primitive and Darwinian than anything seen before. Objectivists know this. What perhaps they do not always appreciate, given their less than fanatical approach to reality, is what turning back the clock would mean. Or perhaps they do not care.

When Alan Greenspan spoke out against building codes, he knew perfectly well what a lack of adequate building and fire codes would mean. Fifteen years before his birth, 146 people, mostly young women, were burned alive or leaped to their death from the fire at the Triangle Waist Factory just east of Washington Square Park in New York City. There was no requirement for employers to provide a safe workplace, so none was provided. Triangle's owners crammed their employees into crowded workspaces without proper exits, and inadequate fire codes meant that the fire stairways were insufficient. The result was that dozens of workers' corpses piled on the sidewalk on March 25, 1911. Anywhere in the world where building codes are inadequate or absent, the result is always the same: Dead people.

In an Objectivist world, the reset button would be pushed on government services that we take for granted. They would not be cut back, not reduced—they would vanish. In an Objectivist world, roads would go unplowed in the snows of winter, and bridges would fall as the government withdrew from the business of maintaining them—unless some private citizen would find it in his rational self-interest to voluntarily take up the slack by scraping off the rust and replacing frayed cables. Public parks and land, from the tiniest vest-pocket patch of green to vast expanses of the West, would be sold off to the newly liberated megacorporations. Airplane traffic would be grounded unless a profit-making capitalist found it in his own selfish interests to fund the air traffic control system. If it could be made profitable, fine. If not, tough luck. The market had spoken. The Coast Guard would stay in port while storm-tossed mariners drown lustily as they did in days of yore. Fires would rage in the remnants of silent forests, vegetation and wildlife no longer protected by rangers and coercive environmental laws, swept clean of timber, their streams polluted in a rational, self-interested manner by bold, imaginative entrepreneurs.

With industry no longer restrained by carbon-emission standards, the earth would bake in self-generated heat, ice-cap melting would accelerate, extreme weather would become even more commonplace, and seacoasts would sink beneath the waves. Communities ravaged by hurricanes, floods and tornadoes would be left to fend for themselves, no longer burdening the conscience of a selfish, guilt-free world.

The poor and elderly, freed from dependence on character-destroying, government-subsidized medical care, would die as bravely and in as generous quantities as in the romantic novels of a bygone era.

Minimum wage laws would come to an end, providing factory owners and high-tech start-ups alike with a pool of cheap labor competitive with any fourth-world kleptocracy.

All laws protecting consumers would be erased from the statute books.

Mass transit would grind to a halt in the big cities as municipal subsidies come to an end.

Corporations would no longer be enslaved by antitrust laws, so monopolies and globe-spanning, price-fixing cartels would flourish. The number of publicly held corporations would be reduced to a manageable, noncompetitive few. Big Pharma would manufacture drugs without adequate testing for safety and efficacy—deterred only by concern for their reputation, as described by Greenspan in 1963. Except that with competition reduced by mergers and legal price-fixing, the market would be a feeble substitute for even the FDA.

Securities laws and stock market regulations would be eliminated. Corporations would operate in secret if they so desired, or with only selective, cursory disclosures to their investors and customers. Only outright fraud would be prosecuted; otherwise the public—a concept no longer recognized as valid—would be on its own.

Insider trading, now legal, would become the norm. Wall Street now would truly be a sucker's game. "Let the buyer beware" would replace the fifty state regulators and the SEC.

Income taxes would end, so the lowest-paid, ten-cent-an-hour, non-OSHA-supervised factory workers would enjoy wages taxed at the same rate—zero—as their billionaire bosses in distant cities and foreign lands. Dynasties of American royalty would arise, as fortunes pass from generation to generation, untaxed.

Nonprofit organizations, apart from those serving the egos and social calendars of the self-indulging rich, would see their funding dry up as government support vanished. The super-wealthy, having repudiated their "giving pledge," would now enjoy their riches without guilt, no longer motivated to share their billions with the poor. Philanthropy would be an obsolete relic of discarded moral codes and forgotten history.

Such is the Ayn Rand vision of paradise: an America that would resemble the lands from which our ancestors emigrated, altruism confined to ignored, fringe texts, grinding poverty and starvation coexisting alongside the opulence of the wealthy. Los Angeles, Chicago, and New York would become like Cairo and Calcutta, with walled enclaves protecting the wealthy from the malnourished, uneducated masses outside.

Yaron Brook was right. What's at stake is not a political issue, but a moral, philosophical issue. In large numbers, Americans have, sometimes unwittingly, abandoned the moral code upon which they were raised. They have done so because of a master storyteller.

Ayn Rand's stories of noble steel barons, fierce railroad magnates and sniveling government bureaucrats formed the basis of her ideology. It is a compelling narrative, and Oliver Stone's abortive approach to *The Fountainhead* suggests a remedy to the Rand narrative: a counternarrative—one that celebrates a creator with a conscience; government not as a Soviet gun but as a builder, a benefactor. It is an optimistic vision, born in an America of hope and not a Russia of despair and privation. This counternarrative can recognize the merit of individuality and self-interest, while rejecting her celebration of the darker impulses—greed and selfishness.

That kind of thinking is required to meet the challenge presented by Rand and her ideas, as they spread from libertarian and Objectivist think tanks to the Tea Party to Congress and, perhaps, the White House.

Those of us who oppose Rand's vision of radical capitalism need to read Rand and understand the flaws in her assumptions and illogic of her vision, just as people during the Cold War studied Communism so as to more effectively oppose it. Having read and understood her books and essays, one is in a better position to identify and then to respond to the right's extremist agenda, and to recognize her ideology when it becomes manifest in society.

We need to understand the basis of her morality, not just its origins but where it doesn't originate—the three great monotheistic religions, the Declaration of Independence, the Constitution, and the other writings and actions of the Founding Fathers. The words "capitalism," "markets," and "free enterprise" appear in none of the founding documents of America. The natural enemies of Ayn Rand are not only Lenin and Roosevelt but Jefferson, Rousseau, and Paine. The Founders were not defenders of oligarchy and selfishness. They sacrificed. They were altruists, and proud of it.

My Objectivist friends are right that morality needs to become part of the national dialogue. However we feel about Rand, we need to ponder her views and think more philosophically. We need to evaluate our own core values, and understand the moral foundations of the social programs and government agencies that are targeted by the right. *Why* do we pay for medical care of the poor and elderly? *Why* do we regulate business? *Why* do we pave roads and maintain parks and build public schools? *Why* do we subsidize public radio, mass transit, family planning clinics, and a host of other programs that don't always benefit ourselves?

We may conclude that we shouldn't do any of those things. Or we may conclude that we cherish those institutions and will sustain them, not because of the clout of special interest groups and the senior vote, not because we can do it if the Democrats control both houses of Congress, but because it's the right thing to do. It's right if we hold a different concept of right and wrong than Objectivists and their allies on the right. It's a question of fundamental moral values, as defined by our national and religious traditions—or by *Atlas Shrugged, The Fountainhead, The Virtue of Selfishness,* and *Capitalism: The Unknown Ideal.*

We need to choose—our heritage or Ayn Rand.

ACKNOWLEDGMENTS

This book originated as an exploration of the mindset that gave rise to the financial crisis of 2008. Over time I realized that all roads lead to Ayn Rand. The catalyst for *Ayn Rand Nation* was my agent at Janklow & Nesbit Associates, Richard Morris. Richard provided invaluable assistance in shaping this book at all stages, in addition to zealously protecting my commercial interests. It really couldn't have happened without him.

At St. Martin's Press, George Witte deserves special thanks for his enthusiasm, editorial wisdom, and keen blue pencil. I also appreciate the good work of Terra Layton at St. Martin's, and Michael K. Cantwell, who vetted the manuscript from a legal perspective. Copy editor Su Wu elegantly corrected my syntax.

My thanks go to all of the people who helped me try to make sense of Ayn Rand's world, past and present. Some are too shy to be thanked by name. They know who they are.

I'm grateful to the members of the New York Ayn Rand Group for taking me under their wing for a few months, heedless of my annoying note-taking, and for their candor and perceptiveness.

Iris Bell, who was Rand's graphic designer, was generous with her time, and I also want to thank her husband, Paul Bell, as well as Benny Pollak, Don Hauptman, Andy George, and the other members of the group for their hospitality. Frederick Cookinham, author of *The Age of Rand: Imagining an Objectivist Future World* (New York: IUniverse, 2005), capably (and literally) showed me the vestiges of Rand's world in New York City.

My thanks go to Richard Behar for very kindly sharing with me tapes of Ayn Rand radio broadcasts from the early 1960s, and to Michael Weiser, my old friend and classmate, for jogging my memory on capitalism as practiced in the Bronx in the 1960s.

I also wanted to single out the following people for their help: John Allison, Peter Boettke, Barbara Branden, Nathaniel Branden, Yaron Brook, Jim Brown, Peter Calandruccio. David Callahan, Barry Colvin, Dr. Robert Flanzer, Gail Flowers, Pamela Geller, Mark Herr, David Kelley, Eugene Kondratov, Kurt Kramer, Mark Meckler, Victor Niederhoffer, Susan Niederhoffer, Jimi Patterson, Lew Prince, Geoff Sayre-McCord, Sally Oljar, Mariella Schlossberg, Oliver Stone, William Thomas, Brad Thompson, and Vickie Towles. This is an alphabetical list, so the proximity of Nathaniel Branden to Yaron Brook is purely coincidental.

And, as always, my heart belongs to Anjali, who stood by me through thick, thin, and Rand.

NOTES

INTRODUCTION

1. Jennifer Burns, *Goddess of the Market: Ayn Rand and the American Right* (New York: Oxford University Press, 2009) and Anne C. Heller, *Ayn Rand and the World She Made* (New York: Nan A. Talese, 2009).
2. Ayn Rand, "Choose Your Issues," *The Objectivist Newsletter*, Vol. 1, No. 1, January 1962, (Irvine Calif: Second Renaissance, 1990), 1.
3. Whittaker Chambers, "Big Sister Is Watching You," *National Review*, December 28, 1957.
4. The *Washington Post* review is quoted in Heller, *Ayn Rand and the World She Made*, 282–83; see also Granville Hicks, "A Parable of Buried Talents," *New York Times Book Review*, October 13, 1957.
5. William F. O'Neill, *With Charity Toward None: An Analysis of Ayn Rand's Philosophy* (Totowa, NJ: Littlefield, Adams, 1972), 3.
6. J. Edgar Hoover letter to Ayn Rand dated January 13, 1966; "Morrell to Wick Memo," undated; Ayn Rand FBI File, provided to author via FOIPA Request No. 1154646-000.
7. Leonard Silk and David Vogel, *Ethics & Profits: The Crisis of Confidence in American Business* (New York: Simon & Schuster, 1976), 219.
8. Ayn Rand with Nathaniel Branden, Alan Greenspan, and Robert Hessen, *Capitalism: The Unknown Ideal* (New York: Signet, 1967), 236. Her denunciation of the Vietnam War can be found in another essay on p. 224.
9. See, e.g., Ayn Rand, "Have Gun, Will Nudge," *The Objectivist Newsletter*, Vol. 1, No. 3, March 1962, (Irvine, Calif: Second Renaissance, 1990) 9.
10. Heller, *Ayn Rand and the World She Made*, 128.
11. Albert Ellis, *Are Capitalism, Objectivism, & Libertarianism Religions? Yes!* (Santa Barbara, CA: Walden Three, 2006).
12. Lizzie Widdicombe, "Talk of the Town: 'Ayn Crowd,'" *New Yorker*, April 13, 2009, 24.
13. "The Ayn Rand Institute: Board Members," ARI Web site: "Board Co-Chair: Arline Mann is an attorney. She is Managing Director and Associate General Counsel of Goldman Sachs & Co.," http://www.aynrand.org/site/PageServer?pagename=staff_board.
14. "Sales of 'Atlas Shrugged' Soar in the Face of Economic Crisis," The Ayn Rand Center for Individual Rights, February 23, 2009, http://www.aynrand.org/site/News2?page=NewsArticle&id=22647.

15. Bennett Cerf, *At Random* (New York: Random House, 1977), 252–53; this was a reference to her essay "The Fascist New Frontier," which was a lecture delivered to the Ford Hall Forum in Boston in 1962. Its text can be found in Ayn Rand, *The Ayn Rand Column* (New Milford, CT: Second Renaissance Books, 1998), 95.
16. "Atlas Felt a Sense of Déjà Vu," *Economist,* February 26, 2009.
17. Santelli said: "I know this may not sound very humanitarian, but at the end of the day, I'm an Ayn Rander." CNBC appearance on February 19, 2009, about a minute into the segment, http://www.cnbc.com/id/15840232?video=1040027101.
18. David Frum, "The GOP's Forgotten History," FrumForum, March 24, 2010, http://www.frumforum.com/the-gops-forgotten-history.
19. Paul Rolly, "Mike Lee and the Big Tent Theory," *Salt Lake Tribune,* July 8, 2010.
20. Craig Gilbert, "Ryan Shines as GOP Seeks Vision," *Milwaukee Journal-Sentinel,* April 25, 2009.
21. Paul Ryan, "The Budget Debate We All Deserve," *Chicago Tribune,* May 16, 2011.
22. Jeff Walker *The Ayn Rand Cult,* (Chicago: Open Court, 1999).

ONE: THE BELIEVERS

1. Cerf, *At Random,* 250.
2. Ayn Rand *Atlas Shrugged* (New York: Plume, 1999), 133, 134.
3. Frederick Cookinham's Web site is http://www.indepthwalkingtours.com/. He is a knowledgeable and suave tour guide, and his tours are a useful introduction to Ayn Rand.
4. Frederick Cookinham, *The Age of Rand: Imagining an Objectivist Future World* (New York: IUniverse, 2005), 226, 227, 228–29. See also Michael S. Berliner (ed.), *Letters of Ayn Rand* (New York: Dutton, 1995), letter to Isabel Paterson, February 7, 1948, 192.
5. Fred takes issue with the ARI at several points in his book, *The Age of Rand,* 384.
6. Berliner, *Letters of Ayn Rand,* 443.
7. More on the old Jewish fraternal societies can be found in Michael R. Weisser's excellent study, *A Brotherhood of Memory: Jewish Landsmanshaftn in the New World* (Ithaca, NY: Cornell University Press, 1985).

TWO: THE PRE-OBJECTIVIST OBJECTIVIST

1. Burns, *Goddess of the Market,* 291–92.
2. Heller, *Ayn Rand and the World She Made,* 361. Interview with Iris Bell in Scott McConnell (ed.), *100 Voices: An Oral History of Ayn Rand* (New York: New American Library, 2010), 227–31.

THREE: THE WINNERS

1. Ayn Rand, *The Ayn Rand Column* (New Milford, CT: Second Renaissance Books, 1998), 24–25.
2. Norman Thomas, the American socialist leader, "reserved some of his most scathing comments for the practices of American business," the *New York Times* observed when

the high school was dedicated. Glenn Fowler, "Dedication Hails Norman Thomas," *New York Times*, May 28, 1976.

3. Leonard Peikoff, *The Ominous Parallels* (New York: Penguin, 1982), 260.
4. Rand et al, *Capitalism*, 45.
5. Orit Arfa, "You Don't Fight a Tactic," *Jerusalem Post*, July 12, 2007.
6. Ayn Rand, *The Virtue of Selfishness* (New York: Signet, 1964), 151.
7. "Medicare's 'Free Market' Facade," Ayn Rand Institute press release, July 18, 2008, http://www.aynrand.org/site/News2?page=NewsArticle&id=19912&news_iv_ctrl=1221.
8. Interview with Evva Pryor, in McConnell, *100 Voices*, 520. Rand's abhorrence of Medicare as "the impending death of the medical profession" is mentioned in another interview on p. 302.
9. Alan Greenspan, "The Assault on Integrity," in Rand et al, *Capitalism*, 118–22.
10. "Powers: UT 'must reinvent how we do business,'" *Austin Business Journal*, May 10, 2011.
11. Form 990 for fiscal year ending September 30, 2009, Ayn Rand Institute, Internal Revenue Service, dated February 5, 2010, 7.
12. Ayn Rand, "Check Your Premises: The Monument Builders," *Objectivist Newsletter*, Vol. 1, No. 12, December 1962, 53.

FOUR: THE BANKER

1. Ayn Rand, *The Fountainhead* (New York: Plume, 1994), 39.
2. Rand, *Atlas Shrugged*, 1,035.
3. "The Ayn Rand Institute FAQ," ARI Web site, http://www.aynrand.org/site/PageServer?pagename=faq_index.
4. David Harriman (ed.), *Journals of Ayn Rand* (New York: Plume, 1999), 24, 66, 68.
5. See William H. Whyte, *The Organization Man* (New York: Simon & Schuster, 1956); Rand, *The Ayn Rand Column*, 112.
6. Ayn Rand, *The Virtue of Selfishness*, 63.
7. Ellis, *Are Capitalism, Objectivism, & Libertarianism Religions? Yes!*, 176.
8. Ibid., 176–77.
9. Ayn Rand, "Moral Inflation (Part II)," *The Ayn Rand Letter*, Vol. III, No. 13, March 25, 1974 (Oceanside, Calif: Second Renassance Books, 1990), 305.
10. Berliner, *Letters of Ayn Rand*, 58.
11. Ayn Rand FBI File, op. cit.
12. Heller, *Ayn Rand and the world she made*, 480.
13. Rand, *The Fountainhead*, 537.
14. Ibid., 242.

FIVE: THE APOSTATES

1. Ron Wertheimer, "TV Weekend: The Ayn Rand Cliffs Notes: Philosophy as Foreplay," *New York Times*, May 28, 1999.
2. Details of this amazingly petty dispute can be found in various Objectivist-leaning Web sites, including Neil Parille's "The McCaskey Schism," *The Objectiblog*, September 19, 2010, http://objectiblog.blogspot.com/2010/09/mccaskey-schism.html. McCaskey's side

of the story can be found on his Web site at http://www.johnmccaskey.com/resignation.html.

3. The e-mail is published in full on John McCaskey's Web site, at http://www.johnmccaskey.com.
4. Ayn Rand, "To Whom It May Concern," *The Objectivist* Vol. 7, issue of May 1968 (dated September 15, 1968). (Palo Alto, Calif.: Palo Alto Book Service, 1982), 449.
5. Walker, *The Ayn Rand Cult,* 193.
6. Nathaniel Branden, *My Years with Ayn Rand* (San Francisco: Jossey-Bass, 1999), 112.
7. Alan Greenspan, *The Age of Turbulence* (New York: Penguin, paperback edition, 2008), 529.

SIX: THE SECESSIONIST

1. Greenspan, *The Age of Turbulence,* 40.
2. Ayn Rand, "Don't Let It Go (Part II)," *The Ayn Rand Letter,* Vol. I, No. 6, December 6, 1971, 19.
3. Ayn Rand, "Brief Summary," *The Objectivist,* September 1971, 1090.
4. "Ayn Rand's Q&A on Libertarianism," ARI Web site, http://www.aynrand.org/site/PageServer?pagename=education_campus_libertarians.
5. Ayn Rand, "Ideas v. Goods," *The Ayn Rand Letter,* Vol. III, No. 11, February 25, 1974, 295
6. David Kelley, *The Contested Legacy of Ayn Rand: Truth and Toleration in Objectivism* (Poughkeepsie, NY: Transaction Publishers, 2000), 11.
7. Peter Schwartz, "On Moral Sanctions," *Intellectual Activist,* Vol. V, No. 1.
8. Kelley, *The Contested Legacy of Ayn Rand,* 15.
9. "ARC on the Tea Parties," Ayn Rand Center for Individual Rights, http://www.aynrand.org/site/PageServer?pagename=media_topic_tea_party.
10. The event invitation can be found at http://www.eventbrite.com/event/415812707. The number of participants is recorded in Form 990 for 2009, Ayn Rand Institute, Internal Revenue Service, dated February 5, 2010, 2.
11. A video of Yaron Brook's speech can be found at the Oxford Libertarian Society blog, http://oxlib.blogspot.com/2010/02/yaron-brook-morality-of-investing-and.html.
12. See IRS Form 990 for 2009, The Objectivist Center, Internal Revenue Service, dated August 20, 2010, 1; IRS Form 990 for 2009, Ayn Rand Institute, op. cit.
13. "The Restriction of Political Campaign Intervention by Section 501(c)(3) Tax-Exempt Organizations," IRS Web site, http://www.irs.gov/charities/charitable/article/0,,id=163395,00.html, updated June 16, 2010.
14. Stephanie Strom, "I.R.S. Moves to Tax Gifts to Groups Active in Politics," *New York Times,* May 12, 2011.
15. IRS Form 990 for fiscal year ending September 30, 2010, Ayn Rand Instute, Internal Revenue Service, January 19, 2011, 1.
16. Rand, *The Virtue of Selfishness,* 34–35.
17. Ellis, *Are Capitalism, Objectivism, & Libertarianism Religions? Yes!,* 101.
18. William K. Stevens, "An Integrated Suburb Thrives in Ohio," *New York Times,* October 18, 1975.
19. Robert Bidinotto, who wrote the review, provided an account of the early stages of the rift on an Objectivist Web site, http://rebirthofreason.com/Forum/ArticleDiscussions/1101_4.shtml#99.

SEVEN: THE COOL OBJECTIVIST

1. Ellis, *Are Capitalism, Objectivism, & Libertarianism Religions? Yes!*, ii.
2. Ibid., 191.
3. "Letter From Nathaniel Branden," *The Objectivist*, December 1967, 379–80.
4. Ellis, *Are Capitalism, Objectivism, & Libertarianism Religions? Yes!*, 193–94.
5. Leonard Peikoff, *Why Businessmen Need Philosophy* (Irvine, CA: Ayn Rand Institute Press, 1999), 11–12.
6. Ayn Rand, "The Money Making Personality," reprinted in Peikoff, *Why Businessmen Need Philosophy*, 29.
7. Ibid., 37.
8. Ibid., 36.
9. Warren Buffett, "My Philanthropic Pledge," *Fortune*, June 16, 2010.
10. Don Watkins and Yaron Brook, "The Guilt Pledge," Forbes.com, September 22, 2010, http://www.forbes.com/2010/09/22/bill-gates-warren-buffett-giving-pledge-opinions-contributors-don-watkins-yaron-brook.html.
11. Andrew Ross Sorkin, "The Mystery of Steve Jobs's Public Giving," *New York Times*, August 30, 2011; "Wozniak on Steve Jobs's Resignation from Apple," telephone interview, *Bloomberg*, August 24, 2011, http://www.bloomberg.com/video/74391682 at approx 8:40
12. For Rand's views on Vietnam, see Rand et al, *Capitalism*, 223–26.
13. See Robert Mayhew (ed.), *Ayn Rand Answers* (New York: New American Library, 2005), 96. Phil Donahue's interview with Rand can be found at various places on the Web, with the portion on Israel extracted at http://www.youtube.com/watch?v=2uHSv1asFvU.

EIGHT: THE AGITATOR

1. Arfa, "You Don't Fight a Tactic."
2. "Bloomberg on Mosque Vote," *Wall Street Journal*, August 3, 2010.
3. Rand, *The Virtue of Selfishness*, 110.
4. The podcast can be found at http://www.peikoff.com/2010/06/28/what-do-you-think-of-the-plan-for-a-mosque-in-new-york-city-near-ground-zero-isnt-it-private-property-and-therefore-protected-by-individual-rights/.
5. Rand, *The Virtue of Selfishness*, 147–57.
6. Interview with Eleanora Drobysheva, McConnell, *100 Voices*, 13.
7. Entry for "Alice Rosenbaum," manifest for the *S.S. De Grasse*, February 19, 1926, accessed via Ancestry.com.
8. Heller, *Ayn Rand and the World She Made*, 56–57.
9. Mayhew, *Ayn Rand Answers*, 96.
10. Peter Schwartz, "On Moral Sanction," *Intellectual Activist*, Vol. V, No. 1, May 18, 1989, available on the ARI Web site, http://www.aynrand.org/site/PageServer?pagename=objectivism_sanctions.
11. See, e.g., Elan Journo and Yaron Brook, "America's Compassion in Iraq Is Self-Destructive," op-ed piece reprinted on the ARI Web site, http://www.aynrand.org/site/News2?page=NewsArticle&id=10775&news_iv_ctrl=1021.
12. Leonard Peikoff, "End States Who Sponsor Terrorism," available on the ARI Web site, http://www.aynrand.org/site/News2?page=NewsArticle&id=5207&news_iv_ctrl=1021.

13. Carey McWilliams, *A Mask for Privilege: Anti-Semitism in America* (Boston: Little, Brown & Co., 1948), 142–43.
14. Irving Spiegel, "Banks Are Urged to End Hiring Bias," *New York Times*, May 21, 1967.
15. Pamela Geller's blog is at http://atlasshrugs2000.typepad.com/.
16. Anne Barnard and Alan Feuer, "Outraged, and Outrageous," *New York Times*, October 8, 2010.
17. Pamela Geller "Even Ayn Rand wouldn't Believe It, Krugman's Nobel," *Atlas Shrugs* (blog), October 13, 2008, http://atlasshrugs2000.typepad.com/atlas_shrugs/2008/10/even-ayn-rand-w.html.
18. See Mayhew, *Ayn Rand Answers*, 13–14, quoting Rand answering an audience question following a 1963 lecture.
19. A compilation of *Little Green Footballs* blog entries on Geller can be found at http://littlegreenfootballs.com/tag/Pamela+Geller.
20. See Pamela Geller, "PayPal Cuts Off Atlas: Truth Is the New Hate Speech," *Atlas Shrugs*, http://atlasshrugs2000.typepad.com/atlas_shrugs/2010/06/paypal-cuts-off-atlas-truth-is-the-new-hate-speech.html for the cutoff on June 12, 2010, and "Paypal Called, Paypal Caved," *Atlas Shrugs*, http://atlasshrugs2000.typepad.com/atlas_shrugs/2010/06/paypal-called-paypal-caved.html for the about-face on June 14, 2010.
21. See Pamela Geller, "Speaker Boehner to Israeli Ambassador Michael Oren . . . 'the United States is committed to standing by our close ally'; Ron Paul to Israel: Drop Dead," *Atlas Shrugs*, February 17, 2010, http://atlasshrugs2000.typepad.com/atlas_shrugs/2011/02/speaker-boehner-to-israeli-ambassador-michael-orenthe-united-states-is-committed-to-standing-by-our-.html; David Horowitz, "Ron Paul Is a Vicious Anti-Semite and Anti-American and Conservatives Need to Wash Their Hands of Him," *NewsRealBlog*, February 17, 2011, http://www.newsrealblog.com/2011/02/17/ron-paul-is-a-vicious-anti-semite-and-anti-american-and-conservatives-need-to-wash-their-hands-of-him/.
22. Corky Siemaszko, "Southern Poverty Law Center lists anti-Islamic NYC blogger Pamela Geller, followers a hate group," *Daily News* (New York), February 25, 2011.
23. Rand, *The Virtue of Selfishness*, vii.
24. Ibid., 38.
25. Ellis, *Are Capitalism, Objectivism, & Libertarianism Religions? Yes!*, 7.

NINE: THE FIRST TEABAGGER

1. Ayn Rand, "The Disenfranchisement of the Right," *The Ayn Rand Letter*, Vol. I, No. 6, December 20, 1971, p. 23.
2. Joseph Farah, *The Tea Party Manifesto: A Vision for an American Rebirth* (Washington, D.C.: WND Books, 2010) 45.
3. See, e.g., Andrew Goldman, "The Billionaire's Party," *New York*, July 25, 2010; Jane Mayer, "Covert Operations," *New Yorker*, August. 20, 2010.
4. Kate Zernike, *Boiling Mad: Inside Tea Party America* (New York: Times Books, 2010), 26–27.

TEN: THE ORGANIZER

1. Dick Armey and Matt Kibbe, *Give Us Liberty: A Tea Party Manifesto* (New York: HarperCollins, 2010), 37–64.
2. Frank Rich, "The Billionaires Bankrolling the Tea Party," *New York Times,* August 28, 2010.
3. Armey and Kibbe, *Give Us Liberty,* 44.
4. Ibid., 47.
5. Scott Rasmussen and Douglas Schoen, *Mad as Hell: How the Tea Party Movement Is Fundamentally Remaking Our Two-Party System* (New York: HarperCollins, 2010), 149–150.
6. Stephanie Mencimer, "Is the Tea Party Movement Like a Pyramid Scheme?" *Mother Jones,* October 19, 2010.
7. Zachary Roth, "Tea Party Leader Was Involved With GOP-Tied Political Firm," *TPM Muckraker* (blog), March 2, 2010, http://tpmmuckraker.talkingpointsmemo.com/2010/03/tea_party_leader_was_involved_with_political_firm.php; Zernike, *Boiling Mad,* 43; Zachary Roth, "FreedomWorks Says Jump, Tea Partiers Ask How High," *TPM Muckraker,* August 11, 2009, http://tpmmuckraker.talkingpointsmemo.com/2009/08/freedomworks_says_jump_tea_partiers_ask_how_high.php.
8. Liz Kellar, "Local lawyer emerges as face of Tea Party movement," *Union,* (Nevada County, CA) February 27, 2010.
9. Benlinen, ed., *Letters of Ayn Rand,* 666.
10. Rand, *The Virtue of Selfishness,* 31.
11. Shannon Travis, "Political Ticker: Conservatives boo GOP congressman as summit attendees push for deeper federal spending cuts," CNN.com, February 26, 2011, http://politicalticker.blogs.cnn.com/2011/02/26/conservatives-boo-gop-congressman-as-summit-attendees-push-for-deeper-federal-spending-cuts/.

ELEVEN: THE VAGUELY DISSATISFIED

1. "About Us," Mid-South Tea Party Web site, http://www.midsouthteaparty.org/about.html.
2. "NAACP Delegates Vote to Repudiate Racist Elements Within Tea Party," NAACP Web site, http://www.naacp.org/news/entry/naacp-delegates-vote-to-repudiate-racist-elements-within-the-tea-pary/.
3. "Mid-South Tea Party Reacts to Racist Accusations," MyFoxMemphis.com, http://www.myfoxmemphis.com/dpp/news/local/071310-mid-south-tea-party-reacts-to-racist-accusations.
4. Associated Press, "Tenn. tea party activists split on GOP relations," *Kingsport Times-News,* April 5, 2010.
5. Mark Herr's Page–Freedomworks Tea Party Group, http://teaparty.freedomworks.org/profile/MarkHerr.
6. Ron Paul, "Commentary: Bailouts will lead to rough economic ride," CNN.com, September 23, 2008, http://www.cnn.com/2008/POLITICS/09/23/paul.bailout/index.html.
7. Paul Krugman, "Armey of Ignorance," *New York Times* blog, November 10, 2009, http://krugman.blogs.nytimes.com/2009/11/10/armey-of-ignorance/.

8. Ayn Rand in a 1964 *Playboy* interview, quoted on the ARI Web site, http://www.aynrand.org/site/PageServer?pagename=faq_index#obj_q7.

TWELVE: THE PERSUADED

1. Rasmussen and Schoen, *Mad as Hell*, 164.
2. Zernike, *Boiling Mad*, 14.
3. Charles Colson, "Atlas Shrugged and So Should You," Chuck Colson Center Web site May 11, 2011, http://www.colsoncenter.org/twominutewarning/entry/33/17003.
4. Zernike, *Boiling Mad*, 129.
5. Marc Lacey, "Tea Party Group Issues Warning to the G.O.P.," *New York Times*, February 26, 2011.
6. Jody Callahan, "Tea Partiers Protest Cohen," *Commercial Appeal*, April 7, 2010.
7. "Transcript of Steve Cohen interview by The Young Turks," *Commercial Appeal*, April 3, 2010.
8. Gregory Korte, "Democrats seize on N.Y. election, make Medicare top issue," *USA Today*, May 25, 2011.

THIRTEEN: THE GREAT DEBATE

1. "Jack H. Skirball" (obituary), *New York Times*, December 10, 1985.
2. Ayn Rand, "Check Your Premises: The Monument Builders," *The Objectivist Newsletter*.
3. The Mike Wallace interview can be found at various places on the Internet, including YouTube and http://www.braincrave.com/viewblog.php?id=383.
4. Edward J. Perkins, *The Economy of Colonial America* (New York: Columbia University Press, 1988), 208.

FOURTEEN: THE MURRAY HILL CANDIDATE

1. Seth Lubove and Oliver Staley, "Schools Find Ayn Rand Can't Be Shrugged as Donors Build Courses," *Bloomberg Markets*, May 5, 2011.
2. Branden, *My Years with Ayn Rand*, 160.
3. Greenspan, *The Age of Turbulence*, 44.
4. Branden, *My Years with Ayn Rand*, 159.
5. Greenspan, *The Age of Turbulence*, 52.
6. Letter from Alan Greenspan, *New York Times Book Review*, November 3, 1957.
7. In my book *Wall Street Versus America* (New York: Portfolio, 2006), I scratched the surface of the unethical practices prevalent on Wall Street, all of which had festered for years because of weak regulation.
8. Letter signed by Allan Blumenthal, Alan Greenspan, Leonard Peikoff, and Mary Ann (Rukavina) Sures, dated September 1968, published as "For the Record," *The Objectivist*, Vol. 7, issue of May 1968, 457.
9. Rand et al, *Capitalism*, 226.
10. Greenspan, *The Age of Turbulence*, 63–64.
11. Soma Golden, "He Stresses Patience to Achieve Goals," *New York Times*, July 24, 1974.

12. Aaron Trask, "Alan Greenspan 'Betrayed' Ayn Rand and Ruined the Economy, Says Rand Institute President," *Daily Ticker*, Yahoo! News, May 9, 2011, http://finance.yahoo.com/blogs/daily-ticker/alan-greenspan-betrayed-ayn-rand-ruined-economy-says-124734929.html.

FIFTEEN: THE BILL FOR COLLECTION

1. Branden, *My Years with Ayn Rand*, 160.
2. Arloc Sherman and Aviva Aron-Dine, "New CBO Data Shows Income Inequality Continues to Widen," Center on Budget and Policy Priorities, January 23, 2007.
3. Jennifer Liberto, "CEOs earn 343 times more than typical workers," *CNNMoney*, April 20, 2011, http://cnnmoney.mobi/primary/_anjlQ1-iwtfhHqTVc; the source was a study by the AFL-CIO, which can be found at http://www.aflcio.org/corporatewatch/paywatch/.
4. Edmund L. Andrews, "Fed Shrugged as Subprime Crisis Spread," *New York Times*, December 18, 2007.
5. Peter S. Goodman, "Taking Hard New Look at a Greenspan Legacy," *New York Times*, October 8, 2008.
6. Remarks by Chairman Alan Greenspan at the American Bankers Association Annual Convention, New York, New York; the Federal Reserve Board, October 5, 2004.
7. Letter to Sen. Michael D. Crapo and Sen. Zell B. Miller, dated September 18, 2002. The letter was signed by Greenspan, Treasury Secretary Paul O'Neill, Securities and Exchange Commission chairman Harvey Pitt, and James E. Newsome, chairman of the Commodities Futures Trading Commission. It is online at http://www.isda.org/speeches/pdf/Derivatives-Letter-to-Sens-Crapo-and-Miller9_18.pdf.
8. Greenspan's testimony can be viewed in the C-SPAN archive, at http://www.c-spanvideo.org/program/281958-1.
9. Rand, *The Virtue of Selfishness*, x.
10. Ayn Rand, *For the New Intellectual: The Philosophy of Ayn Rand* (New York: Signet, 1963), 16.
11. Ayn Rand, "Philosophy: Who Needs It," address to graduating class of the U.S. Military Academy at West Point on March 4, 1974, reprinted in *The Ayn Rand Letter*, Vol. III, No. 7, issue of December 31, 1973, p. 277. (Rand newsletters were commonly dated several months before their actual publication date.)
12. Text of remarks by Alan Greenspan, "Markets and the Judiciary," Sandra Day O'Connor Project Conference, Georgetown University, October 2, 2008.
13. Alan Greenspan, "The Crisis," Brookings Institution, April 15, 2010.
14. "Greenspan: Financial Crisis Doesn't Indict Ayn Rand Theories," *ABC News*, April 4, 2010, http://blogs.abcnews.com/politicalpunch/2010/04/greenspan-financial-crisis-doesnt-indict-ayn-rand-theories.html.
15. This and other FCIC hearings are archived on the Stanford University Web site, at http://fcic.law.stanford.edu/.
16. Goodman, "Taking Hard Look at a Greenspan Legacy."
17. Alan Greenspan, "Activism," *International Finance*, March 2, 2011.
18. Alan Greenspan, "Dodd-Frank fails to meet test of our times," FT.com (*Financial Times*, Web site), March 29, 2011, http://www.ft.com/cms/s/0/14662fd8-5a28-11e0-86d3-00144feab49a.html#axzz1I108nwBH.

19. Henry Farrell, "With Notably Rare Exceptions," *Crooked Timber* (blog), March 30, 2011, http://crookedtimber.org/2011/03/30/with-notably-rare-exceptions/.
20. Paul Krugman, "The Exceptional Mr. Greenspan," *New York Times* blog, March 30, 2011, http://krugman.blogs.nytimes.com/2011/03/30/the-exceptional-mr-greenspan/.
21. Branden, *My Years with Ayn Rand*, 185.

SIXTEEN: THE PROPHECY

1. Alex Epstein, "What We Owe Our Soldiers," *Objectivist Standard,* http://www.theobjectivestandard.com/blog/index.php/2007/11/what-we-owe-our-soldiers-by-alex-epstein-3/.
2. See Heller, *Ayn Rand and the World She Made,* 295–301; Murray Rothbard's essay, "The Sociology of the Ayn Rand Cult," can be found at http://www.lewrockwell.com/rothbard/rothbard23.html.
3. Ron Paul, *End the Fed* (New York: Grand Central Publishing, 2009), 62.
4. Ron Paul, "The Real Lessons of 9/11," Antiwar.com, April 24, 2004, http://antiwar.com/paul/?articleid=2372.

SEVENTEEN: THE VISION

1. Peikoff, *Why Businessmen Need Philosophy,* 14.
2. Stephen Dalton, "Braced for Critical Impact," *Times* (London), September 16, 2006.
3. Lorine Pruette, "Battle Against Evil," *New York Times Book Review,* May 16, 1943.
4. Bosley Crowther, "The Screen in Review; Gary Cooper Plays an Idealistic Architect in Film Version of 'The Fountainhead,'" *New York Times,* July 9, 1949.

EPILOGUE

1. Leonard Peikoff, *Objectivism: The Philosophy of Ayn Rand* (New York: Meridian, 1991), 386.

INDEX